THE FEDERAL DEBT
Structure and Impact

COMMITTEE ON THE FEDERAL DEBT

The special committee listed below,* appointed by the Fund in connection with this project, was asked to study the research findings and to formulate a program of action to deal with the problems disclosed by the research. The Committee's Report, for which the Committee is solely responsible, is given in Part III of this volume. Parts I and II contain the findings of fact and their analysis, for which the Committee has assumed no responsibility.

ARTHUR R. UPGREN, *Chairman*

Professor of Economics and Finance
School of Business Administration, University of Minnesota

HENRY H. HEIMANN

Executive Manager, National
Association of Credit Men

EARL B. SCHWULST

President,
Bowery Savings Bank

NEIL H. JACOBY

Dean, School of Business
Administration, University of
California at Los Angeles

LOUIS STULBERG

Vice President, International
Ladies' Garment Workers' Union

DONALD B. WOODWARD

E. B. MacNAUGHTON

Chairman of the Board,
First National Bank of Portland

Second Vice President,
Mutual Life Insurance
Company of New York

---

* Daniel W. Bell, President, American Security and Trust Company, was prevented by other commitments from attending meetings of the Committee and participating in its conclusions. His views as expressed in correspondence were considered, however, in drafting the report.

Beardsley Ruml, formerly Chairman, Federal Reserve Bank of New York, was a member of the Committee until July 15, 1952 but was unable to take part in any of its decisions.

The Federal Debt

Structure and Impact

By CHARLES CORTEZ ABBOTT

Edmund Cogswell Converse Professor of Banking and Finance
Harvard University Graduate School of Business Administration

With Policy Recommendations of the
Committee on the Federal Debt

New York
The Twentieth Century Fund
1953

vi

FOREWORD

FROM 1895 TO 1916 the United States gross federal debt was fairly stable at a little more than one billion dollars. After World War I it had increased twentyfold—to over $25 billion in 1919. During subsequent years of prosperity it was reduced to around $16 billion, but deficit financing during the depression increased the debt to $36 billion in 1937.

This increase, which was causing grave concern at the time, impelled the Fund to make a study of the debt in relation to the credit of the government.* Commenting on the war's effect on the debt, the report of this study stated that "it would have been considered fantastic to predict in 1914 that the debt would rise from a little over $1 billion to more than $25 billion in five years' time."

Even in 1937 it was beyond the reach of wild imagination to think of a gross federal debt over 200 times as great as before World War I. Yet the figure is now around $260 billion or close to $1,700 for every man, woman and child in the country—vastly more than the authors of the Fund's 1937 report thought the government's credit could possibly bear. Time has proved the contrary, but the existence of this huge debt affects the operation of our entire economy as well as the pocketbook of every American.

In 1948, therefore, the Fund started a study of this whole situation, under the direction of Charles C. Abbott, Converse Professor of Banking and Finance at the Harvard Business School. By the end of 1949 Dr. Abbott had finished a first draft of his report describing the size of the debt, its composition—both in terms of the kinds of obligation it contained and of its holders—the problems of its management and its effects on the economy. However, the Korean War and the rearmament effort, bringing the prospect of further increase in the federal debt, led the Fund to postpone publication of the report while Dr. Abbott revised it to take account of the new situation. The present volume is the result.

As usual with its surveys, the Fund appointed a special committee —the Committee on the Federal Debt—to review the research findings and to formulate a constructive program of action to deal with

* *The National Debt and Government Credit* by Paul W. Stewart and Rufus S. Tucker, assisted by Carolyn Stetson. *The Twentieth Century Fund*, New York, 1937.

the problems which the findings disclose. Under the able chairman-ship of Arthur R. Upgren, Professor of Economics and Finance at the University of Minnesota and formerly Economist of the Minne-apolis Federal Reserve Bank, this distinguished committee has drawn up such a report. It is included as the last chapter of this volume.

The Fund offers this volume to the public in the hope that it will help to clarify a subject difficult for the layman to understand, but one that urgently calls for an enlightened public opinion. The Fund also hopes that the program of action recommended by the Com-mittee will be of special value to those directly concerned with fiscal policies in the United States.

EVANS CLARK, *Executive Director*
The Twentieth Century Fund

330 WEST 42D STREET
NEW YORK 36, N. Y.
NOVEMBER 20, 1952

ACKNOWLEDGMENTS

I should like to record here that no one saw more clearly the need for this study of the management of the federal debt than did the late John H. Fahey. Former Commissioner of the Federal Home Loan Bank Administration, he had a rare personal knowledge of the debt and its significance. One of the original trustees of the Twentieth Century Fund and its President at the time of his death, he knew what the Fund might do to assess the impact of the debt on the nation's economy. This study was inspired by him and the close personal attention he paid to it was warmly appreciated.

The members of the Special Committee for this study have read drafts of the manuscript and their comments have proved of great help in revising the material. I wish to acknowledge my appreciation for the time and effort it has cost them. Comments and suggestions made by other persons, not associated with the Twentieth Century Fund, have also been of great help.

I also wish to express my deep appreciation to Miss Joan Gilbert, my research assistant, and to Mrs. Cecil Bessell, who helped me in preparing charts and tables. Miss Alice M. Inkley has my special gratitude for the large effort of typing and preliminary editing of the manuscript. None of these associates, however, should be held responsible for errors of fact or emphasis which may have been committed here.

CHARLES C. ABBOTT

CONTENTS

Part I: DEVELOPMENT OF THE PROBLEM

Part II: ANALYSIS OF THE PROBLEM

Part III: COMMITTEE REPORT

TABLES

APPENDIX TABLES

FIGURES

PART I

DEVELOPMENT OF THE PROBLEM

Chapter 1

INTRODUCTION

THE SEVENFOLD INCREASE of the federal debt during World War II —from less than $41 billion in June 1939 to nearly $280 billion in February 1946—marked a turning point in the financial history of the United States. The impact of this development on society was tremendous; its effects were to be felt in many ways and in many sectors of the economy.

When hostilities came to an end the federal debt exceeded the total of all other debts in society, exclusive of bank notes, bank deposits and the value of outstanding policies and annuities of life insurance companies. It was greater than the national income; in 1945 it exceeded all income payments by approximately 61 per cent. Interest payments on the debt were larger than the total of the government's ordinary receipts for any peacetime year before 1941. In addition, the government had acquired an enormous contingent liability—and was to acquire a still greater one—through guaranteeing and insuring different kinds of obligations in such fields as housing, and mortgage financing, agricultural credit, commercial banking, business lending and international finance. Thus the direct debt, large as it was, did not represent the total money payments that the government had undertaken to make.

On its face the growth of the debt appeared to be of interest primarily to the financial world. But the fact that so great a debt had come into existence was of consequence to all business concerns, taxpayers and citizens. Procedures used in managing the debt inevitably affect the cash and the administrative budgets of the government, the level of taxation, the volume of credit and the value of the dollar. Consequently debt management is of concern to everyone who pays taxes or uses money—that is, to everyone.

Problems Posed by the Debt

A summary of some of the major problems which the presence of the debt has raised in the economy will suggest its importance.

When a public debt is small compared with the volume of private debt outstanding and with other economic magnitudes, such as national income or the amount of invested capital, Treasury securities can be regarded as simply one type of investment, and the debt can properly be studied in the context of the general capital market. Government obligations have their own characteristics and their price movements have a special significance. But while the debt is comparatively small these facts do not of themselves create special problems.

When the public debt reaches great size, however, and especially if further increases are in prospect, its position in the economy changes. When the total of federal obligations outstanding exceeds that of all other kinds of debt, and when Treasury securities constitute something like half the assets of banks and insurance companies, the debt begins to assume a new character. When it is made up of various kinds of issues which differ among themselves, not only in their rates of interest and the lengths of their maturities, but in other respects, such as marketability, eligibility for purchase by different classes of buyers, the prerogatives attached to them, and the purposes for which they were issued, the debt becomes an object of study in its own right and for its own sake. When certain types of issues are continuously offered at fixed prices, and when all types are immediately convertible into cash, either at fixed or almost fixed prices, federal securities begin to take on, from the point of view of the individual, the characteristics of a bank account. When the federal government holds a large and growing portion of its own obligations in its own investment accounts as reserves against its own liability to pay out sums in connection with social security, unemployment or the claims of depositors of closed banks, the debt takes on a complexion wholly new in the country's experience.

In short, as these things occur, the debt ceases to be simply an outlet for the investment funds of persons and financial institutions. It becomes a vehicle capable of expanding or contracting the deposit structure, quite independently of whether the government has a surplus or deficit on current operating account. It becomes, in some measure, an institution itself. This is increasingly true when a large or increasing volume of Treasury securities are nonmarketable.[1]

1. See the discussion in Carl S. Shoup, "Les Restrictions à la Négociabilité de la Dette Fédérale aux États-Unis," *Revue de Science et de Législation Financières,* July-September 1949.

When the public debt is very large relative to other economic magnitudes it produces effects in an increasing number of economic areas. Deficit financing and the use of surpluses and deficits in the federal budget to affect business activity have long been accepted mechanisms for influencing the course of business and of employment. But when debt—the consequence of deficits—becomes very great, its management acquires a sort of independent significance, as has become abundantly evident since the end of the war, and new problems arise.

For example, debt management, which is the prerogative of the Treasury, impinges on credit regulation and control, which is the responsibility of the Federal Reserve System. Thus the possibility of dispute between two key federal agencies arises. In such a conflict the degree of independence proper for the central bank is necessarily one of the issues at stake. Again, the way in which a large debt is managed affects both the supply of money and the value of money, that is, the purchasing power of the dollar. Since under the Constitution regulation of the value of money is one of the powers given the Congress, new problems regarding the relationship of the legislative and executive branches of the government emerge in this area.

Much economic activity in any field is guided by a certain constancy in the habits of businessmen, investors, employees and officers of financial institutions. These habits are in general founded on sound business and economic beliefs. Banks, for example, typically invest a certain portion of their resources in such a way that these assets can readily be used to satisfy any probable demand for cash on the part of their depositors. Trustees and fiduciary institutions, when managing other people's property, generally give more weight to the safety of the principal of this property than they do to the purchasing power of the principal, or to the value of these assets when compared with real goods and services. When the federal debt is very large, however, the way in which it is managed necessarily affects these business and financial habits. Thus questions sometimes arise as to whether the public interest will be aided or injured if the constancy of behavior by business and financial people is disturbed, either deliberately or inadvertently. In some situations a disturbance may promote the public welfare; under other conditions it may be disastrous. Consequently, the great expansion of the debt during the war set up new considerations in the handling of public affairs.

Another problem which has attracted enormous attention is that of interest policy. This question will be dealt with at greater length further on. It is nevertheless worth while to suggest here some of the issues to be resolved in this area. Traditionally, interest policy has been one of the chief tools used by central banks in regulating credit, in controlling the amount of credit available, and in attempting to mitigate fluctuations in business cycles. But with a large debt the Treasury necessarily is concerned with the interest costs it will have to pay when it sells new securities, either for refunding or for new money purposes. Thus the necessity arises for agreement between these agencies regarding a common policy.

Furthermore, the rates attaching to federal securities are the basic rates in the money market, and movements in the yields of Treasury obligations occasion movements in other rates, such as those attaching to bank loans, corporate bonds, mortgages and agricultural credit. Changes in rates, of course, affect the capital values of these instruments; rising rates bring declines in capital values, and falling rates bring rising values. Rising rates also tend to restrict the amount of credit available, psychologically, if in no other way. Constant or falling rates have the opposite tendency. Consequently it is important that the interest policy formulated by the fiscal authorities give recognition to the needs and requirements of these other markets.

A third element is the weight that should be allowed, in the determination of policy, to the factor of interest costs in the federal budget. Interest paid by the Treasury is a cost to the federal government and to taxpayers, and the higher the rates paid the greater the cost. On the other hand, the greater the amount of interest received by taxpayers, the greater are their tax payments to the government. Consequently, it would appear that the Treasury should be chiefly concerned, not with the gross payments, but with the size of these payments *less* the sums it receives through tax receipts. There is, however, no general agreement on this point.

In the mind of the author the basic problem posed by the existence of a large public debt is that of ownership—ownership of the government securities outstanding. In oversimplified terms, the issue may be stated this way: Over a period of time, what elements in society are to own what portions of the debt, for what reasons, and on what terms? By "terms" is meant here the whole incidence of ownership, not merely the receipt of interest. There are plenty of other problems in debt management, but in reality they are all subsidiary to this problem of ownership. If public authority is not able to achieve and maintain a reasonable degree of stability in the pattern of ownership, there will be little chance of finding desirable solutions to the other questions. Formulation of a sound long-term program for debt management must face squarely this problem of who is to own the debt and why.

Two Settings for These Problems

How any one person will view these problems or answer these questions will depend in large measure on his economic and political beliefs. Yet, as a practical matter, the answers given by him at any particular time will be greatly influenced by his estimate of the future course of events, his appraisal of the likelihood of war or the necessity of maintaining an economy oriented toward military security, as contrasted with the possibility of peace and what may be loosely termed "normal economic conditions."

For what is possible and practicable when the outlook is for peace is radically different from what is required under the hard exigencies of war. When there is little likelihood of an outbreak of hostilities and when the presumption is that economic forces will not be impeded or distorted by military requirements, men are more likely to rely upon some form of the free market process, and to be satisfied with its results, than is the case when war is either imminent or an actuality. Under conditions of war or the threat of war, business and financial processes must be forcibly diverted from their usual channels and used to protect the national security. Consequently the way in which these matters are viewed and the kind of solution advocated for these problems will commonly be colored by the context in which they are placed, whether as problems to be dealt with in times of emergency or as issues to be resolved under less extreme conditions.

The Approach Used in This Study

The immediately succeeding chapters, Chapters 2-5, present the evolution of the debt management problem from the close of World War II to approximately the end of 1948. Here are considered the conditions that existed at the termination of hostilities, the impact of the debt on the Treasury and on Federal Reserve policy, and the interest rate problem.

Chapter 6 discusses the new situation that was precipitated in June 1950 by the invasion of Korea and the action taken by the United Nations in opposing aggression. These actions forcibly and dramatically altered the circumstances in which the United States found itself and produced immediate repercussions on every aspect of the country's financial policies. Most important among the financial consequences was the possibility that the country might, in the near future, be compelled to resume deficit financing on a large scale. The exposition of the situation that developed during the second half of 1950 extends beyond debt management in a narrow sense. In order to place this subject in perspective a considerable number of wider financial issues must be discussed, although generally speaking they centered on the debt and its management. These formed the background for the reorientation of federal financial policies that took place in 1951.

Chapters 7-11 deal with the more technical aspects of the debt and its management, with the maturity schedule, the pattern of ownership and the problems involved in debt retirement and the use of nonmarketable securities. Particular attention is given to the portfolio behavior of particular classes of debt owners, to changes that have taken place in their holdings since the end of World War II. Questions are raised regarding future changes that might take place if, on the one hand, war and extreme boom or depression are avoided and if, on the other hand, an increase in the money supply is not adopted as the easy solution for the problem of ownership. Basically this section is a study in methodology. Thus the figures used are of less consequence than are the concepts and assumptions underlying them.

Though methodology in itself is commonly a barren exercise, the techniques here employed have the virtue of directing attention to certain of the fundamental problems of debt management—problems that must be grappled with whatever the approach employed and irrespective of whether an emergency exists. The issue may be stated as follows: Given the total amount of dollar resources in the economy and their distribution among the various investor groups, what portions of the assets in the hands of each group will willingly be allocated to owning Treasury securities, in view of the financial and business needs of each group, their typical investment behavior and all the tangible and intangible factors that influence the ways in which men manage their own or other people's property? And further, within what ranges can the amounts of assets so allocated be expected to fluctuate, barring the extreme economic dislocations occasioned by war, boom and depression?

The volume of Treasury securities owned over a period of time by one investor or one class of investors will be affected by the yields of Treasury securities, by alternative investment opportunities, by the vagaries of the security markets, and by a host of other considerations. But we must break the circle somewhere. If the truism is granted that *all* the debt must at *all* times be owned by someone, and if the money supply is not increased and the resources needed for debt ownership thereby provided, the answer to the question "Who will own the debt?" must be sought within the economy's existing asset structure. The problem, it is submitted, can be approached by assuming, on the basis of experience, a certain minimum demand for Treasury securities, a certain minimum holding, by each class of investor, almost—but not quite—irrespective of the rates of return attaching to the several classes of federal obligations and to other alternative investments. The suggestion is that from this base it is possible to reason as to how these minimum holdings may be affected by changes in the interest rates and in the other terms of the securities offered to actual or potential holders of the federal debt. It is further presumed that from such a line of reasoning it is possible to draw tentative conclusions regarding the degree of stability in debt ownership that can be induced by adapting the terms of the securities to the needs of the market.

While the situation that resulted from the outbreak of fighting in Korea precluded any expectation of debt reduction in the near future, a chapter on this topic is included, partly to record the country's experience during 1946 and 1947, partly in order that so important an aspect of debt management should not be omitted, partly because debt retirement and the use of nonmarketable issues are, in some respects, related aspects of debt management.

Chapter 12 brings together the major conclusions of this study.

Conclusion

Contrary to much popular belief, the debt does not bring with it a threat of some cataclysm, or even the presumption that national bankruptcy is inevitable. The dangers lie in other directions. If we do not solve our problems skillfully and in accordance with sound principles so great a debt may result in the dilution of the dollar, may enhance the risk of "boom or bust," may undermine the free market process which has brought much of the country's progress and smother the spirit of enterprise thereby leading to a loss of human freedoms.[2] In addition, the very size of the debt implies a concentration of financial power within the federal government much larger than the country has heretofore experienced.

2. See the discussion in *Our National Debt and the National Welfare* (National Debt Series No. 7), Committee on Public Debt Policy, New York, 1948.

Chapter 2

THE SITUATION AFTER WORLD WAR II

IT HAS COMMONLY BEEN SAID that the chief effect of the wartime increase in federal debt was the great growth in purchasing power, as shown by the expansion in demand deposits and currency outside banks, from $60.9 billion in June 1939 to $175.4 billion in December 1945. Yet this development was actually only a part of one still greater, namely, the transformation that debt expansion occasioned in the amount and character of the assets owned by different segments of the economy.[1]

THE CHANGE IN ASSETS

This transformation involved three distinct, though related, types of change. First, the total assets of the leading classes of owners of the federal debt increased sharply. The amount of increase differed, being larger for commercial banks than for other financial institutions, and probably larger for banks than for business corporations or individuals, although data sufficient for exact comparison are not available. Second, as total assets rose, the dollar volume of Treasury securities held by each class of owner increased. Third, the proportion of assets owned by each class of owner that was represented by government securities increased. Thus, the asset structure of each class of owner, or the way in which each class of owner allocated his re-

1. "A cash deficit financed by cash borrowing, other things being equal, increases total liquid asset holdings of the nonbank public, that is, holdings of cash and government securities by others than Treasury investments accounts, Federal Reserve Banks, and commercial banks. To the extent the deficit is financed by direct cash borrowing from the banking system, new money is created by such borrowing and is injected by the deficit expenditures into cash balances held by the nonbank public. To the extent the deficit is financed by cash borrowings from outside the banks, the increase in liquid asset holdings of the nonbank public takes the form of government security holdings. In this case, the cash borrowing lowers the cash balances held by the nonbank public and increases its holdings of government securities. The deficit expenditures, in turn, restore the money supply held by the nonbank public to its previous level." John K. Langum, "Monetary and Public Debt Aspects of Budget Policy," reprinted from the *Proceedings* of the Forty-first National Tax Conference, held at Denver, Colorado, October 4-7, 1948, pp. 4-5.

sources as among different kinds of investment, was substantially altered.

Deficit Spending Caused the Growth

The basic cause of this growth in the amount of assets held by owners of the federal debt, and of the changes in the proportionate amounts of different types of assets, was the deficit spending of the federal government during the war. As Under Secretary of the Treasury Bell said in November 1945:

The tremendous importance of Government buying in the market place during the war period is evident from the fact that Federal Government spending accounted for $323 billion out of aggregate spending of $833 billion during the five-year period. . . . These figures show that the Government accounted for close to 40 per cent of the aggregate spending taking place throughout the country. The remaining $510 billion of spending was accounted for by $428 billion of spending by consumers, $41 billion by business for capital goods, and $41 billion by State and local governmental units.

The Government share of total spending in this war reached a peak of almost 50 per cent in the fiscal year 1945 when the Government accounted for $100 billion out of $211 billion total spending. Contrast this situation with that in World War I when the Federal Government accounted for a maximum of only about one-fourth of aggregate market spending, with the other three-fourths coming from consumers, business, and State and local governments. In the fiscal year 1919—the peak year of Federal spending in World War I —total expenditures in this country amounted to about $75 billion, of which the Federal Government accounted for a little under $19 billion. . . .

Let's look further at that $833 billion of total spending in the five-year period. It is axiomatic that aggregate spending in the country is equal to aggregate income. The head of the coin is the $833 billion of spending while the other side is the $833 billion of income flow. It should be noted that this is a *gross* income flow since it includes such items as funds flowing into business reserves as well as net income in the usual sense.

Who received this gross income flow? We know that the Federal Government received in taxes $133 billion or about 15 per cent of the total income flow, and State and local governments received about $49 billion. Of the remaining $651 billion of income after taxes, about 90 per cent was distributed to individuals and 10 per cent to corporations. Corporations are here treated as a conduit and only the new funds remaining in their hands over the five-year period are counted as being received by them. The corporate income items thus consist of retained earnings plus accretions in reserves, such as depreciation and depletion accounts, over and above what was invested in new capital goods—plant, equipment, and inventories. The income flow to individuals includes dividends received from corporations.

Turn these figures around another way. The Federal Government spent $323 billion and received in taxes $133 billion, leaving a deficit of $190 billion. Individuals and corporations spent $469 billion but had income after taxes of $651 billion. Here was a surplus of $182 billion and if you add in the $8 billion surplus of State and local governments you obtain an exact correspondence with the $190 billion Federal deficit.

One of the major goals of Treasury financing was to try to channel back into the Treasury as much as possible of this $190 billion which people were accumulating as a result of the Federal deficit. From a financing point of view, every means possible had to be taken to persuade people to hold these funds rather than to attempt to spend them, for such an attempt on a large scale would have meant inflation. Direct controls on production, wages, prices, etc., operated on one front to dam up these funds but the Treasury had to operate on another front to see that the funds remained saved. The best way to accomplish this was to get as much as possible of these funds into Government securities.

What were our results? Let's look at the three major forms of liquid assets held by all nonbank investors combined, namely, currency, commercial bank deposits, and Federal securities. These are the significant ways in which the deficit manifested itself. Because of various minor transactions in the economy which we do not need to go into here, the total increase in nonbank holdings of these major liquid assets during the five-year period we are talking about was actually $189 billion, rather than the $190 billion deficit.

Of the approximately $190 billion available, $121 billion was placed in Federal securities by nonbank investors. Individuals were the largest investors, adding $49 billion to their holdings of Government securities over the period. Insurance companies absorbed $16 billion of Government securities and savings banks took $6 billion. Other corporations and associations absorbed $27 billion. State and local governments acquired $5 billion, and Federal agencies and trust funds invested $18 billion—the last representing mostly social security and military insurance funds.

In other words, about two-thirds of the $190 billion of new funds was placed directly in Federal securities and one-third in money savings—that is, currency and commercial bank accounts. The one-third placed in money savings in turn resulted in a corresponding amount of absorption of Federal securities by the banking system. Because individuals and businesses chose to place one-third of their new savings in currency and commercial bank deposits, commercial banks and Federal Reserve Banks absorbed Federal securities of an equivalent amount. Over the five-year period the banks, accordingly, absorbed $68 billion of Federal securities to match the growth of currency and commercial bank deposits. They absorbed also an extra $20 billion of Federal securities as a result of other factors, the most important of which was the growth of the Treasury's cash balance.[2]

2. Daniel W. Bell, Under Secretary of the Treasury, "War Financing—Some Implications for the Future," address at the annual dinner meeting of the Association of Stock Exchange Firms, November 1945.

Variation in Growth

Starting from a comparatively low level in 1939, the debt increased rapidly; in 1945 the growth ceased; in 1946 and 1947 the curve actually turned down slightly; since then the increase has been resumed. Figure 1 indicates growth in the amount of federal securities outstanding—direct and guaranteed—for the fiscal years 1939-1948. The great increase in the debt during the war is clearly shown as com-

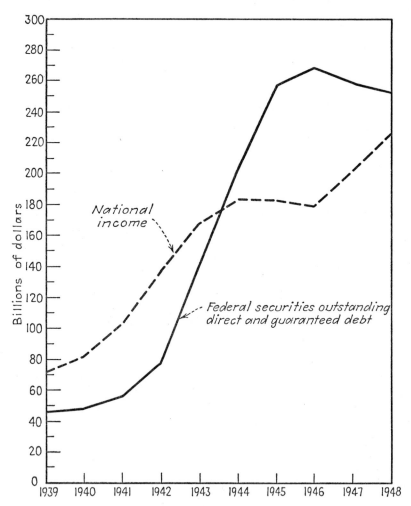

FIGURE 1. GROWTH OF THE NATIONAL DEBT COMPARED WITH THE NATIONAL INCOME, 1939-1948

Source: Appendix Table 1.

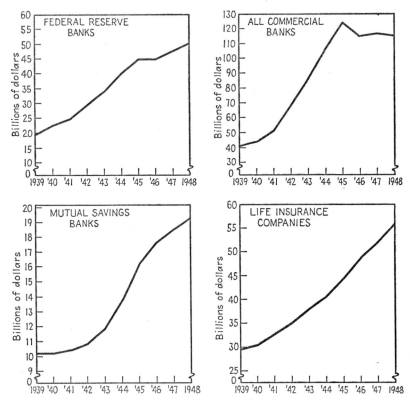

FIGURE 2. ASSETS OF FINANCIAL INSTITUTIONS, END OF DECEMBER, 1939-1948
Source: Appendix Table 2.

pared with the national income and the moderate decline in the total
debt after 1946.

In greater or less degree this S curve was repeated in the behavior
of the total assets of most of the leading types of debt holders.[3]
Total assets of commercial banks, Federal Reserve Banks, savings
banks and life insurance companies all followed this same general
pattern: a rapid growth during the war and a less rapid growth—or
even a slight decline—in the postwar period. In Figure 2 are shown
the annual amounts of total assets (or major segments of the totals)
for these institutions, in order that the similarity between the behavior of the total debt and the behavior of the resources of these
institutions may be traced.

3. The chief exception, as among "leading" types of debt holders, were United
States government agencies and trust funds, for reasons that will be indicated later.

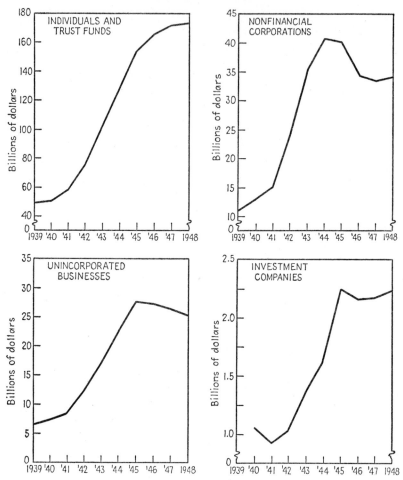

FIGURE 3. LIQUID ASSET HOLDINGS OF INDIVIDUALS AND TRUST FUNDS, NONFINANCIAL
CORPORATIONS, UNINCORPORATED BUSINESSES, AND TOTAL NET ASSETS
OF INVESTMENT COMPANIES, ANNUAL TOTALS, 1939-1948

Source: Appendix Table 3.

Liquid assets of individual persons and trust funds, unincorporated businesses and financial business corporations repeated this pattern. Even the net assets of investment companies showed this same
behavior, although security prices as well as a larger volume of government holdings affected these valuations. Figure 3 reveals this situation. The growth of the federal debt thus increased either the total
or the liquid assets of virtually every segment of the population.
When moderate or large-scale deficit financing is resumed by the fed-

eral government we can expect to see the assets of financial institutions behave in a similar way.

How Money Was Created

The methods of deficit financing give rise to this additional monetary wealth. During the bond-selling campaigns the commercial banking system expanded credit in order to buy bonds—"created money," if you like. The government quickly paid out these funds to persons and to business concerns throughout the land. As the recipients went about their daily tasks they spent the funds, which passed from hand to hand again and again. A large portion came back as deposits to the commercial banking system (indeed, a considerable part never moved outside the system); another substantial portion was saved by individual persons and deposited in savings banks or used to purchase savings bonds, life insurance or other types of investments, or was held in the form of currency; another portion was retained by non-financial business concerns in the form of larger bank accounts needed to carry on the greater volume of business made necessary by the military requirements of the government. Whatever the channels traveled by these funds, they increased either the total assets or the liquid assets of virtually every sector of the population.

Despite the growth of these figures on the books, the country was not made "richer" by them, at least not to the extent of the apparent gain. A very large part of the production financed by the growth of the debt was "expendable" and was shot away during the war. No permanent results were left except the increase in purchasing power, the possibility that purchasing power might expand further in the future if debt management was maladroit, the obligation to pay the debt, and such war plants as could be converted to peacetime production. Furthermore, the increase in purchasing power, in the number of dollars outstanding, tended to raise prices, especially after the end of hostilities. Insofar as the price level was forced onto a new and higher plateau, the "real" value of every dollar diminished.

On the other hand, against all the evils of war, financial and otherwise, can be set two beneficial results: the idle men and idle plant capacity that existed in the country in 1939 were called into production during the war and greatly increased the country's output of goods and services; and the stimulus to production given by war requirements, together with the great volume of needs for houses, machinery, clothes and other items that accumulated during the war, served to keep the economy operating at a very high level during the immediate postwar period.

THE NEW IMPORTANCE OF GOVERNMENT SECURITIES

At the end of the war, not only did virtually each segment of society hold a larger dollar volume of government securities than before but, in addition, this amount was a greater percentage of total assets than in 1939, as may be seen in Table 1. For example, in December 1939 all member banks combined owned $14,328 million

TABLE 1

U.S. GOVERNMENT SECURITIES HELD BY LEADING CLASSES OF OWNERS, AS OF DECEMBER 1939 AND DECEMBER 1945

(Dollar Amounts in Millions)

	Holdings as of December 1939			Holdings as of December 1945		
Class of Owner	Amount	Percentage of Total Assets	Percentage of Liquid Assets	Amount	Percentage of Total Assets	Percentage of Liquid Assets
All member banks	$14,328	25.9		$78,338	56.7	
Other personal[a]	5,700		12.6	41,600		30.0
U. S. government agencies and trust funds[b]	5,605	e		27,031	e	
Legal reserve life insurance companies	5,373	18.4		20,583	46.0	
Trust funds[d]	3,100		68.9	14,000		88.1
Federal Reserve Banks[b]	2,551	13.5		24,262	53.8	
Nonfinancial business corporations	1,600		14.2	18,600		46.2
Unincorporated business	1,100		17.2	10,000		35.8
Financial business corporations[e]	500		29.4	2,700		56.3

Sources: Federal Reserve Bulletin, March 1940, p. 249; June 1946, p. 632; June 1948, p. 658. Board of Governors of the Federal Reserve System, Annual Report, 1945, p. 62. *Treasury Bulletin,* December 1945, p. 47; March 1946, p. 49. *Life Insurance Fact Book, 1948,* Institute of Life Insurance, New York, 1949, pp. 46-50.

a. Includes holdings of farmers and professional persons.

b. Government agencies and trust funds holdings consist of public marketable and special issues. Federal Reserve Bank holdings consist of public marketable issues. Guaranteed debt held by these two classes together as of December 1939 was $286 million.

c. Holdings of United States government securities are virtually 100 per cent of total assets.

d. Includes only amounts administered by corporate trustees.

e. Includes real estate companies, finance and credit companies, insurance agencies (not carriers), investment trusts, security brokers and dealers, holding companies not otherwise classified, etc.

of Treasury securities; the comparable figure in December 1945 was $78,338 million. Thus the net increase was $64,010 million. Between December 1939 and December 1945, federal obligations increased from 25.9 per cent of total assets of member banks to 56.7 per cent. Whereas in December 1939 only 14.2 per cent of the liquid assets of nonfinancial business corporations was represented by Treasury securities, the comparable figure at the end of the war was 46.2 per cent. These comparisons reveal in striking fashion one of the major impacts of the debt on the private economy and the new position attained by Treasury securities in the financial and business worlds.

The growth in holdings of Treasury securities meant, for certain classes of holders, that interest received on such investments became a much more significant part of their income than heretofore. Data are not readily available to give a clear picture of this aspect of the debt in relation to the economy as a whole, but in 1945 the earnings on direct and guaranteed United States government securities received by Reserve Banks, amounting to $139.5 million, exceeded their net earnings of $92.6 million by some 50 per cent. The $997 million of interest on Treasury obligations received by all member banks in that year exceeded their net profits of $794 million by 25.6 per cent. It has been estimated by the author that roughly 46 per cent of the "total interest and other income" received by life insurance companies in the same year was in the form of interest on their portfolios of government securities.

INTEREST BURDEN AND RATES

The interest burden of the debt was one aspect of this whole problem that attracted great attention at the end of the war; indeed, it has continued to receive much emphasis. As of September 1945 the computed annual interest charge on the whole debt amounted to $5,044 million, which represented a computed annual rate of 1.943 per cent. This figure of $5,044 million was 2.8 per cent of the 1945 national income of $182.7 billion. But some of the interest paid went back to government institutions, to the government's own investment accounts, and did not swell the national income in the hands of persons and businesses. The amount of interest paid, exclusive of that paid on securities held by government agencies and trust funds, is considerably less than the total paid, and is for many purposes a more significant concept.

The interest charge for the several types and maturities of debt differed considerably. In accordance with the government policy of "stabilized" interest rates, established in 1942 for public marketable securities, rates at the end of the war ranged from ⅜ per cent for the shortest-term debt, Treasury bills, to 2½ per cent for the longest-term bonds. Rates for nonmarketable debt—that is, for savings bonds and special issues—were somewhat higher. The coupon rates of some unredeemed issues sold before the war were considerably above these levels—in some instances higher than 3 per cent, and in the case of one issue, which had been sold in 1922, as high as 4¼ per cent. The market prices of these high-coupon securities, of course, rose sufficiently to bring their yields to new purchasers into substantial conformity with the wartime pattern of rates.

The yields of Treasury securities as of September 29, 1945 which, taken together, formed the so-called "Treasury yield curve," are shown in Figure 4. This curve shows how yields rose from the short-term to the long-term securities, the rise being more rapid in the short-term brackets.

THE MATURITY SCHEDULE AND THE PATTERN OF OWNERSHIP

Persons charged with managing the debt should take into consideration not only interest policy and the interest burden of the debt but also the maturity schedule of the debt and the "pattern of ownership"—the amounts and types of debt held by the leading classes of owners. The significance of the maturity schedule lies in the fact that it outlines, in chronological form, the sequence of problems that the debt managers must solve; that is, it shows by successive time periods the volume of obligations coming due that must either be paid off or refunded if the government's credit is to be preserved. The pattern of ownership indicates as of a given time the answer that has been found to the question: Who is to own how much and what kinds of government debt? Establishment and maintenance of the desired and desirable pattern of ownership is perhaps the chief problem of debt management. Study of the changes that take place in the pattern is one of the most revealing ways of analyzing debt management policy. These two facets of debt management, the maturity schedule and the pattern of ownership, are complementary and must be studied together.

The maturity schedule of the federal debt as of September 30,

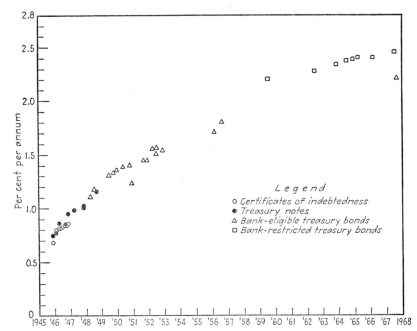

FIGURE 4. YIELDS OF TAXABLE TREASURY SECURITIES, SEPTEMBER 29, 1945
Source: Appendix Table 4.

1945, which at that time totaled $262,565 million, is shown on the left-hand side of Table 2. The right-hand section of the table presents the pattern of ownership, the portions of each class of debt then held by the several categories of owners: commercial banks, savings banks, insurance companies, Federal Reserve Banks, government agencies and trust funds, and all others.

The maturity schedule is divided chronologically into subheadings: short-term securities; intermediate securities; long-term securities; other securities. The "short-term securities" classification includes securities due within one year and securities payable on demand; the classification "intermediate securities" includes those with a maturity of longer than one year but coming due before January 1, 1951; "long-term securities" are defined as those maturing on January 1, 1951 or thereafter; in the category "other securities" are the obligations of the postal savings system, the Panama Canal loan and guaranteed securities. The dollar amounts of the individual maturity classes are also shown as percentages of the total debt.

In the pattern of ownership are presented the proportional amounts

TABLE 2

MATURITY SCHEDULE AND PATTERN OF OWNERSHIP OF THE FEDERAL DEBT, AS OF SEPTEMBER 30, 1945

	Maturity Schedule of the Federal Debt		Pattern of Ownership: Percentage of Each Maturity Class Held by Class of Owner[a]				
Security Class	Amount, in Millions	Per Cent	Commercial Banks	Stock Savings and Mutual Savings Banks	Life, Fire, Casualty and Marine Insurance Companies	U.S. Government Agencies and Trust Funds and Federal Reserve Banks	All Other Investors
Total direct and guaranteed debt	$262,565	100.00	30.20	4.02	8.35	19.20	38.40
Short-term securities							
Securities due within one year							
Bills	$ 17,018	6.48	11.91	.06	—	77.90	10.11
Certificates	35,072	13.36	46.10	.70	1.41	20.60	31.10
Total bills and certificates	$ 52,090	19.84	35.00	.49	.95	39.40	24.23
Other marketable issues due within one year							
Notes	$ 10,147	3.86	66.40	.50	1.00	13.75	18.30
Bonds	541	.21	43.00	.37	2.96	3.33	50.30
Conversion bonds	16	.01	20.60[b]	—	—	—	79.40[b]
Total notes and bonds	$ 10,704	4.08	65.20	.49	1.10	13.21	20.30
Special issues due within one year[c]	11,971	4.56	—	—	—	100.00	—
Total securities due within one year	$ 74,765	28.47	33.80	.41	.82	45.40	19.75

Securities payable on demand						
United States savings bonds	$ 46,741	17.80	1.77	.44	.57	.02	97.10
Treasury notes (savings series)	9,021	3.44	.64	.02	.16	.19	98.60
Depository bonds	516	.20	92.30	—	—	—	7.75
Matured debt	305	.12	—	—	—	—	—
Debt bearing no interest	2,086	.79	—	—	—	—	—
Commodity Credit Corporation	490	.19	46.90	—	—	—	53.10
Total securities payable on demand	$ 59,159	22.53	2.82	.37	.50	.05	96.50
Total	$133,924	51.01	20.30	.39	.68	25.80	52.80
Intermediate securities						
Securities due Oct. 1, 1946—Sept. 30, 1947						
Notes	$ 9,603	3.66	64.10	2.05	4.65	3.01	26.20
Conversion bonds of 1947	13	—	—	—	—	—	—
Special issues^e	2,893	1.10	—	—	—	100.00	—
Total due Oct. 1, 1946—Sept. 30, 1947	$ 12,509	4.76	49.50	1.58	3.58	25.00	20.15
Securities due Oct. 1, 1947—Sept. 30, 1948						
Notes	$ 3,748	1.43	77.20	1.36	.86	7.99	12.50
Bonds	5,250	2.00	71.50	2.00	3.46	4.44	18.55
Special issues^e	2,148	.82	—	—	—	100.00	—
Total due Oct. 1, 1947—Sept. 30, 1948	$ 11,146	4.25	59.50	1.39	1.92	24.02	12.95
Securities due Oct. 1, 1948—Sept. 30, 1949						
Bonds	$ 819	.31	44.40	.98	5.74	10.62	38.60
Special issues^e	1,718	.65	—	—	—	100.00	—
Total due Oct. 1, 1948—Sept. 30, 1949	$ 2,536	.96	14.20	.31	1.86	71.25	12.49

23

TABLE 2 (continued)

Maturity Schedule of the Federal Debt			Pattern of Ownership: Percentage of Each Maturity Class Held by Class of Owner[a]				
Security Class	Amount, in Millions	Per Cent	Commercial Banks	Stock Savings and Mutual Savings Banks	Life, Fire, Casualty and Marine Insurance Companies	U.S. Government Agencies and Trust Funds and Federal Reserve Banks	All Other Investors
Securities due Oct. 1, 1949—Dec. 31, 1950							
Bonds	$ 4,322	1.65	58.00	1.87	2.34	2.01	35.80
Special issues[c]	1,790	.68	—	—	—	100.00	—
Total due Oct. 1, 1949—Dec. 31, 1950	$ 6,113	2.33	41.00	1.32	1.65	30.60	25.30
Total	$ 32,304	12.30	48.50	1.37	2.50	29.60	18.10
Long-term securities							
Bonds due Jan. 1, 1951—Dec. 31, 1955	$ 46,485	17.70	62.20	6.85	9.10	2.95	18.20
Bonds due Jan. 1, 1956—Dec. 31, 1960	10,034	3.82	33.10	15.30	16.45	7.05	28.20
Bonds due Jan. 1, 1961—Dec. 31, 1965	7,688	2.93	20.00	19.02	13.02	4.34	43.80
Bonds due Jan. 1, 1966—Dec. 31, 1970	17,746	6.76	.36	12.11	46.20	12.67	28.50
Bonds due Jan. 1, 1971—Dec. 31, 1975	14,164	5.39	9.85	8.30	35.20	12.80	34.10
Total	$ 96,117	36.61	36.90	9.90	20.82	6.74	25.50
Other securities							
Postal savings system	$ 117	.04	11.10	.86	.86	30.80	56.40
Panama Canal loan	50	.02	2.00	—	—	—	98.00
Guaranteed securities[d]	53	.02	32.40	5.41	35.19	16.20	10.80
Total	$ 220	.08	12.72	1.47	6.86	20.60	58.40

Sources: Treasury Daily Statement, October 1, 1945, and Treasury Bulletin, December 1945, pp. 51-53.

a. Based on Treasury Survey of Ownership.
b. Includes all conversion bonds.
c. Maturities of special issues are in some cases assumed.
d. Other than Commodity Credit Corporation.

of each maturity class owned by the several classes of owners.[4] For example, the second line of Table 2 indicates that as of September 30, 1945, Treasury bills were outstanding in the amount of $17,018 million; this amount was about 6.5 per cent of the total debt. Of this total, commercial banks held 11.9 per cent, savings banks 0.06 per cent, United States government agencies and Reserve Banks together 77.9 per cent and all other investors 10.1 per cent.

From Table 2 we may see that on September 30, 1945, $74,765 million, or about 28.5 per cent of the debt was due within one year and that securities payable on demand amounted to another $59,159 million, or 22.5 per cent of the total. The sum of these two categories was $133,924 million, or 51 per cent of the total. On the same date only $96,117 million, or 36.6 per cent, of the debt had a maturity in excess of five years, that is, matured after January 1, 1951. The heavy concentration of maturities in short-term and demand obligations that then existed and that has continued to exist was a result of the wartime financing policies of the Treasury.

The fact that so large a proportion of the debt would mature quickly, coupled with the fact that prospective federal budgets evidently would not yield sufficient surpluses to retire all of the short-dated debt as it fell due, meant that the Treasury during the five years following V-J Day would be faced with difficult refunding problems. The additional fact that some 22 per cent of the debt was redeemable on demand—notably the E, F, and G savings bonds—meant that the refunding problem might at any time become acute.

Whether the refunding problem of the Treasury was to increase, to decrease or to stay the same was evidently going to depend in large measure on the length of maturities of new securities offered by the Treasury, the general fiscal policies of the government, and the business and financial needs of the owners of federal obligations.

As may be seen from the ownership pattern shown in Table 2, commercial banks held 30.2 per cent of the total debt on September 30, 1945, savings banks about 4 per cent, insurance companies 8.4

4. The percentages computed in the pattern of ownership are based on the data in the Treasury Survey of Ownership of securities issued by the United States government and by federal agencies. These data cover approximately 95 per cent of the amount of such securities owned by all banks and insurance companies in the United States. Thus the picture presented in the computations of the pattern of ownership in this study is not completely accurate. It is believed that they are sufficiently accurate, however, to permit the kinds of use made of them and the types of conclusions drawn from them in this study.

per cent, Federal Reserve Banks and government agencies and trust funds together 19.2 per cent, and all other investors 38.4 per cent. Reserve Banks and "government agencies and trust funds" (actually the Reserve Banks) owned 77.9 per cent of the Treasury bills outstanding and 45.4 per cent of total securities due in one year. They were the largest holders of these classes of debt, although commercial banks were the largest owners of Treasury certificates and of "other marketable issues due within one year." The bulk of the securities owned by savings banks and insurance companies, as would be expected, were long-term bonds. "All other investors"—including individuals, business concerns and private trusts—held over 97 per cent of the savings bonds and Treasury notes (savings series). Government agencies and trust funds held 100 per cent of the special issues.

Pattern of Ownership Not Accidental

The form and the character of the pattern of ownership at any given time are not accidental. The pattern is the result of a host of forces, among which are Treasury policy, Federal Reserve policy, the fiscal requirements of the government, the volume of assets possessed by various segments of society, the financial needs and investment behavior of the several classes of owners, and business and political prospects. In an over-all sense the pattern of ownership is, on the one hand, the end product of debt management and, on the other, a fundamental part of the frame of reference within which debt management policies must be formulated. Consequently this pattern is a basic element in an appraisal of the impact on the private economy of a huge government debt and of the policies followed in managing it.

THE MOST DISCUSSED QUESTIONS

The various problems that center around the question of ownership were not, as of V-J Day, the subject of as much comment as were some others, and have not since then been the object of as much controversy. It therefore seems desirable to outline briefly the major issues that have been in the forefront of public thinking and often a matter of dispute. The purpose in presenting this summary is not to offer definitive judgments, but simply to present a background for the theme of this book.

Should Rates Be Frozen?

The Treasury and the Federal Reserve authorities indicated to the financial world in 1942 that the market for federal obligations would be stabilized for the duration at the then existing level. Thus, the so-called "Treasury yield curve"—the rates of return yielded by Treasury securities of different maturities—came to be frozen. In 1942 the yield curve ran from ⅜ per cent for ninety-day Treasury bills—the shortest-term obligation employed—through ⅞ per cent for twelve-month Treasury certificates, up to 2½ per cent for the longest-term obligations. These rates continued throughout the war and were maintained at the termination of hostilities.

Almost immediately after V-J Day a controversy broke out regarding the desirability of continuing, under the new situation that developed with the return of peace, conditions that had been found useful in financing the war. Interest in the question became keen after the termination of the eighth—and last—war loan drive in the final months of 1945. As the financial community realized during 1946 that the Treasury was likely to have a budgetary surplus, rather than a deficit, the altered outlook still further stimulated interest in the topic.

Three major elements—as well as a multitude of minor ones—entered into the picture. There was the question of the desirability of fixed interest rates in a country that was, except in wartime, predominantly a free market economy. This question raised the problem of the functions that interest rates might or should perform in contemporary society. Even if it were agreed that a fixed, or at least a "regulated," interest rate was desirable, there remained the question whether the level of rates as fixed during the war was appropriate for the new conditions of peace.

Closely allied to this question were two others: First, was the shape of the wartime interest curve correct? That is, were the several rates of return obtainable from Treasury obligations of differing maturities "right," in view of the different risks and other characteristics of these maturities? Second, conceding that a regulated level of interest rates was appropriate, was it necessary that the curve be rigid? More specifically, might it not be desirable either to permit some fluctuation throughout the curve or at least at one end of it? Actually, of course, it was through the development of flexibility, particularly at the short end of the curve, that a way was found to shift slightly away from the rigid conditions of wartime.

Finally, since the control of interest rates was accomplished jointly by the Treasury and the Federal Reserve authorities, the very fact of their cooperation raised many questions regarding the duties and responsibilities of each, not only in respect to their joint undertakings in this area but, more importantly, in other areas where only one or the other was directly involved.

In particular, it was argued that the Reserve's policy of market support for the prices of Treasury obligations precluded the Reserve authorities from effectively exercising their statutory responsibility of credit control. The repeated requests of the Reserve authorities for new legislation that would increase their powers lent strength to this view. In turn, the Reserve authorities felt that so long as the policy of market support continued, their existing mandate was inadequate for the performance of their duties.

The Free Market Process Involved

The question of the appropriateness of fixed interest rates ultimately involved the whole issue of fluctuating prices and free markets in the contemporary American economy. Proponents of continued regulation seem to have relied chiefly on two lines of reasoning. It was argued that, in view of the overwhelming need for the continuance of a high-level economy in this country, government authority should employ every available means to this end, and regulation or manipulation of interest rates was, admittedly, an important tool for achieving this purpose. It was also contended that in view of the very large government debt and the catastrophic consequences that would follow from its mismanagement, not only to the financial institutions that were its chief owners but to the entire population, it was simply too dangerous to let the prices of Treasury obligations be influenced by the whims of "nervous holders" or fluctuate with the vagaries of the market place. Typical of these views is Seltzer's statement:

. . . a moderate rise in interest rates, reflecting a moderate restriction of bank credit, would be ineffective for precautionary purposes, and would be ineffective as an attack even upon the actual development of an inflationary rate of spending if the latter did not owe much to an expansion of direct bank lending to business or of new capital flotations.

Yet even a moderate rise in interest rates would be very unsettling and capable of quickly getting out of control. Once the movement became well started, no one would know in advance that it would be confined to moderate proportions (unless this were officially announced, in which case much of the efficacy would be sacrificed). All anyone could be sure of was that the long-established policy of low or declining interest rates had been withdrawn. Disorderly selling in considerable volume might develop, necessitating large-scale market support by the Federal Reserve System to avoid sharp price declines.

While a moderate rise in interest rates, reflecting a moderate restriction in the availability of credit, would be likely to be ineffective in curtailing the aggregate rate of spending, a sharp and substantial rise—say, to a level of 5 or 6 per cent for governments—would be another matter. Such a rise might well dampen inflation both because of the effects of the rate rise as such and because of the degree of credit restriction it would reflect. It is also capable of having the opposite result, however, if the rise were widely interpreted as reflecting upon the credit of the federal government.[5]

Opponents of fixed interest rates also presented two major arguments. First, it was asserted that rigidity of this character in the financial system inevitably led to numerous unforeseen results, both undesirable and far-reaching. The difficulty in which the Reserve System found itself in regard to credit control was but one example. The supposition that pegged prices for government securities made "all Treasury securities as good as money, or even better, because they bore interest" illustrated another type of difficulty. As Chandler said later, discussing the postwar situation:

. . . in pursuing its present policy [of stabilizing the yields of Treasury securities] the Federal Reserve cannot refuse to buy and monetize governments even if it disapproves of the purpose for which the new money will be used. Holders may exchange their securities for money to be used for (1) consumption, (2) purchase or construction of capital goods, (3) repayment of debt, (4) purchase of other securities, new or old, or (5) increase of idle balances. The Federal Reserve is powerless to prevent monetization of the government debt at the selected pattern of interest rates even if the new money is used directly to inflate spendings for consumption or capital goods or is used to supply liberal low-cost loans for these purposes.

In short, we are now on what may be called a "low-yield government security standard," for the Federal Reserve stands ready to monetize all the debt that others are unwilling to hold at the selected pattern of yields.[6]

Second, many opponents of the policy of fixed rates believed that controls inevitably spread in an economic system, and that a fixed

5. Lawrence H. Seltzer, "Is a Rise in Interest Rates Desirable?," *American Economic Review,* December 1945, pp. 843-44.
6. Lester V. Chandler, "Federal Reserve Policy and the Federal Debt," *American Economic Review,* March 1949, pp. 418-19.

money market would ultimately be found incompatible with free commodity markets or a free labor market. They feared that rigidities in one sector would necessarily lead to rigidities in others, and that measures originally taken to protect and stabilize the government's credit would finally result in regulated commodity prices, controlled wages and a minutely regimented economy. Their argument in effect was that when and as inflationary pressures developed in the economy—an eventuality which they considered inevitable sooner or later—public policy, instead of relying upon indirect measures to check price increases and boom tendencies, would readily turn to a reliance upon price ceilings, wage freezes, materials allocations and all the other direct controls that characterize a rigid and regimented economy. Many of the events of the latter part of 1950 and 1951 substantiated this position, albeit this was a period of national emergency.

The questions of the "correctness" of the level of rates and of the shape of the interest curve at any particular time necessarily involve judgment as to the goal of economic policy and appraisal of whether existing economic forces are compatible with the achievement of that goal. While there was general agreement that maintenance of a high-level economy was the proper objective of policy, this agreement did little more than sharpen the differences of opinion as to how that goal should be gained, and whether the character of the prevailing interest structure helped or hindered its attainment.

Differences of opinion existed as to whether this end could be achieved more readily through higher or lower taxes, more or less investment in business enterprise, free or controlled commodity prices, more or less welfare expenditure, an increased or a decreased volume of equity capital investment. Yet all these matters must be considered in deciding upon the "correctness" of any level and structure of interest rates. In short, the desirability of the interest curve—or, more properly speaking, the succession of curves—that the country has had since the end of the war is an extremely technical matter that cannot be resolved without an appraisal of the existing economic situation and a forecast of future economic conditions.

Other Considerations

For reasons that will be made evident later, the new conditions greatly enhanced the importance of the traditional legal and administrative powers of the Treasury. In the postwar period the powers became of far greater fiscal and monetary significance than had been the case in the prewar period. This circumstance, coupled with the policy of controlled interest rates, raised a question of the prospective position of the Reserve System itself in the postwar financial world. What is the function of a central bank in a controlled money market? The question has both theoretical and practical implications; a political as well as an economic meaning.

The fact that all financial institutions emerged from the war with very large holdings of Treasury obligations suggested that these institutions might have a new social responsibility—that of repository for a large segment of the public debt. This responsibility, if it existed, had to be assessed in the light of the widely differing sets of governmental regulations that controlled the operations of these institutions. The fact that the regulations did differ so widely assumed a new aspect in view of the common ownership of Treasury securities by these institutions.

The ability of financial institutions to increase or decrease their holdings of Treasury obligations at will, in a market pegged by the fiscal authorities themselves, raised new and puzzling problems of credit expansion and contraction. These problems induced the suggestion that the federal government should sponsor a far-reaching investigation, with the object of studying the structure of financial institutions, public and private, and determining whether the existing structure was well suited to the needs of the country. Considerable evidence was cited indicating that the structure was deficient in a number of respects.

Against this background may be traced the financial developments and the policies that were pursued after the return of peace in the summer of 1945.

Chapter 3

DEBT IMPACT ON THE TREASURY

ANY GREAT POLITICAL EMERGENCY, particularly that of war, necessarily magnifies the influence and authority of the executive branch of the government. The most important effect of the wartime growth of the debt on the Treasury was greatly to increase its fiscal and monetary powers, in a real if not in a legal sense. Its position was enhanced not so much by a mandate of the Congress as by the logic of the situation. The Treasury was the major creditor in the country, able to determine the rate of interest it was willing to pay, and thereby influence the rates that all other borrowers would pay. Its obligations exceeded those of all others combined, and its financial stability was fundamental to the stability of all banking institutions. Its power was buttressed by the fact that the federal government was a political and not a commercial borrower.

As Under Secretary of the Treasury Wiggins stated:

> No matter how jealous we may be of the freedoms of private enterprise, nor how abhorrent to our concept of such freedom that control and management by central government may be, the hard facts are that the management of our large public debt is such a dominant factor in the financial and economic life of the Nation that it is imperative that firm control of debt management be exercised by the Federal Government. This must continue as long as the public debt continues at its present relative size and proportions. . . .[1]

Thus, big debt produced, as it must, "big government," and the financial powers of the executive branch of the government grew at the expense of those of the legislative branch, of the central bank and of the private financial system.

TREASURY POLICIES AND THEIR IMPLICATIONS

Interest Policy

The preponderance of Treasury securities in the portfolios of all types of financial institutions on V-J Day has been discussed in the

1. A. L. M. Wiggins, Under Secretary of the Treasury, "Fiscal Policy and Debt Management," address before the Academy of Political Science, April 1, 1948.

preceding chapter. The solvency of these institutions depended upon the continued soundness of these assets, and the interest received on government debt had now become the major source of income for most financial institutions. Thus the earning power of capital invested in financial institutions was largely dependent upon Treasury policy.

The importance of the federal government's interest policy, however, was not limited to its influence on the profitability of financial institutions. As the basic interest rate in the money market, the yield on Treasury securities regulated, if it did not control, all other types of rates.

The Treasury's choice of maturities of new and refunding offerings exercises an important influence on the level of interest rates in different sectors of the money and investment markets, because of the great volume of federal securities outstanding and the frequency and size of the Treasury's refunding operations.[2]

On the one hand this control influenced the volume of credit and, on the other hand, the cost of funds for business, agriculture, home financing and other purposes. Furthermore, the interest burden in the budget, in excess of $5 billion annually (see Figure 5), was a fixed charge on the federal revenues, not directly susceptible to congressional control. Slight variations in the average rate necessarily led to substantial changes in the dollar charge. Finally, the policy pursued jointly by the Treasury and the Federal Reserve System in supporting the government bond market—which in turn meant a "frozen" pattern of rates for short-, intermediate- and long-term funds—signified that the central bank had, in the interest of maintaining "an orderly government bond market," sacrificed important methods of regulating credit conditions.

Debt Retirement

The policies followed by the Treasury in retiring debt were perhaps even of greater moment than interest policy. Moreover, so many variables entered into the whole subject of debt retirement that the general public could not grasp the complexities of the matter, even though subject to the far-reaching repercussions of debt redemption.

In analyzing this matter, it is necessary to make a distinction be-

2. *Monetary Policy and the Management of the Public Debt,* Replies to Questions and Other Material for the Use of the Subcommittee on General Credit Control and Debt Management [Reply by the Secretary of the Treasury], Joint Committee on the Economic Report, 82d Cong., 2d sess., Joint Committee Print, 1952, Part I, p. 115.

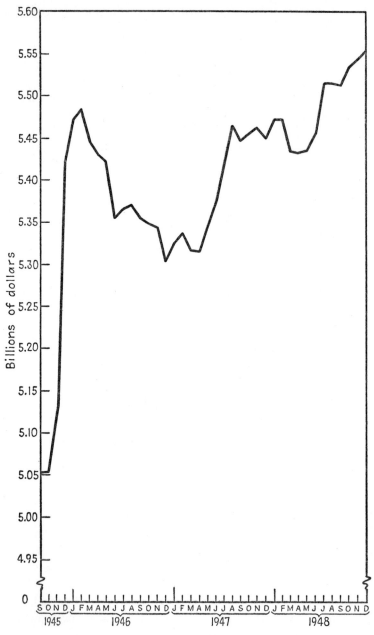

FIGURE 5. COMPUTED ANNUAL INTEREST CHARGE ON THE PUBLIC DEBT AND GUARANTEED OBLIGATIONS, SEPTEMBER 1945—DECEMBER 1948

Source: Appendix Table 5.

tween the marketable and the nonmarketable but redeemable debt. Granted the existence of surplus funds in the Treasury, the amount of the marketable debt repaid within a given time period was largely a matter of Treasury discretion, whereas the amount of nonmarketable savings bonds redeemed lay with the owners, since such obligations were repayable on demand.

In the first years after V-J Day four types of funds were available for repayment of the marketable debt, and each possessed different economic implications. During 1946 the excess borrowing of the eighth war loan was largely used for debt reduction. During 1947 and the early part of 1948 the Treasury surplus of tax receipts over expenditures was used for this purpose. Here a distinction must be made between the cash surplus and the surplus in the administrative budget, a point discussed further elsewhere. Finally, throughout the postwar period funds received from the sale of nonmarketable obligations were employed in reducing the volume of marketable debt outstanding; this operation must, of course, be viewed as refunding rather than as debt reduction.

Treasury Balances and Bank Reserves

The timing of debt retirement, as well as the Treasury's discretion in shifting its funds from the war loan accounts in the commercial banks to the government's accounts in the Reserve Banks, intimately affected the reserve position of the commercial banking structure. As the Secretary of the Treasury has stated, "The main objective of Treasury deposit policy is to smooth out the seasonal or other fluctuations in Treasury cash receipts." But he has also said that "On occasion, Treasury deposits . . . are used with the longer-run objective of tightening bank reserves in periods of inflationary pressure and easing them when the situation is reversed."[3]

Periods in which Treasury balances in the Reserve Banks were rising more rapidly (or falling less rapidly) than balances in the depositories, for example, January and October–November 1948, reveal the application of pressure on the reserve position of commercial banks. In periods when balances in commercial banks were growing at the expense of balances in the Reserve Banks, for example, August–September 1947, February–April 1948 and September 1948, the position of commercial banks tended to ease. This pressure, which

3. *Ibid.,* p. 43.

the Treasury was in a position to put on the commercial banks, probably equaled or exceeded, potentially, the power of the Reserve Banks to influence the reserve position of the commercial banks through open-market operations—at least so long as the Reserve Banks supported the prices of Treasury securities. Figure 6 shows the course of

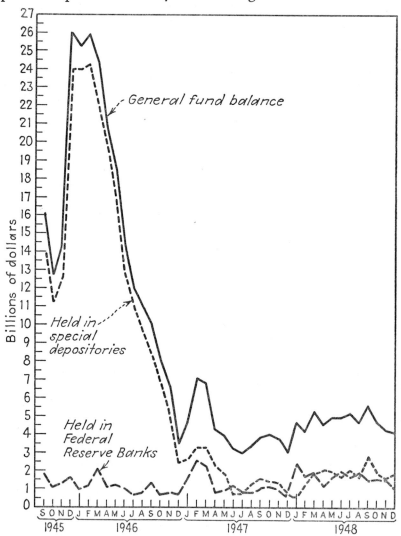

FIGURE 6. GENERAL FUND BALANCE OF THE U.S. TREASURY AND PORTIONS HELD IN SPECIAL DEPOSITORIES AND IN FEDERAL RESERVE BANKS, SEPTEMBER 1945—DECEMBER 1948

Source: Appendix Table 6.

the Treasury's general fund balance during the period September 1945—December 1948 and the portion of it held in special depositories, mostly commercial banks, and in the Federal Reserve Banks.

We should note in passing that quite different economic effects follow from retirement of debt held by one class of owners than from retirement of debt held by another. Repayment of debt is not necessarily deflationary, except in the case of obligations held by Federal Reserve Banks. Throughout the immediate postwar period fiscal authority endeavored, so far as possible, to retire bank-held debt. As regards Federal Reserve holdings this policy was directly deflationary; as regards commercial bank holdings it can better be described as reducing the possibilities of further inflation in the future. Chapter 11 discusses this point more fully.

Offering Policy

In addition to interest policy and debt retirement policy, the offering policy of the Treasury was a powerful instrument of fiscal control. The types of securities offered by the Treasury to the public, either for refunding purposes or to raise new money, of course exerted a compelling influence on the character of the portfolios of federal securities held by the several classes of owners. Of even greater consequence, perhaps, was the fact that the Treasury's offering policy was the chief mechanism for regulating the maturity schedule of the debt. Assuming that all maturing securities could not be repaid as they came due, the Treasury's offering policy thus determined the character and magnitude of the refunding problem in the future.

The official Treasury view since the end of the war has been that new offerings have been carefully gauged to meet the needs of investors and that the debt structure has been "tailored" to their requirements. Subsequent to the completion of the eighth war loan in December 1945, new offerings through June 1949 were virtually confined to three types: nonmarketable savings bonds, chiefly series E, F and G; nonmarketable special issues sold only to government agencies and trust funds; and marketable securities of a maturity no longer than twelve months (or, in one or two instances, thirteen months). The effect of this policy was to maintain the twelve-month, floating debt at high levels and to reduce the proportionate amount of the debt represented by intermediate- and long-term securities. This offering policy was pursued during periods when there was a federal deficit as well as when there was a surplus, during periods when inflationary pressures were present as well as when deflationary tendencies were uppermost, during periods when the prices of government securities rested on the "pegs" as well as when they were above the supported prices. Whether in fact it tailored the debt to the needs of those who must own it appears doubtful.

With the return of deficit financing in 1949, and faced with very large amounts of refundings in the three years 1950-1952, the Treasury began to deviate from this policy and to offer some obligations of somewhat larger maturity. The major change, however, came in the spring of 1951, and is discussed in Chapter 6.

DEBT MANAGEMENT AS SEEN BY THE TREASURY

We now are in a position to turn our attention to the major issues in debt management raised by Treasury spokesmen.

In the summer of 1945, just before the end of the war, Secretary of the Treasury Morgenthau summarized the borrowing principles followed by the government during the war as follows:

> The necessary funds should be raised in such a manner as to minimize the risk of inflation.
> The securities offered should be those best suited to the needs of investors.
> The cost of financing the war should be kept at a reasonable level.[4]

This was hardly a complete statement. No mention was made of the steady decline in the average maturity of the debt, of the large and growing use made of nonmarketable obligations, of the elimination of tax-exempt securities and the rapid growth in the number and types of securities outstanding. Only indirect reference was made to the steady decline in the average interest cost of the debt.

Regard to Needs of Investors

Some months later, in November 1945, Under Secretary of the Treasury Bell, in a speech that surveyed the financing of the war, made a more explicit statement regarding the ways in which different types of debt had been adapted to the needs of investors and to the results achieved under that policy.

4. *Summary Report of the Secretary of the Treasury,* 1945, p. 34.

First of all we have arranged the debt so that each investor class holds securities which are appropriate to it. Over 60 per cent of the securities held by the commercial banks are due or callable in less than five years. On the other hand, insurance companies hold only about 10 per cent of their portfolios in the form of securities due or callable within five years, and 90 per cent in longer categories. Individuals largely hold Series E, F, and G savings bonds, which they may either cash when the need arises or continue to hold at an ascending rate of interest. About half of the holdings of individuals is in the form of Series E bonds, a security designed exclusively for the average small investor.

Corporations other than banks and insurance companies hold close to one-third of their Government securities in the form of savings notes—a highly flexible instrument which may be turned in on taxes, redeemed for cash or held for investment at increasing rates of interest. The bulk of the remainder of corporation holdings is in the form of short-term securities, largely certificates of indebtedness.

This "tailoring" of securities to the needs of the investor is a healthy thing for the economy.[5]

Mr. Bell's remarks gave as comprehensive recognition to the needs of the investor as an important factor in debt management as, perhaps, any pronouncement by an official spokesman. His statement also seems to have recognized, at least by implication, the importance of the pattern of ownership and the way in which the debt was distributed among the several classes of owners. Whether the policy of tailoring the debt to the needs of investors—and of the economy—was pursued as meticulously during the next three years as Mr. Bell's statement implied it had been during the war is questionable.

Secretary Vinson on Interest Rates

During the autumn of 1945 Secretary of the Treasury Vinson made a series of statements regarding the future course of interest rates. Speaking at Peoria, Illinois, on September 3, he said:

Interest rates . . . should continue low for a long time to come. It is self-evident that this is in the interest of people as taxpayers. Not as evident, but just as valid, is that low interest rates—what the economists call a "cheap money policy"—benefits the people as consumers, as workers, and as citizens.[6]

5. Daniel W. Bell, Under Secretary of the Treasury, "War Financing—Some Implications for the Future," address at the annual dinner meeting of the Association of Stock Exchange Firms, November 19, 1945.

6. Fred W. Vinson, Secretary of the Treasury, address at Peoria, Illinois, September 3, 1945.

A week after Under Secretary Bell's speech, Secretary Vinson, speaking at Indianapolis, again touched on the subject:

The interest burden or carrying charge on the debt is well within the ability of the economy to bear; but it is large and it should serve as a constant reminder to us that the burden of the debt will be far greater if we permit our national income to fall. It should be remembered also that the burden would be much greater if the level of interest rates were only slightly higher.[7]

And again:

A policy of low interest rates clearly benefits the taxpayer by making possible a lower level of Government expenditures and, consequently, a lower level of taxation than would otherwise be possible. More important, low interest rates will be a stimulating force in the economy generally . . .[8]

These statements, which were among the earliest indications in the postwar period of the Treasury's thinking on this point, clearly showed that the wartime pattern of rates—originally frozen as a war measure—would be continued on the return of peace. No aspect of debt management and no policy of the Treasury was subsequently discussed more, and none proved more controversial.

It is perhaps significant that in these early statements Secretary Vinson emphasized two aspects of the interest problem: the burden that interest charges imposed on the budget and the supposedly self-evident virtues of a "cheap money." To many persons these virtues were not self-evident, particularly in the inflationary situation that prevailed during the immediate postwar period—although in all fairness it must be stated that at the time Secretary Vinson spoke, the official Washington view was that deflation was more to be feared than inflation. In any event, it was a new development in the economy for the Treasury rather than the Federal Reserve System to assume publicly—in a situation other than that of an emergency—the responsibility for interest policy; and no mention was made in Secretary Vinson's speeches of the monetary effects and other implications of a controlled money market in peacetime.

Five months later, in May 1946, shortly after the end of the boom in government bonds that followed the eighth war loan, Assistant Secretary of the Treasury Foley explicitly called public attention

7. *Idem,* "Transition from War to Peace and Prosperity," address before the Indiana State Chamber of Commerce, November 27, 1945.
8. *Ibid.*

to the level of rates prevailing and to the fact that the wartime rate structure had not changed.

The interest rates at which the Treasury borrows money have not changed, maturity-for-maturity, since Secretary Vinson took office. They are low, measured by most historical standards—although long-term rates are not so low, for example, as those prevailing in Great Britain in the last decade of the Nineteenth Century, nor are short-term rates as low as those prevailing in the United States during most of the thirties.[9]

Secretary Snyder on Interest Rates

Six months later Secretary of the Treasury Snyder was prepared to argue that higher interest rates would be of no aid in controlling inflation.

Let us turn now for the moment to the subject of interest rates. It is sometimes urged that higher interest rates would aid in the control of inflationary forces.

It is my view that, for the present, no anti-inflationary purpose would be served by increasing interest rates. This is because it would interfere with the stability of the Government bond market and would introduce uncertainties, which themselves might contribute to inflation. The immediate effect of higher interest rates might very well be to increase rather than to decrease the volume of currency and deposits. This is because the typical investor's reaction to the higher rates might be "wait and see," rather than "run and invest."[10]

So, within so short a space as ten months, two Secretaries of the Treasury told the American people that low interest rates "will be a stimulating force in the economy generally" but that "no anti-inflationary purpose would be served" by higher rates. During the controversy between the Treasury and the Federal Reserve System in the autumn of 1950 and the spring of 1951, Treasury spokesmen reiterated, with ever-greater emphasis, views virtually identical with those cited.

A captious critic would be justified in concluding that the Treasury was uncertain about the effects of a flexible interest rate, or that flexible rates were a one-edged but not a two-edged weapon, or that the Treasury, focusing its attention on the budgetary burden of the interest charge, was unwilling to assume the responsibilities

9. Edward H. Foley, Assistant Secretary of the Treasury, address before the National Association of Mutual Savings Banks, May 16, 1946.
10. John Snyder, Secretary of the Treasury, "The Budget and the Problems of Managing the Public Debt," address before the American Bankers Association, September 24, 1946.

entailed in its new postwar power to regulate interest rates. During the next twelve months a few cautious increases in rates were undertaken. But attention was mainly concentrated, both then and later, on the desirable level of rates, rather than on the underlying problems—the size of the floating debt, the Treasury's refunding problem and the desirability of a controlled money market in a purportedly free economy.

Bank Debt Retired, Savings Bonds Sold

In his speech of May 1946, Assistant Secretary Foley also dealt with two other Treasury policies that were to be of increasing importance—the reduction in the debt held by commercial banks and the continued sale of savings bonds.

It has been our desire to concentrate the reduction in the debt, as far as possible, upon securities held by banks. It has, consequently, been gratifying to the Treasury that the government security holdings of the Federal Reserve Banks and weekly reporting member banks—the only banks concerning which data are available—have declined by $4.3 billion since the end of the year—a decline equal to almost three-quarters of the net reduction in the total debt occurring during this period.[11]

Almost all the funds used for debt reduction during the spring of 1946 were the excess borrowings of the eighth war loan in November and December 1945. Thus the debt retired during the spring of 1946 was in substance a "refunding in reverse"—first money was borrowed, and then debt was retired—though it may be doubted if the Treasury planned it that way. Since a large part of the funds raised in the eighth war loan were borrowed at the higher, long-term rates, and since the obligations redeemed in the spring of 1946 were mostly short-term funds carrying low rates, this "refunding in reverse" tended to raise the interest cost and was not in accord with the Treasury's announced aim of minimizing the interest burden. Furthermore, since it was Treasury policy at this time to retire only short-dated, maturing obligations, and since the banks were the largest holders of this type of security, it was not surprising that debt reduction was concentrated in the bank-held debt. In view of the fact that Treasury policy called for retirement of bank-held debt, the Treasury's gratification regarding this fortunate confluence of circumstances was understandable.

11. Foley, *op. cit.*

In connection with the continuance of sales of savings bonds Assistant Secretary Foley said:

An important aspect of the Treasury's policy with respect to debt management at the present time is to encourage the people to buy and hold savings bonds. We are sometimes asked, "With a steadily declining debt, why is the Treasury continuing to push the sale of savings bonds?"

The answer is, of course, that the Treasury is pushing the sale of savings bonds, not to obtain money to finance the deficit but to combat inflationary pressures which are still continuing from the war, and which will continue a while longer, and to secure a better distribution of the debt.

Every dollar of savings bonds sold today permits us to retire a dollar of debt held by banks. Every dollar which is used to purchase savings bonds and which would otherwise be spent is a dollar removed from the present inflationary markets for consumers' goods, and a dollar added to our backlog of purchasing power saved up against the day when goods will be plentiful.[12]

These general sentiments were frequently repeated. For example, in October 1946, Secretary Snyder said:

The Treasury has two main objectives in promoting the sale of savings bonds. The first is to continue and, if possible, to further the wide distribution in the ownership of the public debt. In doing this we maintain an important element of stability in our economy . . .

The second major objective of the savings bond program is to aid in combating inflation. It does this by drawing purchasing power off the market at a time when goods are scarce. . . .

The purchase of savings bonds also helps to combat inflation by making possible the retirement of additional amounts of bank-held debt.[13]

Results of Refunding Policy

These statements merit some attention. During the immediate postwar period, when inflationary pressures were strong, the continuing sale of savings bonds was undoubtedly a beneficial policy. Such sales absorbed purchasing power that might otherwise have flowed into the markets for goods and services, as Secretary Snyder pointed out. They also served to widen the ownership of the debt, unquestionably a desirable objective, in that they helped to refund bank-held debt and to place a part of the debt in the hands of individuals, a "counterinflationary" procedure. Funds received from the sale of savings bonds over and above the volume of redemptions,

12. *Ibid.*
13. John Snyder, Secretary of the Treasury, "The Role of the Savings Bond Program in Today's Economy," address at a savings bond rally sponsored by the Federal Reserve Bank of St. Louis, October 23, 1946.

during periods when the Treasury had a cash deficit, also helped to cover such a deficit. Assistant Secretary Foley did not mention this, perhaps because the Treasury was operating with a surplus at the time he spoke. But in a comprehensive survey of results to be achieved by the sale of these bonds, this purpose is surely to be mentioned. The fact that the results achieved by the continuous sale of savings bonds change as the condition of the federal budget changes is an interesting element in this operation and an aspect of debt management that merits consideration.

On the other hand, in view of the comparatively high rate of interest carried by savings bonds, their sale did not work in the direction of minimizing the interest burden. Indeed, when the entire postwar offering policy of the Treasury is considered, the suspicion arises that the regulation of the rate of interest paid to particular classes of debt holders was an underlying, unacknowledged policy that was as influential as the objective of minimizing the burden as a whole. Finally, notwithstanding the fact that the continuous offering of savings bonds has, with the passage of time, become entrenched in our financial structure, it seems legitimate to inquire whether these sales are necessarily desirable as a permanent fixture. If the sale of savings bonds is admittedly a useful device for combating inflation, might not the temporary cessation of such sales be helpful in checking deflation? On this point the fiscal authorities have been silent.

The Maturity Schedule in Theory and Fact

In his speech of September 24, 1946, Secretary Snyder also made one of the few official references to the maturity schedule of the debt and to its suitability to the needs of the investing public.

One aspect of public debt management which is frequently discussed has to do with the size of the short-term debt. The distribution of the debt by maturity classes is primarily a function of the distribution of ownership— that is to say, securities are tailored to the needs of the various investor classes as much as possible. Thus short-term securities go to the banks and to business organizations. Almost half of bank holdings of securities are due or callable in less than one year. In the case of nonfinancial corporations four-fifths of United States Government security holdings are either presentable on demand or fall due within one year.

In contrast, longer-term securities are designed for long-term savings investors, such as insurance companies, savings banks, and individuals. Three-fourths of the Federal securities held by insurance companies and savings banks are not due or callable for more than ten years. In the case of individuals, more than two-thirds of United States securities held are savings bonds, which were designed to avoid the risk of market fluctuations. . . .

Accordingly, this tailoring of securities to meet investors' needs sets the maturity structure almost automatically; and has resulted in a substantial volume of short-term securities.[14]

This statement hardly did justice to the influence exercised by the Treasury's offering policy on the maturity schedule of the debt. After the completion of the eighth war loan in December 1945, the Treasury ceased offering marketable securities of longer than twelve months' maturity, and maturing obligations that were not redeemed were refunded into this short-term paper. Thus the public was not given the opportunity to buy marketable issues with a maturity longer than twelve (or, in one or two instances, thirteen) months.

From September 1945 through March 1947 the volume of ninety-day bills outstanding was maintained virtually constant, at $17 billion; between April 1947 and December 1948 the total of bills outstanding gradually declined, to $12.2 billion. From December 1945 to December 1948 the total short-term debt maturing within twelve months—bills, certificates, notes and bonds, including special issues—ranged between $80.2 and $61.6 billion, or between 28.6 and 24.4 per cent of the total debt; marketable twelve-month debt (i.e., exclusive of special issues) ranged between $68.6 and $42.3 billion.

During this period market conditions would have permitted successful offerings of marketable federal securities of a maturity longer than twelve months to have been made on a number of occasions. Thus the maintenance of so large a volume of short-term, floating debt was a direct result of Treasury policy, not of the compulsion of the market. The usefulness to investors or to the economy of the country of so large a volume of short-term obligations has not been demonstrated, or ever even argued by the Treasury authorities in any explicit fashion. And certainly some of the problems experienced by the Treasury in 1950 and 1951, following the outbreak of fighting in Korea, were immediately traceable to this policy.

14. Snyder, "The Budget and the Problems of Managing the Public Debt."

Changes in 1947

In 1947, for the first time since the end of the war, some slight shifts in the interest structure were engineered, the volume of Treasury bills outstanding began to decline, and a few changes were made in the amount and type of marketable securities offered for public purchase. Sufficient time had also elapsed for Treasury spokesmen to be able to review the not inconsiderable accomplishments since V-J Day. Speaking in July, Secretary Snyder said:

During the fiscal year just ended the public debt—including guaranteed obligations held outside the Treasury—was reduced by $11,522 million, of which $754 million was the result of the budget surplus. The total amount outstanding on June 30 was $258,376 million. This compares with $279,764 million at the postwar peak which was reached on February 28, 1946. The major part of this reduction in the debt has been accomplished by reducing the Treasury cash balance from its postwar peak to its present level. Future reductions in the debt can occur only from budget surpluses.

Practically the entire decline in the debt since the peak has been in the holdings of the commercial banking system. Holdings of debt by nonbank investors as a whole have remained practically constant. This concentration of debt reduction in bank holdings has been in accordance with the Treasury policy of spreading the ownership of the debt as broadly as possible, and has helped to alleviate inflationary pressures during the reconversion period. This debt reduction program was made possible by the Treasury's policy of maintaining a substantial portion of the debt in short-term securities.

This policy maintained the liquidity of the banking system and put a large portion of the debt in a form in which it could be easily retired. As a consequence of the liquidity of the banks' Government security portfolios, the large turnover of funds incident to the debt reduction program occurred without disturbance to the money market. The reduction in the debt has naturally resulted in a substantial decline in the proportion of short-term securities, as well as in the proportion held by banks. The two-fold character of this decline has consequently resulted in keeping the maturity distribution and the form of the debt well adjusted to the character of its ownership.[15]

This was one of the first instances in which a Treasury spokesman dwelt explicitly on the different sources of cash available for debt retirement.

Under Secretary of the Treasury Wiggins made the operational side of debt retirement still clearer, and designated the several phases of postwar debt management. Speaking of the situation that

15. John Snyder, Secretary of the Treasury, "Financial Operations of the United States Government during the Fiscal Year 1947," *Treasury Bulletin,* August 1947.

existed in February 1946, when the debt was at its peak and the Treasury had cash balances of $26 billion, he said:

With these factors, the correct policy of debt management was clear. It was to utilize the excess cash balance beyond budget needs for the retirement of the debt. The proper place for such retirement was in the commercial banking field. This policy was followed, with the result that by the end of December, 1946, when cash balances had been brought down to a peacetime working level, the total debt had been reduced by over $20 billion, of which $19 billion were taken out of the commercial banking system. . . .

We then moved into the second phase of postwar debt management. From January 1, 1947, through June 30, 1947, there was a budget surplus of approximately $3/4 billion. This represented the reduction of the public debt which it was possible to achieve during this six-month period from an excess of receipts over expenditures. However, during this same period, it was possible to reduce the holdings of the commercial banking system by $6 billion through the application of this surplus, through the use of the proceeds from the sale of Savings Bonds to the public, and through the use of the excess of the cash operating surplus over the budget surplus. The inflationary pressures had increased during the period and, therefore, the economic objective of an anti-inflationary debt management policy was paramount.[16]

Secretary Snyder's Review

In May 1948, Secretary Snyder gave a still more complete exposition of the Treasury's program during the preceding three years. Speaking before the National Association of Mutual Savings Banks, he said:

I should like to review the history of the management of the debt since the debt reached a peak of $280 billion in February, 1946. The Victory Loan of two months earlier had been our last great drive for funds. War costs had begun to taper off, and we no longer needed a Treasury cash balance of the proportions for which the emergencies of the preceding years had called. A debt pay-off program was therefore inaugurated. It has brought the debt down to the current total of $252 billion. This pay-off program which we have carried out fell into three periods. From the end of February, 1946, to the close of the year, the debt was reduced by $20 billion through the application of cash funds received from the Victory Loan. During the calendar year 1947, the next phase of the pay-off program, we were able to cut the debt by $2.5 billion. The cash left over from the Victory Loan had been expended by this time, so that debt reduction during 1947 had to come from the budget surplus —and was, in fact, just about equal to that surplus. The third phase of the debt pay-off program occurred during the first four months of this year. In those few months, we reduced the debt by $4.7 billion—almost twice the re-

16. Wiggins, *op. cit.*

duction for the entire calendar year 1947. The money for this program came from our budget surplus of $6 billion accumulated since January 1, 1948. The rest of the surplus has been added temporarily to the cash balance. Part of this remainder may eventually be used for debt reduction—although some of it will be needed to meet new requirements for national defense and international aid during the months to come.

As bankers, I am sure that all of you are familiar with the policy behind the debt pay-off program as it has been conducted. Increasing inflationary pressures in the economy during the past two years have made it imperative that fiscal and monetary policy be directed to combating further increases in prices. The very fact that the Treasury was receiving more money in taxes than it was paying out through its expenditures was of major anti-inflationary importance. Hand in hand with this development has been our Treasury policy, during the period, of aiming at a reduction in the Federal security holdings of the commercial banking system. In seeking to achieve this objective, we have found that our wartime program of fitting securities to the needs of the various investors has paid dividends. You will remember that during the war we issued a large volume of short-term bills and certificates to the banking system. As a result, our job of paying off the debt held by banks has been considerably simplified. It is gratifying to us that, since the peak of the debt, nonbank holdings of Federal securities have gone up by about $3 billion, so that the reduction in holdings by commercial and Federal Reserve Banks has actually been greater than the reduction in total public debt. On February 28, 1946, commercial and Federal Reserve Banks held $117 billion of Federal securities. At the present time, they hold $86 billion. This decline of $31 billion represents a reduction of more than 25 per cent in commercial and Federal Reserve Bank portfolios of Government securities in just a little over two years. This is a substantial achievement. We could hardly have laid out, and we certainly would not have dared forecast, a program as successful as this when we stood at the threshold of debt pay-offs back in 1946. . . .

This nonmarketable part of the debt may go up by something like $3 billion during the year ahead, thus permitting a reduction in the total of the marketable debt. This is due primarily to the intensity with which we are pressing —and will continue to press—our savings bond campaign. It is also because of the further accumulation of social security money and other Government trust fund receipts.[17]

CONCLUSION

The necessities of war finance so magnified the importance of debt management that in the postwar period it became a major concern of the Treasury and of the economy as a whole. In the long run, the budgetary situation was, of course, the controlling factor

17. John Snyder, Secretary of the Treasury, "Mutual Savings Banks and the Public Debt," address before the National Association of Mutual Savings Banks, May 24, 1948.

in the retirement or the growth of the debt; but for considerable periods of time the effect of surpluses or deficits could be concealed, reinforced or counteracted by variations in the size of the general balance, by employment of the resources of government trust funds and by the administrative flexibility that derives from the distinction between the administrative and the cash budget. The complete discretion of the Treasury to set the terms of new offerings, and hence the maturity schedule of the debt, its ability to use the resources of the government trust funds in buying and selling marketable securities and its freedom to vary the amounts of the general fund balance carried in the Reserve Banks and in the commercial banking system gave it immense power.

The growth of the debt transformed the legal authority and traditional administrative discretion of the Treasury into a concentration of monetary controls. The failure of the Congress to give some general indication of its wishes regarding the maturity schedule of the debt, the level and structure of interest rates, the types of obligations to be issued and the principles to be pursued in managing the debt left unimpaired the influence and authority that accrued to the Treasury as a result of wartime developments.

On the whole, Treasury policy during the immediate postwar period was reasonably clear, even though explanations of policy did not always appear entirely consistent. Interest rates were held within a relatively narrow range. As was often stated, this policy had the virtues of stabilizing the market for federal securities and, in a technical sense, of preserving confidence in the government's credit. It also had the result of continuing, under peacetime conditions, a regulated money market and of minimizing any difficulties inherent in the continuous refunding process that went on.

Because the rate structure was frozen at a low level early in the war, stabilization of interest rates had the effect of minimizing the interest burden imposed on the budget. But "cheap money" was also defended on other grounds: as a stimulative influence when business recession was in prospect and as a matter of no consequence when inflationary pressures were present.

The desirable objective of spreading the ownership of the debt was furthered by continuing sales of nonmarketable securities, supplemented by special drives to increase the sales of such securities. In September 1945, for example, the total of nonmarketable debt—savings bonds and special issues—amounted to about 25.5 per cent of the total debt; by December 1948 it had grown to 34.3 per cent. Yet this policy did not tend to minimize the interest burden, since many of these securities carried the highest rates of any obligations issued. An equally important result of the continuing sales was the money they provided to offset the continuing flow of redemptions of E, F and G bonds, and thus to give this block of demand debt the semblance of a self-sustaining character.

Offerings of marketable securities were almost entirely confined, before 1949, to short-term obligations. While it was alleged that this procedure was designed to "tailor" the maturity schedule to the needs of the investing public, it has not been demonstrated that this was the result. There can be no doubt, however, that this policy shortened the average maturity of the debt, increased the volume of refundings above the level that would have prevailed had longer maturities been employed and—since short-term paper carried the lowest rate of return—worked in the direction of lowering the interest burden. Debt retirement, as was proper in an inflationary situation, was concentrated in the bank-held debt. Since the commercial banks and the Federal Reserve Banks held the bulk of the short-term, maturing debt, this result was not difficult to achieve.

Finally, the record shows an extreme reluctance on the part of the Treasury to abandon wartime policies or to yield any of the powers or prerogatives devolving upon it as a result of the emergency. If the Congress had imposed some general limits on Treasury discretion—narrow or confining limitations would, of course, not have been practicable—or if the Treasury itself had pursued different policies, its enhanced monetary powers would not have remained so large. At the least, the prospect for the indefinite continuance of these powers would have diminished, and the natural tendency for big debt to produce big government could have been moderated.

In the absence of some official expression as to the desirability in the future of flexible interest rates, of a long-term program of debt retirement, of some sort of maturity schedule other than one in which half of the debt was payable on demand or due within twelve months, the supposition must be that the executive branch looked forward to an indefinite continuance of the regulated money market that began during the war and to the continued concentration of monetary powers in the Treasury.

Chapter 4

DEBT IMPACT ON THE FEDERAL RESERVE[1]

WHAT IS THE PROPER FUNCTION of a central bank in a controlled money market? What should be the relation of a central bank to the sovereign political power under conditions that require stability in the prices of the obligations of the state? What is the proper sphere of activity and course of action for a central bank when more than half of its assets consist of government securities and when its portfolio policies will inevitably be one of the major forces influencing not only the market prices of such securities, but also the level of interest rates, the availability of credit and, perhaps, the general course of business activity?

The correct answers to these questions were not evident on the termination of hostilities. Nor are they entirely clear now. When at some future date experience with debt management and the re-examination of central banking theory have combined to produce a body of doctrine applicable to this new situation, the position and the function of central banks will probably be seen to have changed substantially since 1939.

If we are not as yet able to formulate precisely the proper duties and responsibilities of central banks in the new, postwar situation, it is, nevertheless, possible to describe the policies actually pursued by the Federal Reserve System. In general the Reserve authorities sought to control the inflationary situation inherited from the war while maintaining a reasonable degree of stability in a number of markets simultaneously, particularly the market for Treasury securities. Stability in the market for federal obligations meant, on the one hand, stability in the whole interest structure; on the other hand, it meant that the amount of credit available could be controlled only with great difficulty if at all. It is in this connection that the possibility of contradiction in Reserve policy appeared. The question has repeat-

1. A revision and elaboration of the author's paper, "Notes on Federal Reserve Policy, August 1945—June 1948," published in the *Journal of Finance*, June 1949. Permission to use this material is gratefully acknowledged.

edly been raised whether frozen interest rates might not make impossible effective control of credit conditions and of the price level. While Reserve operations in the money market have received the most consideration, that should not detract attention from the steps taken to maintain reasonable stability in the stock market, in commodity prices, in the volume of credit outstanding—particularly consumer credit—and even in the labor market.

Before tracing changes in Reserve portfolios of government securities, in the amount of Reserve credit available, in alterations in interest rates and in the use made of direct credit controls, it is desirable to mention briefly a number of elements present in the postwar situation. Hitherto in this study they have either not been commented on at all or have been mentioned only in passing. They nevertheless formed important parts of the economic environment within which Reserve policy was formulated.

THE ENVIRONMENT OF FEDERAL RESERVE POLICY

One of the chief elements in the formation of Federal Reserve policy was the necessity that the Treasury be continuously able to refund its maturing obligations on favorable terms. During the four years ended in December 1948, debt due within twelve months continuously amounted to between 24 and 29 per cent of the total debt, and debt redeemable on demand was at all times only a slightly smaller percentage. The two classes of debt together were continuously about half of the total securities outstanding. Under such circumstances a regulated, stable market for government securities was, at least in the eyes of persons carrying the responsibility for debt management, a necessity.

Other Agencies of Control

Another element in the environment within which Reserve policy operated was the rise of significant mechanisms of monetary and credit control that lay outside its competence. This development, which began before the war, was accelerated in the postwar period, and falls into a number of distinct parts.

In the first place there was the enhanced position of the Treasury in the money market, a result of the growth of the debt and of the budget. The nature of its position was made manifest by the importance adhering to the interest rates attached to new issues of government securities, by its administrative discretion regarding the use of budgetary cash surpluses and by its ability to influence the investment policies of government agencies and trust funds. These agencies and trust funds held a large and growing volume of resources. Moreover, these resources, at least in part, could be and at times were used to influence the prices of marketable government securities. Such operations largely paralleled the powers inherent in the Reserve System's open-market operations and affected the reserves of commercial banks.

A number of expanding governmental agencies were in a position to extend credit, or to insure credit extended by others. The policies and operations of these agencies were not subject to control by the Reserve authorities. Though these agencies operated in virtually every type of lending—business, agriculture, housing, consumer credit, etc. —they were of special significance in the mortgage field and the market for agricultural credit. In the aggregate, these circumstances meant that the portion of the financial system directly sensitive to Reserve credit policy was much smaller than twenty years earlier.

Business Needed Financing

A third factor in the environment was the great demand on the part of business for credit and capital in the immediate postwar years. This demand had not been anticipated, particularly in view of the large liquid assets held by business concerns at the end of the war. Nevertheless, the commercial and agricultural loans of member banks more than doubled, growing from $8.2 billion in June 1945 to $19.4 billion by the end of 1948. The bulk of this rise took place in 1946 and 1947; during this period the growth reached almost $8.2 billion, an amount equal to the total outstanding in June 1945. During the years 1946, 1947 and 1948 the volume of securities sold by business corporations to raise new money amounted, respectively, to $3.3, $4.6 and $5.6 billion. These totals greatly exceeded the volume of new money security flotations for any previous year since 1929.

This demand for financing was especially significant in view of the wartime growth of Treasury obligations in the hands of persons and business concerns and the uses to which these holdings were put. The appearance in private hands of such great holdings of governments, together with the fact that the prices of federal obligations were stabilized, in effect introduced a new element into investment and property management. The combination of these two circumstances meant that for many portfolio managers, trustees and treasurers of business concerns, the government portfolio became virtually a second cash account. The easy access to cash afforded by holdings of government securities whose prices were pegged and, conversely, the inducement offered by a stabilized market to convert cash—ordinarily a nonearning asset—into an earning asset, widened the range of procedures feasible in private financial management. Not the least consideration was the lack of risk involved in placing temporarily surplus funds in the government securities market. One consequence of this broadening of the alternatives open to the private financial manager was to make more difficult and uncertain the adjustment of credit to the legitimate needs of the economy. Another result was to make probable large-scale liquidation of Treasury securities by "nonbank" holders when and as more attractive investment outlets appeared.

The Economy Had to Be Strong

Finally, great political importance was attached to the monetary and economic stability of the United States in the years immediately following the war. The United States emerged from the conflict the only major power that had not been devastated, and it had a manifest obligation for leadership in international reconstruction.

Its financial position had to be unquestioned and its economy had to operate at a high level. These were necessary conditions for "winning the peace," and in both respects this country was notably successful in the period immediately after V-J Day. Aside from the fact that postwar prices advanced more than was desirable, seldom has the economy performed as satisfactorily as in the three or four years after the peace. The rise in the price level during this period was chiefly caused by three factors: shortages resulting from the war; the increased money supply; and the world-wide drought in 1947. The rise in prices that followed the outbreak of fighting in Korea, however, had other causes and should be viewed differently.

FEDERAL RESERVE POLICIES

We turn now to the behavior of the Federal Reserve System's portfolio of Treasury securities, the major source of Reserve credit and the major instrument of Reserve policy. For present purposes Federal

Reserve credit may be defined as the funds furnished to commercial banks when the Reserve Banks acquire certain assets, primarily Treasury securities and loans to member banks.

Reserve Credit Behavior

Between September 1945 and December 1948 total Federal Reserve credit outstanding, with the exception of two months, remained within the relatively narrow range of $21.6 and $24.8 billion. Even in the two months when total Reserve credit outstanding moved outside these limits—in December 1945 upward and in April 1948 downward—the deviation was not significant. Figure 7 shows the behavior of Federal Reserve credit and of the Federal's portfolio of government securities during this period.

The relative stability in Reserve credit, however, may be subject to misinterpretation unless it is considered in conjunction with other concurrent developments. Between February 1946, when the federal debt reached its peak of about $279 billion, and December 1948, the

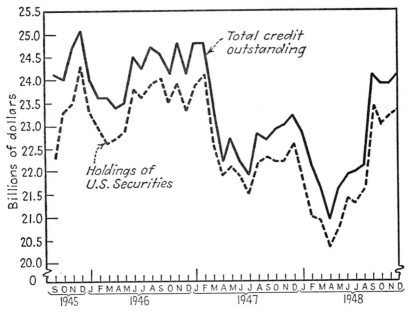

FIGURE 7. TOTAL FEDERAL RESERVE CREDIT OUTSTANDING AND FEDERAL RESERVE BANK HOLDINGS OF U.S. GOVERNMENT SECURITIES, END OF MONTH, SEPTEMBER 1945—DECEMBER 1948

Source: Appendix Table 7.

gross debt was reduced approximately $26 billion. Of the debt retired, a considerable portion was represented by securities held by the Reserve Banks. The redemption of Reserve-held debt, however, did not commensurately reduce the Reserve System's portfolio of government securities, since obligations redeemed were replaced with Treasury securities purchased from other classes of holders. Many of the purchases, of course, were made as a result of the System's policy of market support for federal obligations. Thus, debt redemption and the policy of market support for Treasury obligations combined to keep the Reserve portfolio of governments within the limits indicated in Figure 7.

Reserve Balances of Member Banks Grew

The fact that Reserve credit did not increase, however, did not keep the reserve balances of member banks from growing. In September 1945 they amounted to $15.4 billion, and by the end of 1948 they had risen to nearly $20 billion. The major source of the growth, as is indicated in Table 3, was the importation of gold. Other mone-

TABLE 3

CHANGES IN MEMBER BANK RESERVE BALANCES AND RELATED ITEMS,
SEPTEMBER 1945–DECEMBER 1948

(*In Millions*)

Member bank reserve balances, September 1945			$15,414
Increased, September 1945—December 1948, by:			
Increases in Reserve Bank credit outstanding	$ 269		
" " monetary gold stock	4,128		
" " Treasury currency outstanding	363		
Decreases in Treasury cash holdings	942		
" " nonmember bank deposits	448		
		$6,150	
Decreased, September 1945—December 1948, by:			
Increases in money in circulation	$ 658		
" " Treasury deposits with Reserve Banks	789		
" " other Reserve accounts	130		
		1,577	
			4,573
Member bank reserve balances, December 1948			$19,987[a]

Source: *Federal Reserve Bulletin,* Monthly Averages of Daily Figures.

a. The *Federal Reserve Bulletin* gives member bank reserve balances as $19,990 million in December 1948.

tary factors contributed to this result, as did the Reserve's purchases of federal securities, but the basic element was the gold inflow.

In an inflationary situation, if traditional central bank procedures had been followed, the central bank would have endeavored to offset the stimulative effects of gold imports on the reserve position of the commercial banks through open-market sales of government obligations. But such selling was not possible under the policy of market support for Treasury securities, and sales were not made. Insofar as the effects of gold imports were offset, they were counteracted in 1948 by raising the reserve requirements of member banks. Such advances added perhaps $3 billion to the reserve requirements; but, except for the increase in September 1948, the increase in requirements was confined to central reserve city banks.

The raising of reserve requirements compelled the banks to find additional reserve funds. These they obtained by selling government securities to the Reserve System, and the advances in legal reserve requirements, particularly that of September 1948, simply led to a transfer of Treasury obligations from the commercial banks to the Reserve Banks in amounts approximately equal to the increase in required reserves. Since sales of securities were made in a pegged market, and since the commercial banks thereby acquired sufficient reserves to support their outstanding loans, the effect of raising legal requirements was hardly as deflationary as it might otherwise have been. Had the sales been made in a fluctuating market, so that the banks' portfolios either showed book losses before the transfer or actual losses after the transfer, the banks probably would have sought to acquire reserve funds in ways other than through the sale of governments—for instance, through borrowing at the Federal or through curtailment of loans—and the deflationary results of higher reserve requirements would then have been much greater. The most immediate effect of the operation, as it actually took place, was the reduction of bank earnings that resulted from converting securities, which were earning assets, into cash, a nonearning asset.

The Composition of the Portfolio Changed

If the relative stability in the Reserve System's total government portfolio is to be seen in proper perspective, it is necessary to examine also important changes in its maturity pattern, changes which were concealed behind the aggregate figures.

Until December 1947, when the support prices for Treasury securities were lowered on Christmas Eve, virtually all of the Reserve's holdings of government securities had a maturity of less than twelve months. Before that time Treasury bonds at no time amounted to as much as 5 per cent of total holdings, and bonds with less than a year to run were a substantial fraction of this 5 per cent. This short-term type of portfolio was in accordance with the traditional view that central banks should not hold paper with a maturity in excess of one year. The few occasions before the entrance of the United States into World War II when the Federal Reserve Banks purchased substantial quantities of long-term governments, notably in 1937 and 1939,[2] are probably better viewed as aberrations from tradition than as the establishment of precedents.

In December 1947, however, the System's holdings of intermediate-and long-term bonds advanced sharply from less than a billion dollars to $2.9 billion, and the totals continued to rise, almost without interruption, throughout 1948. By the end of that year virtually one half, or $11 billion, of the total portfolio of $23.3 billion was in the form of bonds. Of this $11 billion, more than $7 billion had maturities in excess of fifteen years. Clearly, 1948 marked a turning point in Reserve practice regarding the type of portfolio that it was proper for a central bank to hold. As Guthman states:

. . . the greatly changed picture . . . at the end of 1948 reflects a development of profound importance that marks an extreme swing from the original policy of the Federal Reserve Act.[3]

These acquisitions were, of course, undertaken in connection with the Reserve's policy of stabilizing the government securities market. Here two significant observations can be made. So long as the traditional central bank policy of holding no long-term paper prevailed, the Reserve Banks were not in a position, in their own right, to regulate directly the long end of the government market. Conversely, if long-term security prices rose and long-term interest rates threatened to drop below the desired range, the Reserve Banks were not in a position to check such a price rise by selling long-term securities from

2. See the discussion in Lester V. Chandler, "Federal Reserve Policy and the Federal Debt," *American Economic Review*, March 1949, and in the Annual Reports of the Board of Governors for 1937 and 1939.

3. Harry G. Guthman, "Financial Institutions as a Factor in Fiscal Policy," in *Fiscal Policies and the American Economy*, Prentice-Hall, New York, 1951, p. 281.

the System's portfolio, since they did not own such securities.[4] The Reserve Banks, in short, did not have the "ammunition" required to enforce their policy of stabilized government security prices. Thus the policy of keeping the prices of long-term governments within a relatively narrow price range led to a change in the character of the Reserve Banks' portfolio—and to a change in the traditional concept of central bank operations.

Government Trust Funds Enter the Scene

It is in connection with these considerations that purchases and sales of marketable securities for the account of government agencies and trust funds achieve particular significance. These purchases and sales, it must be assumed, were made at the direction of the Treasury pursuant to the policy of market support for federal securities. The operations were of sufficient moment to justify a brief digression.

The volume of marketable Treasury bonds in the hands of government agencies and trust funds following the eighth war loan rose to a peak of $6.9 billion in December 1945. Thereafter they remained relatively constant during the first three months of 1946. Between April and December 1946, however, they declined nearly $700 million. The sales began virtually at the same moment that the dramatic post-eighth-war-loan boom in the government market came to an end. Presumably the sales contributed to the ending of this boom and the weakening in long-term bond prices that continued throughout 1946. More than two thirds of the bonds sold in the operation were thought to have come from the Government Life Insurance Fund.

Again in 1947, during the first three months of the year, the volume of marketable securities in the hands of government agencies and trust funds remained comparatively constant, but in April heavy sales began. This selling, which continued during June and July when the fixed rate of ⅜ per cent on Treasury bills was abandoned, did not come to an end until October, at which time approximately $1.9 billion of long-term obligations had been sold, most of which seem to have come from the Federal Deposit Insurance Corporation and the Postal Savings System.

4. The supply of long-term securities available could have been increased at any time if the Treasury had changed its offering policy and used longer-term securities for refunding purposes.

This liquidation terminated virtually at the same time that other moves in the money market were undertaken, in September and October, which raised the certificate rate to one per cent. Almost as soon as selling of bonds for the account of government trust funds ceased, the movement was reversed and heavy purchases began. Between October and December more than $900 million of bonds were bought back, and the buying continued after the turn of the year as the market felt the impact of the lowering of the support prices on Christmas Eve. By February 1948, government agencies and trust funds held $5.3 billion of marketable Treasury securities, an increase of $1.1 billion since October. Much of this buying seems to have been done for the account of the Federal Old-Age and Survivors Insurance Trust Fund and the Unemployment Trust Fund.

The sales of long-term marketable securities from the trust funds in 1946 and 1947 were made at a time when the Reserve System did not have in its locker the type of ammunition needed to check the rise in long-term bond prices. The purchases of bonds made for the account of the trust funds at the end of 1947 and the beginning of 1948 unquestionably were of substantial aid to the Reserve authorities in their support of government security prices. The use of government investment accounts for the manipulation of the prices of the government's own security prices was a new and very significant phenomenon in the postwar money market. The fact that government agencies, because of technical accounting reasons, do not need to be as greatly concerned as do private institutions with the profits and losses that result from purchases and sales of Treasury securities in some measure presumably facilitated the operation. Whether the resources of the trust funds will continue to be used for this type of market operation remains to be seen. Such purchases and sales of marketable issues for the account of the trust funds largely parallel the open-market operations of the Reserve authorities. The relationship of these two types of control is one of the unsettled questions in the postwar money market.

Interest Rates

The "interest rate problem" in its larger aspects is discussed in another chapter. Here we are concerned simply with the extent and the timing of interest rate changes between V-J Day and the end of 1948.

At the end of the war the interest rate structure that had been frozen in 1942, as an aid in financing the war, still obtained. This structure ranged from ⅜ per cent on ninety-day Treasury bills, through ⅞ per cent on twelve-months' paper, up to 2½ per cent on the longest-term taxable bonds. The general pattern is indicated in Table 4 under the date October 1945.

The eighth war loan in November and December 1945 signified that the deficit financing was, at least temporarily, at an end. Despite the return of peace and the new prospect of budgetary surpluses, the fiscal authorities gave no indication that there was any immediate intention of changing their interest policies. This circumstance, together with the expected cessation of new issues of Treasury securities, presumably was the basic cause for the rapid rise in the government securities market that marked the final weeks of 1945 and the opening months of 1946. The yields of government securities as of March 1946, shown in Table 4, indicate approximately the high point of the advance, and a comparison of these figures with the corresponding data for the preceding October indicates the magnitude of the change that took place in less than five months.

The termination of this rise corresponded with the initiation of sales of long-term bonds from the trust funds that continued throughout 1946. At the same time a number of other minor steps were taken by the Reserve authorities that tended to stiffen rates, such as the withdrawal of the ½ per cent preferential discount rate on borrowings secured by short-term Treasury obligations and the right of nonmember banks to borrow on government securities at the one per cent rate. Slight as these monetary moves were, in retrospect it is evident that they marked the turning point in the long decline in interest rates that had begun in 1932. As such, this turning point in April 1946 was of considerable significance in the financial world. By November of that year a new pattern of rates for government obligations had been established and the question was whether the almost imperceptible stiffening of interest rates was to continue.

President Sproul on Interest Rates

In December, President Sproul of the New York Reserve Bank, made one of the most significant speeches of the immediate postwar period concerning debt management, credit conditions and interest rates. In the course of his remarks he said:

TABLE 4

YIELDS OF TREASURY SECURITIES,
SELECTED DATES, OCTOBER 1945–DECEMBER 1948

(Per Cent Per Annum)

Security Class	October 1945	March 1946	November 1946	August 1947	December 1947	February 1948	May 1948	December 1948
Bills[a]	.375	.375	.376	.748	.950	.996	.997	1.154
Certificates—9-12 months[a]	.83	.79	.84	.85	1.04	1.10	1.09	1.21
Bonds—3-5-year taxables[a]	1.17	.99	1.28	1.31	1.54	1.63	1.51	1.64
Bonds—7-9-year taxables[b]	1.50	1.28	1.60	1.54	1.86	2.08	1.89	1.94
Bonds—15-years and over taxables[b]	2.35	2.09	2.25	2.24	2.39	2.45	2.42	2.44
2½s of 9/15/67-72[c]	2.16	1.98	2.20	2.10	2.43	2.42	2.31	2.37
2½s of 12/15/67-72[c]	d	2.19	2.38	2.32	2.48	2.48	2.45	2.47

Sources:

a. "Open Market Rates in New York City," *Federal Reserve Bulletin;* monthly figures are averages of weekly prevailing rates; 3-month bills—rate on new issues offered within period.

b. "Bond Yields," *Federal Reserve Bulletin;* averages of daily figures for the period.

c. "Market Quotations," *Treasury Bulletin;* for over-the-counter closing quotations in New York market for last trading day of the month, as reported to Treasury by Federal Reserve Bank of New York.

d. Not issued as of this date.

We came out of the war with short-term rates still pegged where they were when we went in, but with the longer term rates under steady downward pressure. So long as differences in maturity, and the risks which longer maturities are supposed to involve, are deprived of their significance, the tendency of interest rates is to come together at one figure for all maturities. If the short end of the rate curve is fixed, that means that the long end will tend to decline. So much for the loss of control over the cost of credit. . . .

Nor should there be any reason for Treasury concern, if short-term rates are unfrozen. The Treasury would still be able to sell its short-term securities for refunding purposes just as it does now. Banks and other investors would hardly prefer to hold idle funds, from month to month, in anticipation of a minor change in rates which might not be forthcoming. The market for intermediate securities would be subject to greater uncertainty and therefore less attractive, especially to banks, but the Treasury's long-term market need not be affected.[5]

These observations foreshadowed coming events.

In the summer and early fall of 1947 a further series of moves were undertaken, designed to raise short-term, but not long-term, interest rates. In July the Reserve authorities eliminated the ⅜ per cent posted rate for Treasury bills, with the purpose of letting the yield on bills seek its own level relative to the certificate rate. By August the short-term pattern had substantially adjusted itself to the new situation—as shown in the column headed August 1947 in Table 4—and in September and October a further series of moves were initiated that raised the twelve-months' certificate rate to one per cent. On Christmas Eve the support prices for long-term securities were lowered; in January the New York discount rate was raised to one per cent; and by February a new pattern of rates for both short-term and long-term securities emerged. Speaking in January, President Sproul said:

. . . our present program of modest restraints involving a combination of debt management and credit policy is the best course to follow in trying to achieve our objective, which is to prevent bank credit from adding further to inflationary pressures and, if possible, to reduce somewhat the supply of money.[6]

During the early part of 1948 the yields on intermediate Treasury securities eased off, the low point in the decline being reached in

5. Allan Sproul, "Money Management and Credit Control," address before the eighteenth midyear trust and banking conference, New Jersey Bankers Association, December 6, 1946, as reported in *Commercial and Financial Chronicle,* December 12, 1946.

6. *Idem,* address at the midwinter meeting of the New York State Bankers Association, as reported in the *New York Times,* January 27, 1948.

May. The pattern of rates existing in that month is shown in Table 4. The movement was promptly reversed, however. In August the New York discount rate was raised to 1½ per cent and the Secretary of the Treasury let it be known that the rate on new certificates issued October 1 would be raised from 1⅛ to 1¼ per cent. By the end of the year this change had tightened short rates appreciably, and a new structure of rates had been established.

The Changes Were Important

While in the long view it may appear that changes in the level and structure of yields of Treasury securities during the period covered by this study were not appreciable, such an opinion is likely to be misleading. Slight as the rise in the general level of rates was, the change that came in the spring of 1946 marked a turning point in a fourteen-year decline in rates that was of great significance. The change in the structure that took place during 1947 was the first substantial change in the wartime pattern that had been established in 1942. Although the rate on ninety-day money had not risen above one per cent even as late as June 1948, it was then nearly three times as high as it had been in August 1945, and by the end of the year it was well above one per cent. And, even though the variations in yields in terms of basis points were small, in view of the tremendous dollar magnitudes involved these small percentage variations were of enormous consequence to portfolio managers in financial institutions, as well as to the Treasury itself. In the light of these considerations the turning point in April 1946 was of real moment in the postwar financial history of the country, even though the stiffening of rates in 1946 and 1947 was not accompanied by a shortage of loanable funds, as has generally happened in the past when rates turned up.

Availability of Credit

Behind the stability in the Reserve Banks' total portfolio, however, behind the shifts in the proportionate amounts of short- and long-term securities held, and behind these moderate changes in interest rates lay a deeper question. This was whether the Reserve Banks, so long as they stood ready to buy Treasury securities at virtually fixed prices in what might prove to be very large amounts, could exert any effective pressure on the reserve position of the commercial banking system and hence on the deposit structure. That is, would not such a policy, if faithfully adhered to at times when holders of Treasury obligations other than the Reserve Banks were insistent sellers, lead to a loss of control of the money supply by the responsible agency?

Background of the Problem

This was not entirely a new problem. During the depression of the 1930's, when commercial banks accumulated unprecedentedly large excess reserves, the Reserve System found that it was, in some measure, losing its ability to influence banking practice. During the war, when stability in the government securities market was a necessary war measure, it became evident—with the growth of the debt —that this issue at some future time might become acute.

In its 1945 Annual Report the Board of Governors called attention to the situation.

> The creation of unnecessary bank credit by the commercial banking system is the particular concern of those charged with monetary responsibilities. It can not be a matter of indifference that at present the country's central banking mechanism lacks appropriate means, that may be needed, to restrain unnecessary creation of bank credit through continued acquisition of Government or other securities by the commercial banks. . . .
>
> One of these [circumstances inherited from the war financing] is the Reserve Board's assurance to the Treasury that the rate of 7/8 per cent on one-year certificates will be maintained, if necessary, through open-market operations. This means in practice that the Federal Reserve stands ready to purchase short-term Government securities in the open market to prevent short-term interest rates from rising. . . .
>
> This policy makes it possible . . . in the absence of effective restraints, for commercial banks to sell short-term, lower-yield Government securities to the Reserve System and thus acquire reserves which, on the basis of reserve requirements, can support a sixfold expansion of member bank credit. To the extent that commercial banks use these reserves, either for their own account or in loans to customers . . . the money supply can thereby be increased *on the volition of the banks irrespective of national monetary policy*. . . .[7]

Although Reserve authorities here focused attention on short-term securities, this line of reasoning could almost equally well have been applied to long-term obligations. Indeed, from the end of 1947 on, it was the long-term Treasury securities that became the focus of attention, and it was on the desirability of supporting the long-term

---

7. *Thirty-second Annual Report of the Board of Governors of the Federal Reserve System*, 1945, pp. 3-4. Italics supplied.

2½ per cent rate that the Treasury and the Federal Reserve authorities split most sharply. In 1949 Mr. Eccles made the nature of the problem explicit in testimony before the Douglas Committee:

> To maintain a very low rate pattern when there is a strong demand for credit, the System cannot avoid supplying Federal Reserve credit at the will of the market.
>
> Under these conditions it can hardly be said that the Federal Reserve System retains any effective influence in its own right over the supply of money in the country or over the availability and cost of credit, although these are the major duties for which the System has statutory responsibility. Nor can it be said that the discount rate and open-market operations of the System are determined by Federal Reserve authorities, except in form. . . . This will be true as long as the System is not in a position to pursue an independent policy but must support in the market any program of financing adopted by the Treasury even though the program may be inconsistent with the monetary and credit policies the System considers appropriate in the public interest.[8]

Proposed Solutions

Generally speaking, three types of solution for the dilemma of the fiscal authorities have been advanced. The first type looks to a change in the Federal Reserve Act and an increase in the statutory powers of the Reserve authorities. The second emphasizes the fact that the Reserve System has no explicit legal obligation to support the market for Treasury obligations and notes that there were various times in the postwar period when, in view of the condition of the market, the Reserve authorities seemingly could have modified or withdrawn their support policies without producing any serious results, at least at the moment. The third point of view assumes that the ultimate solution lies in the federal budget, in controlling expenditure and eliminating all unnecessary expenses. If the Treasury and the Reserve authorities coordinate their policies, it is argued, the dilemma need not become acute during times when there is a federal surplus, when the budget is balanced on a cash basis, or when there is a prospect of a cash balance. If this line of reasoning is extended it would appear to follow that in times of deficits or prospective deficits some concessions may need to be offered security holders to induce them to retain their holdings and refrain from forcing them on the market.

8. *Monetary, Credit, and Fiscal Policies,* Hearings before the Subcommittee on Monetary, Credit, and Fiscal Policies of the Joint Committee on the Economic Report, 81st Cong., 1st sess., 1950, p. 223.

New Federal Reserve Powers

In its 1945 Annual Report the Board of Governors outlined three measures designed to cope with the situation. One would have empowered the Board to place a limit, proportionate to the size of a bank's demand deposits, on the amount of long-term securities that it might hold. The second would have permitted the Board to require all commercial banks to hold a stipulated amount of Treasury securities as a secondary reserve against deposit liabilities, in addition to the existing required cash reserve. The third would have allowed the Board to raise reserve requirements above the existing legal maxima. None of these found favor with the Congress, although the third was adopted, on a limited basis, as an emergency measure in 1948. In addition, other devices centering around the manipulation or redefinition of bank reserves have been suggested by various persons at different times, but none have been adopted.

Relaxation of Market Support

Few responsible persons have suggested that the Reserve authorities completely abandon the practice of market support, even though the System has no statutory obligation for this policy. Rather, the question has turned on the rigidity of the support and the way in which the policy should be implemented. A publicly acknowledged, meticulously enforced policy of market support, it is pointed out, effectively precludes the central bank from exerting any restraint on the money supply. If holders of Treasury obligations wish to sell, the central bank must buy at the support prices, and stability in the prices of government securities is achieved at the cost of expanding the volume of deposits. Under these conditions financial institutions can, in effect, use their government portfolios as a second cash account since they are assured that these obligations can be converted into cash, at any future time, without fear of loss. Thus they know that whenever some alternative use of funds appears they will be in a position, immediately, to take advantage of it by selling governments.

Critics have pointed out that, from the end of the war till about October 1947, long-term Treasury securities did not require support; that in connection with the lowering of support prices on Christmas Eve, 1947, the first publicly admitted "peg" came into being; and that there were times in 1948 and particularly in 1949 when the long-term securities were above the support prices. The periods when the securities were not supported, it has been noted, afforded opportunities to the Reserve System to indicate that their policies were changing, and thereby create both some uncertainty in investors' minds and some leeway in their own operations. Although the Reserve authorities issued a statement in June 1949 that was perhaps designed to have some such effect, numerous opportunities for a step of this kind had already been passed by, and the statement was not universally interpreted in the manner intended.

The Third Approach

The course of events since the end of the war suggests that the most practical approach to these problems is one based on very close working arrangements between the Treasury and the Reserve authorities, a recognition of the importance of monetary as well as fiscal policy, and a flexible attitude toward the changing needs of the economy. The other approaches suggested have not proved feasible, either politically or economically. Implicit in this view is the importance of a balanced budget and recognition of the necessity of making ownership of federal securities attractive under conditions of deficit or prospective deficit financing. While all the implications of this approach have not been, and probably cannot be, foreseen, the logic favoring evolution of this type of procedure seems so strong as to make further developments in this direction appear a probability.

Specific Credit Regulations

Maintenance of a relatively constant volume of Reserve credit outstanding, changes in member bank reserve requirements and moderate shifts in interest rates did not exhaust the scope or purpose of policy as the Reserve authorities sought, on the one hand, to preserve reasonable stability in *general* credit conditions and, on the other, to find solutions to the problems just discussed. In addition, individual kinds of credit, particularly consumer credit and credit used in the stock market, became objects of Reserve policy. These moves, implemented through alterations in Regulations W, T, U and D, were designed to check directly inflationary tendencies in the stock market and the market for consumer goods. It was perhaps hoped, also, that they would indirectly have deflationary repercussions elsewhere, in wholesale commodity markets and in the labor markets.

Consumer Credit Changes

What was accomplished in the area of consumer credit by the sequence of changes in Regulation W is not entirely clear. The relaxation of these controls in the autumn of 1945 came at a time when the fear of a postwar depression was real. The changes made in the summer and fall of 1946 were intended to check the expansion of consumer credit, but their over-all effect is doubtful. The expiration of consumer credit controls in November 1947, which was contrary to the expressed wish of Reserve authorities, occurred in the midst of a long series of moves that, after advancing the rate for one-year money in September and October, culminated on Christmas Eve in the lowering of the support prices for Treasury bonds.

Their expiration was followed on November 24 by the much-publicized joint statement of the Board of Governors, the Federal Deposit Insurance Corporation, the Comptroller of the Currency and the Executive Committee of the National Association of Supervisors of State Banks that urged commercial banks to pursue conservative lending policies. Reimposed in the autumn of 1948, these controls were again relaxed in the spring of 1949, as business activity receded, and again imposed after Korea.

Margin Trading Changes

The reasons that led, in January 1946, to the increase in margin requirements to 100 per cent were, presumably, to be found in the behavior of the stock market, although this change in Regulations T and U took place during the dramatic rise of the government bond market that followed the eighth war loan. Presumably the reduction in margin requirements to 75 per cent thirteen months later, in February 1947, was partially induced by the break in the stock market the preceding fall. Their further reduction in the spring of 1949 to 50 per cent came at a time when fears of a business recession were beginning to outweigh fears of a resumption of the inflationary spiral. After the break in the stock market in the autumn of 1946, there was at no time evidence of any appreciable amount of stock market speculation, and the high level of margin requirements can be justified only as a preventive, not as a remedial mechanism.

THE NET RESULT

The three and a half years that immediately followed V-J Day presented to the Reserve authorities a new problem, that of determining appropriate central banking policy at a time when the federal government had an enormous debt, half of which was represented by short-term or demand obligations. The essence of the situation lay in the fact that under the conditions existing the authorities did not believe it practicable to terminate their wartime policy of market support, even though deficit financing had, at least temporarily, come to an end. This decision in turn raised a second problem. Under these circumstances, what mechanisms could the Reserve System employ to control the inflationary situation inherited from the war? Critics alleged that inflationary pressures were perpetuated, if not made more acute, by the System's policy of market support for Treasury obligations.

The answer found was an eclectic one. Use was made of a variety of control measures, including the psychological one of market uncertainty, although this was not pushed to any great extent. Even though the prices of government obligations were stabilized, this operation did not lead to any substantial expansion either of the Reserve's own portfolio of Treasury securities or of Reserve credit outstanding, largely because the Treasury was able during this period to reduce its debt some $26 billion. Had this reduction not taken place the financial history of this period would have been radically different. The policy of stabilization, however, brought into play a new mechanism of money market control—namely, the use of funds in the hands of government agencies and trust funds—and led to an almost revolutionary change in the maturity pattern of the Reserve System's own portfolio of government obligations.

But if the Reserve authorities were able to pursue a policy of market support without expanding the volume of Reserve credit, the maintenance of this policy precluded them from offsetting the effects of gold imports and of other monetary developments that tended to ease the reserve position of commercial banks. Insofar as these developments were counteracted, they were met partly by advancing the legal reserve requirements of member banks (and by an emergency grant of statutory authority to raise them still further), and partly by permitting a moderate advance in short-term rates.

The increases in reserve requirements in 1948 added something like $3 billion to the volume of nonearning assets that member banks were required to carry. Since these funds were largely obtained by the banks through the sale of government obligations to the Reserve Banks—at pegged prices—it is probable that bank earnings were affected more directly than was the availability of credit.

The advances in short-term rates, which brought to an end a fourteen-year decline in interest rates, were a cautious departure from wartime rigidities but did not mark the end of the controlled market and had only a moderate deflationary significance.

Where possible, the mechanisms designed to affect the general availability of credit were supplemented by measures intended to restrict the uses of funds in specified markets, notably the stock market and the market for consumer goods.

The combination of expedients employed by the Reserve System during this period, however, did not furnish a permanent solution to the fundamental problem presented to it by the growth of the federal debt. In particular, they did not show how the availability of credit could be limited if prices of government securities were stabilized, especially in the event of renewed deficits.

Chapter 5

THE INTEREST RATE PROBLEM

WITH THE ADVENT of an enormous federal debt the interest policy of the government at once became a matter of controversy. This was the point at which policies of credit control most immediately came into conflict with debt management procedures. Although the diverse interests did not appear in open opposition until after the outbreak of fighting in Korea in 1950, the possibility of such a collision was inherent in the situation from V-J Day on. For this there were several reasons.

Traditionally, interest policy has been an instrument for the regulation of credit conditions. In the postwar period, however, with the growth of the debt, it became a key factor in debt management. Thus, interest rates occupied a strategic position in two major areas of public policy, and the way was opened to possible conflicts of objective.

The monetary authorities found themselves in the difficult position of attempting to control the postwar inflationary boom at a time when they were committed, through their market support policy, to furnishing the banks with an almost unlimited volume of reserve funds. Heretofore a dilemma of this nature had not appeared, partly because the Reserve Banks had never before embarked on so rigorous a policy of support for Treasury obligations, and still more because the federal debt had never been so large.

The sheer magnitude of the debt also meant that the burden of interest payments, upwards of $5 billion, raised issues that were, or might be, of political consequence. At the same time, the low level of Treasury rates, because of their strategic position relative to all other types of rates, necessitated a re-examination of the role of interest in a free market economy. Thus the respective roles of monetary and of fiscal policy were involved. As a consequence, the debate over rates proceeded in an atmosphere charged with political overtones and ideological positions.

72

INTEREST POLICY

Postwar interest policy embraced two distinct elements, which in discussion were commonly confused. The first was the fact that the federal government stabilized interest rates; the second, that rates were stabilized at a low level.

Stabilization was first undertaken as a war measure. The low level at which rates were pegged, however, was in large part a historical accident, induced by the circumstance that World War II closely followed the Great Depression, when the government embarked on a low interest, cheap money policy as a recovery measure.[1] A feeling in some quarters that the financial community had benefited unduly from the interest policy followed in World War I also was used as a justification of this action. But how different would post-war financial history have been, and how altered the debate over interest policy, if rates during hostilities had been pegged at a higher point!

The low level at which rates were set meant, so far as the controversy regarding flexible rates was concerned, that at the outset the argument chiefly turned on the advantages and disadvantages of a higher level. This was a somewhat different point from the fact that rates were stabilized. Moreover, the pattern that was frozen, in which short rates were lower than long, was an unusual pattern. Since 1900 it had been more common for long rates to be below short than for the reverse situation to prevail. We cannot determine exactly the way in which this circumstance affected postwar conditions. But there is no question that the shape of the interest curve and its "correctness" as regards "realities" were of critical importance at various times in the postwar period, particularly when viewed with reference to the objectives of fiscal authority, to the differing risks attaching to securities of different maturities, and to the needs of investors.

At a later stage in the argument less attention was paid to the level and the stability of rates and more stress was placed on the availability of credit, a much more important question. Stable rates, as has been pointed out, in effect signified that bank credit was available in virtually unlimited amounts. As inflationary pressures

1. For a more complete discussion of the establishment of the wartime pattern of rates see Henry C. Murphy, *The National Debt in War and Transition*, McGraw-Hill Book Company, New York, 1950, Chapter 8.

increased it became less a question whether rising interest rates would or could check increasing prices and more a question whether any way could be found to check credit expansion so long as stable rates indicated that credit was readily obtainable.

Before examining the significance of stabilized rates and of low rates it will be desirable to survey the behavior of the yields of government securities in the immediate postwar period.

THE BEHAVIOR OF RATES

Immediately on the outbreak of hostilities in 1941, fiscal authority announced that prices of Treasury securities would be stabilized for the duration, and on December 8, 1941 the Board of Governors issued the following statement:

> The System is prepared to use its powers to assure that an ample supply of funds is available at all times for financing the war effort and to exert its influence toward maintaining conditions in the United States Government security market that are satisfactory from the standpoint of the Government's requirements.[2]

This meant, in practice, that yields on the different maturities of federal obligations then existing would be maintained throughout the war. This pattern extended from ⅜ per cent on ninety-day Treasury bills, through ⅞ per cent one-year certificates, to 2½ per cent on the longest-term bonds.

The same scale still held in September 1945, after the end of hostilities. Prices of intermediate- and long-term securities rose following the eighth war loan, but the rise came to an end in April 1946. In July 1947 short rates were advanced, with repercussions on the yields of intermediate- and long-term securities as the spread between the rates on short- and long-term obligations narrowed. During 1948 the continued rise in short rates was not reflected in the behavior of the long-term obligations, as these maturities were supported "on the pegs" by the Reserve Banks. (See Figure 8.) Figure 9 shows the level and shape of the yield curve of Treasury bank-eligible bonds, as of December 1945, 1946, 1947 and 1948. The changes in these curves from one date to another reflect the results of the support policy on this substantial portion of the debt. Changes in both the level and the configuration of this curve brought by the advance in short rates in 1947 are clearly illustrated.

2. *Federal Reserve Bulletin,* January 1942, p. 2.

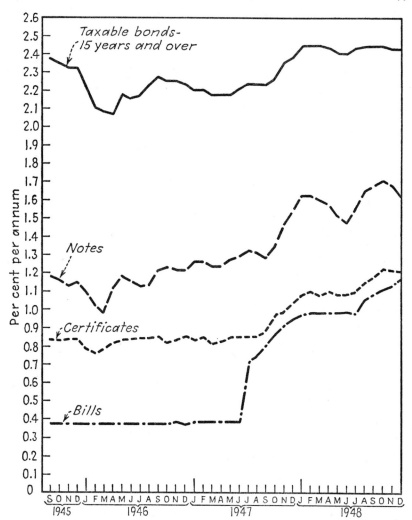

FIGURE 8. INTEREST RATES ON U.S. GOVERNMENT SECURITIES,
SEPTEMBER 1945—DECEMBER 1948

Source: Appendix Table 8.

The over-all picture presented by these charts is one of stability. There is little doubt that, except for the intervention of the authorities, rates would have broken out of this range, either upward or downward, on several occasions. The authorities took steps in the early months of 1946, for example, to halt the rise in intermediate- and long-term securities, and in 1947, between April and September, heavy sales of bonds were made by the Reserve Banks and gov-

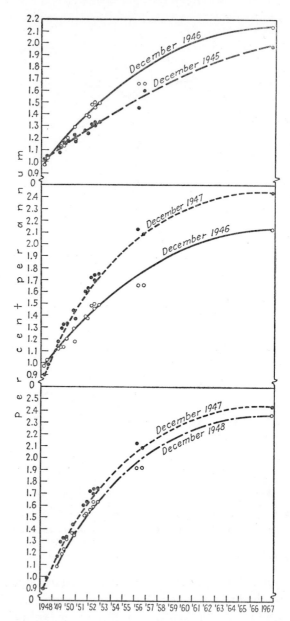

FIGURE 9. YIELDS TO EARLIEST CALL DATE OF TAXABLE ISSUES OF U.S. TREASURY BANK-ELIGIBLE BONDS, AS OF DECEMBER 31, 1945, 1946, 1947, 1948

Source: Appendix Table 9.

ernment trust funds to check the threatened advance in prices. Again, in the last few months of that year and in the early part of 1948, almost equally heavy purchases were made to support the market.

STABILIZED YIELDS

The significance of stabilized yields for government securities is best approached by summarizing some of the traditional thinking of economists regarding the functions of interest rates. This material sets the stage for understanding the views both of those who advocated a meticulously regulated market for government securities (and yields) and those who took a somewhat different position.

Savings and Investment

In an oversimplified sense, interest has often been regarded as a price—the price demanded by the saver if he is to transfer his savings to someone who wishes to spend them, either for consumption or investment purposes. In this view a higher rate will ordinarily make a larger supply of savings available and, conversely, will reduce the demand for savings and the purchasing power or command of resources represented by them.

Two considerations have largely destroyed the usefulness of this concept when applied to government borrowing during the war and, in some measure, in the postwar period. The first is the recognition, given increasing emphasis by economists during the last twenty years, that decisions to save or to invest are the result of many and often complex reasons. Other factors, such as business prospects, institutional habits, the level and character of taxation, the desire for capital gains, expectations regarding future price movements and the availability of funds for particular kinds of investment are of great importance. Moreover, the critical or dominant motives for saving vary among different types of business concerns and among the several income brackets in the economic pyramid, and differ in the various stages of the business cycle.

Thus high rates do not necessarily induce a larger supply of savings of an amount that can be predetermined, at the same time checking the demand for savings; nor do low rates necessarily, or in any predictable way, encourage investment and discourage saving. This is not to say that *high enough* rates will not stifle investment, particularly in some fields, such as housing or the construction of public utilities, where the cost of financing is an important part of the total expenditure. It does mean, however, that when rates are in a "moderate" range other considerations often outweigh interest in decisions to save or to invest.

The second consideration turns on the position of the government, particularly in wartime. Military requirements will not be checked by interest rates. Thus high rates will not reduce the government's demand for funds and, within "reasonable" limits, are not likely to increase the supply of savings appreciably. Furthermore, when—as in wartime—the government is the largest user of materials, savers cannot find any substantial quantity of outlets for their funds other than federal securities. Thus they are unable to put pressure on the government to set a higher rate, competitive with what other borrowers might be willing to pay.

Consequently the concept of interest rates as a price, the movement of which tends to balance the supply of savings and the demand for them, has only limited validity in wartime, in periods when the government is a large borrower of money and purchaser of supplies and at times when the rationing and allocation of materials limits the possibility of investment.

Loans and Deposits

In monetary theory the level of rates attaching to short-term borrowing, as influenced by the central bank, and the availability of credit, as influenced by the central bank, are traditionally regarded as the principal mechanisms for affecting the volume of bank loans, and hence of deposits and of purchasing power. The generally accepted purpose of central bank operation in this field is the stabilization of business activity at a high level.

While we speak of the availability of credit and the level of rates as being twin methods of control, the former is the more basic of the two. A plentiful supply of credit relative to the demand for it will tend to result in a low price, that is, a low rate of interest; a restricted supply, on the other hand, will force insistent borrowers to raise their bids. Logically, the level of rates is the result of the demand-supply situation, although changes in rates, through the psychological effects they produce on lenders and borrowers, can in turn alter this relationship. It is at this point that the necessities of credit control and the requirements of debt management can come into conflict, particularly under conditions of "full employment" and increasing inflationary pressures.

The Case for Low, Stabilized Rates

The position of those persons favoring a continuance of the low, stabilized wartime pattern of rates, which in effect has been the position of the Treasury, may be summarized as follows:

First, there is little evidence that a rise in interest rates, unless severe, exerts an important deflationary effect and is an important weapon in fighting inflation. Particularly is this the case when banks and other investors hold large quantities of Treasury bills that mature and can be turned into cash every week. This regular inflow of cash reduces the likelihood that a debt holder needing funds will either be forced to sell his government securities in a weak market, or borrow against them. This point of view, as generally presented, fails to make clear that it was the Treasury's offering policy which made the large quantities of bills available.

The argument goes on to state that there is little evidence that higher rates, unless the advance were extreme, would either check the demand for financing because of cost considerations, or lead to a larger volume of savings and more investment funds willing to hold Treasury obligations. Extreme increases in rates, however, must be out of the question, partly because of the danger that they might precipitate a serious recession, partly because they would bring appreciable declines in the prices of outstanding government securities. These declines would, in turn, injure the holders of such securities, particularly financial institutions. Falling prices might also deter potential buyers of government securities from their purchases because of the expectation of a further reduction in prices. If inflation becomes a serious menace, the direct regulation of particular kinds of credit and the lending activities of financial institutions and, even, the control of inventories and the allocation of materials are preferable methods of fighting it. In Secretary Snyder's words:

It has been argued that if the Government had permitted higher interest rates on its long-term securities at the end of the war . . . inflationary pressures would have been lessened.

I do not agree . . . that if the support prices of Government securities had been lowered below par, sales of these securities to the Federal Reserve would have been stopped and inflationary pressures would have been lessened.

It seemed to me that, under the circumstances which existed, we would have taken the risk of impairing confidence in the Government's credit if the prices of Government bonds had been permitted to go below par; and that as a result the Federal Reserve might have had to purchase more bonds below par than at a par-support level. This, of course, would have increased bank reserves and to that extent would have been inflationary rather than anti-inflationary.[8]

And again:

High prices in special areas are most effectively dealt with by specific measures applied directly to those areas.[4]

Second, when interest rates rise the prices of outstanding securities fall. Such a fall might have unpredictable consequences. If it took place on a large scale it might necessitate very heavy acquisition of Treasury securities by the Reserve Banks, which would increase an already swollen volume of bank deposits. Furthermore, the refunding problems of the Treasury would be greatly complicated by a weak or falling market. These difficulties would, of course, be enhanced if the Treasury should come into a period of heavy deficit financing and needed to sell securities in order to raise new money. The fact that the Treasury's refunding problems have been largely of its own making is, of course, overlooked in this argument.

Third, rising rates would increase the interest burden in the federal budget, and such a use of taxpayers' funds would not be warranted in view of the results likely to be achieved. How rapidly the interest burden would in fact rise would depend upon how rapidly the debt were refunded at the higher rates, although this point is sometimes omitted in simplified statements of this argument. It should be noted, also, that the higher interest payments would result in higher tax payments, so that some part of the increased burden would be offset. This argument, as commonly stated, often implicitly assumes that higher rates would exert no deflationary effects, and hence, in an inflationary situation, there would be no compensation in that direction for the larger interest charge in the budget.

The Case for Flexible Rates

Those persons who have mistrusted the consequences of a long-continued policy of stabilized rates at a low level have, in part,

3. Reply by John W. Snyder, Secretary of the Treasury, *Monetary, Credit, and Fiscal Policies*, Joint Committee Print, printed for the use of the Joint Committee on the Economic Report, 81st Cong., 1st sess., 1950, p. 10.
    4. *Ibid.*

argued along other lines and, in part, have interpreted the available data somewhat differently, as follows:

First, the prices and yields of government securities were stabilized in the postwar period by the actions of the Federal Reserve System. This policy, in a sense, was a voluntary one since the System has no legislative mandate to stabilize prices of government securities.

Second, the policy of stabilizing the market when private holders wish to sell securities means that the Federal Reserve must stand ready to buy all securities not desired by other segments of the economy. When business is active and expanding, when prices are rising and when there is an insistent demand for financing, such purchases inevitably lead to an expansion of deposits. Thus the central bank, charged by law with regulating credit conditions, loses control of the volume of deposits and of credit conditions. In that event market demand determines the money supply, not the responsible authority. This consequence might not be deleterious in a situation in which there were unemployed men and resources; but when the economy is running close to capacity an increase in the money supply almost inevitably leads to a growth of inflationary pressures and further price advances.

Third, the situation is made more difficult when financial institutions, particularly commercial banks, hold large quantities of Treasury securities. This circumstance, coupled with the policy of supporting the prices of Treasury securities, renders ineffective the System's principal methods of controlling a credit expansion, namely, sales of government securities, changes in rediscount rates and changes in the reserve requirements of member banks. The reasons are plain. A policy of supporting the prices of federal securities obviously precludes the System from selling these same securities. So long as banks have plenty of government obligations to sell to the Reserve System they need not borrow from it to replenish their reserve funds and, indeed, are not likely to borrow so long as the loss of income on the securities sold is less than the interest they would have to pay if they borrowed. And, again, so long as the banks have plenty of government securities, an increase in reserve requirements simply leads to a transfer of these obligations to the Reserve System, since the banks sell to get funds needed to meet their requirements.

Fourth, an increase in interest rates is not especially to be desired for its own sake, or because interest cost is an important element to most borrowers in making investment decisions. What is desired is the restriction on the availability of credit that can be accomplished only through lowering the prices at which the Reserve Banks stand ready to purchase Treasury obligations. True, interest rates will rise as a consequence of the fall in prices, but that is an incidental result, not the primary goal.

The availability of credit will be restricted by lowering the support prices in a variety of ways, of which only two will be mentioned. In the first place, institutions will not be so ready to convert governments into cash—to use them as a second cash account—in order to reinvest in other and seemingly more attractive ways if their sale entails incurring some loss as against the purchase price. The attitude of those persons making investment decisions is likely to be quite different in such a situation than when governments can be sold at no loss or, even, perhaps a slight profit. Banks and other potential lenders are reluctant to sell securities at a book loss, and as the book loss becomes greater this reluctance deepens.[5] In the second place, the new investment will need to be especially attractive in order to induce the lending institution to take advantage of it if a portfolio loss must first be absorbed, and this fact will of itself lead to a more careful screening of credits, to a form of rationing of financing.

Fifth, the expectations of lenders and borrowers regarding future financial conditions have an independent effect on the demand for and supply of credit. The prospect of stable rates for the indefinite future leads to one type of decision; but the anticipation of changing rates and the belief that the future contains some uncertainty leads to another type of decision. This is true even though we cannot generalize regarding the types of action that result from these two kinds of situations.

Some of these points were made explicit in a letter written by Governor Eccles of the Federal Reserve Board to Senator Douglas in the winter of 1949.

A very fundamental dilemma confronts the Federal Reserve System in the discharge of the responsibilities placed on it by Congress. The System has by statute the task of influencing the supply, availability, and cost of money

---

5. *Monetary Policy and the Management of the Public Debt,* Replies to Questions and Other Material for the Use of the Subcommittee on General Credit Control and Debt Management [Reply by the Chairman of the Board of Governors of the Federal Reserve System], 82d Cong., 2d sess., Joint Committee Print, 1952, Part I, p. 371.

and credit. In peacetime, the objective is to do this in such a way that monetary and credit policy will make the maximum possible contribution to sustained progress toward goals of high employment and rising standards of living. Federal Reserve System powers for carrying out this responsibility are at present basically adequate. But the System has not, in fact, been free to use its powers under circumstances when a restrictive monetary policy was highly essential in the public interest. It has been precluded from doing so in the earlier postwar period in part because of the large volume of Government securities held by banks, insurance companies and others who did not view them as permanent investments. Reasons for supporting the market under these conditions I have already presented before your committee.

This policy of rigid support of Government securities should not be continued indefinitely. The circumstances that made it necessary are no longer compelling. But the Federal Reserve would not be able to change these policies as long as it felt bound to support debt-management decisions made by the Treasury, unless these were in conformity with the same objectives that guide the Federal Reserve. The Treasury, however, is not responsible to Congress for monetary and credit policy and has had for a long time a general easy-money bias under almost any and all circumstances. As long as the Federal Reserve policy must be based upon this criterion, it could not pursue a restrictive money policy to combat inflationary pressures.

Decisions regarding management of the public debt set the framework within which monetary and credit action can be taken. As the size of the debt grew through the period of deficit finance in the thirties and particularly over the war period, Treasury needs came to overshadow and finally to dominate completely Federal Reserve monetary and credit policy. When the Treasury announces the issue of securities at a very low rate pattern during a period of credit expansion, as it did last Wednesday, the Federal Reserve is forced to defend these terms unless the System is prepared to let the financing fail, which it could not very well do. To maintain a very low rate pattern when there is a strong demand for credit, the System cannot avoid supplying Federal Reserve credit at the will of the market.

Under these conditions it can hardly be said that the Federal Reserve System retains any effective influence in its own right over the supply of money in the country or over the availability and cost of credit, although these are the major duties for which the System has statutory responsibility. Nor can it be said that the discount rate and open-market operations of the System are determined by the Federal Reserve authorities, except in form. They are predetermined by debt-management decisions made by the Treasury. This will be true as long as the System is not in a position to pursue an independent policy but must support in the market any program of financing adopted by the Treasury even though the program may be inconsistent with the monetary and credit policies the System considers appropriate in the public interest.[6]

6. Letter dated December 1, 1949, from M. S. Eccles to the Hon. Paul H. Douglas, in *Monetary, Credit, and Fiscal Policies,* Hearings before the Subcommittee on Monetary, Credit, and Fiscal Policies of the Joint Committee on the Economic Report, 81st Cong., 1st sess., 1950, pp. 222-23.

Finally, there is the belief, firmly held in some quarters, that the presence of governmental controls in one market inevitably leads to the extension of these controls into other markets. Thus a closely regulated money market—which admittedly is a key element in the economy—will, if long continued, almost certainly lead to the growth of similar regulations in the commodity and labor markets.

Comment

In the monetary, as in other fields, strict regimentation is by its nature incompatible with administrative flexibility. Once a policy of meticulous control is undertaken the efficacy of the powers of the regulatory agency is in some measure lost, since authority can thereafter be exerted in only one direction, that of relaxation. *Complete* exercise of regulatory discretion, paradoxically, leaves the regulating agency powerless. If it wishes to re-establish its flexibility and maneuverability it must endeavor to do so either by retreating or by acquiring authority over new segments of the economy. When money rates are closely controlled, fiscal authority will—almost necessarily—attempt to expand the scope of business activities over which it has discretion and the regulatory powers it may employ. The efforts of the Reserve System in the postwar period to obtain new legislative authority is a case in point, as is the frequently voiced suggestion that credit controls should be directly extended to particular kinds of financing and to the lending activities of financial institutions. The idea of regulating investment by specifically limiting investment opportunities through the allocation of resources and the rationing of materials also reflects, in part, the loss of flexibility of existing powers.

Low Yields

The fact that the level of rates established subsequent to Pearl Harbor was, historically, a rather low one complicated these problems inherent in a policy of a stabilized rate.

Whether the interest structure established in 1941 was or was not a suitable one for financing the war need not concern us. Very likely it was the best that could be developed under the conditions then prevailing. More important is the question whether the wartime pattern was suitable after the return of peace, in view of the high level of employment that continued to prevail and all the other changes brought by the cessation of hostilities. On a priori grounds one might suppose that a level and structure of rates proper for war conditions and large deficits would not be ideally adapted for peacetime and the possibility—even the temporary actuality—of balanced budgets.

Yet fiscal authority was slow to make changes. One reason, no doubt, was that the cheap money policy was combined with the policy of stability, and a policy of stability inevitably leads to a defense of the existing situation, even though underlying conditions change. Indeed, the cautious advances made in short rates in 1947 and 1948 can be interpreted as recognition—but only a grudging recognition—that the interest pattern must be adapted to a shifting economic scene.

Rates on government securities are, of course, the basic rates in the money market. Hence the maintenance of a low yield on Treasury securities meant that all other types of interest charges—on home mortgages, on corporate bonds, on foreign loans, on agricultural credit, on stock exchange loans—would also remain at moderate levels. Yet even if the government were entitled to a low rate it did not necessarily follow that all borrowers should also have had the benefit of it.

The cheap money policy was, to be sure, valuable from the budgetary point of view. It limited the interest burden at a time when there was much talk—more talk than action—regarding the necessity of reducing unnecessary expenditures. And for this, as well as for other reasons, the cheap money policy had, as it always has, much political appeal.

Whether the level of rates maintained during the war and immediate postwar period was well adapted to the needs of those persons and institutions whom the logic of the situation called upon to hold federal securities is another matter. Here opinion divided sharply. Life insurance companies, with many of their outstanding contracts based on the expectation of 3 per cent or 3¼ per cent earnings, believed that 2½ per cent, the highest rate obtainable on long-term governments, and the only slightly better rates obtainable on corporate issues, were inadequate for their needs. Commercial banks, faced with rising operating costs and higher reserve requirements, felt a lack of earnings, even though the income received on their portfolios of government securities was very nearly "costless," so long as the prices of these securities were supported. Substance was given to this view by the fact that stocks of many banks had, since the early 1930's, sold at considerable discounts from their book or liquidating values, principally because bank earnings were not large enough to support market prices equal to these break-up values.

Whether these beliefs were entirely justified is not the immediate point at issue. The important consideration is that their existence would lead many institutions, when and as the opportunity arose, to liquidate government securities in order to reinvest at higher returns.

STABILIZED YIELDS AND THE PATTERN OF OWNERSHIP

Did the interest policy pursued during the war and in the immediate postwar period enhance or diminish stability in the pattern of ownership, which must always be one of the primary goals of debt management?

So long as outlets for investment funds other than federal securities are limited, and in particular so long as these outlets are not adequate to absorb the moneys available for investment, low and stabilized rates are not incompatible with stability in the pattern of ownership. Such conditions prevail in peace, when the economy is running at less than capacity, and in wartime, even though output is then close to the possible maximum. In this type of situation persons and institutions with funds to place have no alternative other than to accept the terms offered them by fiscal authority, although the lower the yields received the greater their compulsion to seek new and higher paying outlets.

When other opportunities open up, however, or even when there is only an expectation that such opportunities will open up, the logic of the situation shifts. Under such conditions holders of federal securities have a real motive for selling, in order to make what they consider more advantageous use of their money. Particularly is this the case when the prices of Treasury obligations are supported at such a level that no loss is involved in their sale.

A high-level, expanding economy, the pursuit of which is now national policy, is very likely to provide a large number of attractive outlets for investable funds. Indeed, active and expanding business conditions, marked by something like full employment, are commonly defined in terms of plentiful and profitable investment opportunities. And if these conditions are characterized by rising prices, the possibilities of investment will be further enhanced, since with advancing prices and costs a larger volume of capital is required by business concerns to carry on the same volume. Thus a high-level economy, if rates of Treasury securities are stabilized, is likely to induce instability in the pattern of ownership as holders of these obligations sell them in order to acquire other investments.

It is, of course, possible even under these conditions for the central bank to hold rates steady, by buying at fixed prices all the securities offered. But it can do this only at the cost of expanding bank deposits. This in turn is likely to push the price level still higher and thereby further stimulate the transfer of federal securities. The counteracting move, of course, is to impose a penalty on the sale of these securities, which can be done by lowering the price at which the central bank buys. Thus we reach the conclusion that, under peacetime conditions of high activity in the economy, a rising level of rates is likely to be necessary simply to maintain stability in the pattern of ownership of government securities, irrespective of the effects advances in rates may have on saving and investment or the creation of bank loans and deposits.

CONCLUSION

The dissension regarding interest policy has combined within itself two types of disagreement. On the one hand there has been the theoretical or ideological disagreement. On the other hand there has been the conflict of interests among the parties involved.

The ideological split has centered around the diverse views regarding the function of interest rates in the economy and the presumed effects of high or low rates on savings, investment, the behavior of government bond holders and the expansion of deposits.

The conflict of interests among the parties involved has turned on more concrete issues. The Treasury, charged with managing a tremendous debt, confronted with a serious refunding problem and living always under the shadow of having to raise new money when and as deficits return, found a low and stable interest policy ideally suited to its needs. Such a policy kept the interest burden at a minimum and greatly aided the refunding of government securities as they fell due or moved within the call period.

The market support policy of the Reserve System, on the other hand, largely emasculated its traditional mechanisms of monetary management—open market operations, changes in the discount rate and alterations in bank reserve requirements—and took control of the money supply from it. Under conditions of active business, when the economy is running close to capacity and inflationary pressures are imminent, this result raises the question whether the System properly fulfills its legislative responsibility if it persists indefinitely in the policy of market support for government obligations. At the same time, important portions of the debt-owning public, feeling the need for higher returns, are very likely to shift their government holdings to the Federal when more attractive investment opportunities open up, and thereby increase inflationary pressures.

We need not attempt to resolve the theoretical controversy, even were that possible in the present state of economic knowledge. What is clear, on the basis of experience since the war, is that a controlled market for government securities, which enforces a low and stable rate structure, is not compatible with stability in the pattern of ownership when business activity is at a high level and is giving indications of attempting to rise still higher. The policy may be compatible with reasonable stability in the ownership of Treasury obligations when the economy is operating below capacity, or under the compulsions of war, but conditions change as capacity is approached under conditions of peace. In such a situation more attractive uses for funds lead to selling of government securities, and as the central bank acquires them purchasing power is expanded and inflationary tendencies are again enhanced. To check this movement a reduction in the bank's buying price is necessary. This raises interest rates and leads to market uncertainty. Thus a restriction in the availability of credit and a reduction in the transfers of government securities brings a rise in rates. But this is a result of the restrictive situation that develops, not the cause; nor is it the primary objective of such a policy.

Chapter 6

THE EFFECT OF KOREA

THE RESISTANCE of the United States to aggression in Korea in June 1950 immediately altered the circumstances surrounding debt management and, in some degree, the nature of the problem. This was so partly because of the new political outlook, partly because of the public interpretation of it and the actions that followed this shift in expectations.

IMMEDIATE REPERCUSSIONS

Public Reaction

In broad outline the public, following the lead of various governmental pronouncements, almost at once reached the conclusion that the cold war was likely to continue for a long time, perhaps ten or twenty years, that a great increase in federal expenditure for armaments was imminent and that shortages of many kinds were just around the corner. The response to this prospect was rapid. Private expenditures spurted, bank loans increased sharply and commodity prices, which were already high, advanced rapidly. The shadow of a severe inflation fell across the country and the danger was enhanced as persons and business concerns took actions designed to protect themselves, or to profit, from the developments they anticipated.

Treasury Refunding

These developments had a sharp impact on the problems of debt management. In the first place, they occurred at a time when the impending volume of refunding of Treasury securities was very large. As of June 30, 1950, there were $35,339 million of fixed maturity issues coming due in the next six months, another $15,736 million in the following six months, and an additional $11,997 million of maturities became callable during the first half of 1951— a total of $63,072 million. (See Table 5.) In the second place, the

TABLE 5

MATURITY SCHEDULE OF INTEREST-BEARING PUBLIC MARKETABLE
SECURITIES ISSUED BY THE U.S. GOVERNMENT
FOR THE PERIOD JULY 1950–DECEMBER 1951,
AS OF JUNE 30, 1950

(*In Millions*)

| Year and Month of Maturity | Description of Security | Amount of Maturities | |
		Fixed Maturity Issues	Callable Issues, Date of First Call
1950			
July	Bills	$ 3,905	
	1¼% Certificates	5,601	
August	Bills	5,516	
September	Bills	4,112	
	1⅛% Certificates	1,197	
	2½% Bonds	1,186	
	2% Bonds	4,939	
October	1⅛% Certificates	6,248	
December	1½% Bonds	2,635	
Total		$35,339	
1951			
January	1⅛% Certificates	$ 5,373	
June	2¾% Bonds		$ 1,627
July	1¼% Notes	8,445	
September	2% Bonds		7,986
	3% Bonds		755
October	1¼% Notes	1,918	
December	2¼% Bonds		1,118
	2% Bonds		510
Total		$15,736	$11,997
Summary			
Fixed maturity issues			
1950			$35,339
1951			15,736
Issues coming within first call date			11,997
			$63,072

Source: Treasury Bulletin, August 1950, p. 21.

Note: Totals will not necessarily add because of rounding of figures.

enlarged military needs meant, presumably, that the Treasury would issue some securities for the purpose of raising new money in the not-too-distant future, which would be in addition to any obligations sold in connection with refunding maturing debt. In the third place, in view of the enhanced demand for financing by the private segment of the economy, the Federal Reserve's policy of market support became even more controversial than formerly since, so long as it continued, control of this demand for credit seemed difficult if not impossible to many persons, including a portion of the Reserve Board itself. Yet abandonment of the policy in the face of the Treasury's requirements seemed to other persons more hazardous than ever.

The Split of Opinion

This combination of circumstances made debt management critically important. While there was general agreement that an increase in taxation was immediately necessary, divisions of opinion appeared elsewhere in the financial field. There were those who, in Leffingwell's phrase, wished to "get our debts in order," and this view generally implied some long-term refunding and a rise in interest rates. There were those who felt that continuance of existing debt policies was essential, and that the way to make them workable was by the use of various kinds of direct controls. To oversimplify the divergence, the split was between those who wished to place chief reliance on indirect controls and taxation, with a minimum of direct controls, and those who put their confidence in an elaborate system of direct controls, taxation and a perpetuation of the debt policies pursued during and since World War II. The compromise view, and the view which largely prevailed, wished to use both direct and indirect controls.

These differences of opinion had been inherent throughout the whole postwar period, but the outbreak of hostilities brought them to a head. Their most dramatic manifestation was the open break in the relations of the Treasury and the Federal Reserve System that developed in August 1950 in connection with the terms of the issues offered for refunding obligations coming due in September and October. This difference regarding debt and credit policy continued in an acute form throughout the autumn of 1950 and into the spring of 1951.

Before considering this dispute in detail we must survey the course of economic, business and financial developments during the second half of 1950.

DEVELOPMENTS DURING THE SECOND HALF OF 1950

In the second quarter of 1950 Gross National Product was at an annual rate of $271.6 billion; by the end of the year it had risen to an annual rate of $300.2 billion, an increase of about 11 per cent, although the advance was less than appeared if the figures were deflated for price changes.

This expansion was reflected both in production and in price indices. In June the Federal Reserve index of production stood at 199; by December it was 218, roughly a 10 per cent advance. The index of durable manufactures rose even more rapidly, roughly 13 per cent in the second half of 1950. The wholesale commodity price index shot up from 157.3 to 175.3, a rise of nearly 12 per cent, and some sensitive prices, such as hides, textiles and chemical products, climbed even faster. These developments were accompanied by a comparable increase in personal income which, by the end of the year, was at an annual rate of $241.0 billion, approximately a 10 per cent advance since June.

The Influence of the Budget

These manifestations of a boom and an inflationary situation took place notwithstanding the distinctly deflationary influence exerted by the federal budget. On September 23 the Revenue Act of 1950 became law. Current estimates were that this act would raise federal tax receipts by some five to six billion dollars. Furthermore, a promise was given that the Congress would apply itself to a retroactive excess profits tax law immediately it reconvened in January. In addition, and most important, during the last half of calendar 1950 the Treasury had a net cash operating income, in excess of cash outgo, of $796 million. But the rise in prices took place despite this withdrawal of purchasing power, and it was this fact as much as any which gave rise to apprehensions regarding the strength of the inflationary forces.

The Explanation: Private Expenditures

The explanation of the advance in prices in the face of this deflationary situation lay in the behavior of private spending, particularly on the part of business concerns. New plant and equipment expenditures, which in the first quarter of the year had amounted to $3,700 million, rose in the second quarter to $4,330 million, and in the final quarter of 1950 to $5,830 million. Business inventories, which in June were $54.2 billion had, by the end of the year, increased by more than $7 billion to $61.5 billion, more than 13 per cent. All this resulted in a sharp spurt in gross private domestic investment from $47.7 billion in the second quarter of 1950 to $60.2 billion in the fourth quarter. These expenditures were financed partly by a rise in the turnover of money, partly by a reduction in certain kinds of liquid assets, but chiefly by an increase in borrowing.

Debits to total deposit accounts in all reporting centers advanced from $119.4 billion in June to $140.0 billion in December. Although some of this rise was seasonal, it nevertheless brought an appreciable increase in the rate of deposit turnover as compared with December 1949.

Evidence of the reduction of liquid assets can be found in various places. Total time deposits, for example, fell about half a billion dollars during the latter half of the year; many open-end investment companies discovered that redemptions of outstanding shares exceeded new sales; and cash-ins of United States Government Savings Bonds, Series E, consistently ran ahead of new sales.

These developments, of course, reflected an increase in consumer spending. But the rise in consumer debt was not great, partly because of the use of direct credit controls by the Federal Reserve. Total consumer credit, for example, increased only $2.4 billion between June and December 1950, as compared with a rise of $2.7 billion during the comparable period in 1949, and total installment credit rose only $1.4 billion in the latter half of 1950, as compared with an increase of $1.8 billion in the second half of 1949.

Increased Borrowing

Thus, far and away the most important source of the spending was the increase in business borrowing, as concerns endeavored to ready themselves for the situation that they saw ahead. Loans of all insured commercial banks rose nearly $7.5 billion between June and December, in the most rapid increase on record, and commercial loans constituted the great bulk of this advance. Much the same picture was presented by the insurance companies. Assets of the 49 major life insurance companies that account for approximately 90 per cent of the assets of all life insurance companies, rose $2.1 billion during the second half of 1950. At the same time their holdings of government obligations declined $1.2 billion. One may surmise that the funds represented by the asset increase, plus the funds released by sales of governments—a total of about $3.3 billion

—was invested in the private segment of the economy, in mortgages and in corporate obligations. The reductions in the holdings of Treasury securities by the leading lending institutions covered by the Treasury Survey of Ownership are summarized in Table 6. These decreases are indicative of the extent to which sales of federal securities provided funds sought by private borrowers.

TABLE 6

PORTFOLIOS OF GOVERNMENT SECURITIES HELD
BY LEADING LENDING INSTITUTIONS,
JANUARY AND DECEMBER 1950

(*In Millions*)

Institution	January	December	Net Reduction
Total	$85,943	$77,783	$8,160
Commercial banks	60,504	54,893	5,611
Life insurance companies	14,590	12,746	1,844
Mutual savings banks	10,849	10,144	705

Source: Appendix Tables 18, 22, 24.

Commenting on the current situation in November 1950, the Federal Reserve Bank of New York stated:

. . . in the period since the start of the war in Korea, Government receipts have exceeded disbursements, and the accentuated inflationary pressures have clearly been the direct result of accelerated private spending, much of it financed by credit. It is true, of course, that such spending has been stimulated by fears of later shortages of civilian goods as a result of the national defense program, and to some extent by fears of further inflationary price advances growing out of Government deficit financing.[1]

Federal Reserve Credit

During this period Federal Reserve credit, with few interruptions, expanded persistently, notwithstanding the manifestly inflationary situation. Standing at $18.2 billion at the end of June, it had, by the last week of December, risen to $20.3 billion, a two billion dollar advance. This increase, in view of the rising prices, brought the Reserve System under heavy criticism, since this behavior appeared directly contrary to orthodox central banking procedure. The ex-

1. *Monthly Review of Credit and Business Conditions,* Federal Reserve Bank of New York, November 1950, p. 126.

planation, of course, lay in the price support which the Federal Reserve gave to government securities—although at declining levels—at a time when other holders, for reasons already indicated, wished to sell. This policy, and the changes which occurred in it, was one of the root causes of the dispute between the Federal Reserve and the Treasury, to which we will now turn.

THE TREASURY-FEDERAL RESERVE DISPUTE

Prior to the Korean invasion it had appeared that the Treasury was in the process of cautiously departing from its postwar practice of refunding all maturing securities into short-term obligations, and this change was consistent with the Federal Reserve's efforts in the spring of 1950 to exercise a restraining influence. The government securities maturing in December 1949, for example, had been refunded into five-year notes. Although the certificates coming due in January had been replaced with one-year paper, longer-term obligations had been used to refund the certificates maturing in February and March, and the bond issue coming due on March 15 and the note issue maturing April 1 had been refunded into five-year obligations. During the spring of 1950 a moderate program of selling federal securities lowered the total amount of Federal Reserve credit outstanding, from a peak of $18,829 million in January to $17,290 million in the third week of May.

This decline in Reserve credit came to an end shortly after the Treasury's announcement on May 4 of the terms to be offered in connection with the maturities of June 1 and July 1. In exchange for the certificates then payable the Treasury offered 1¼ per cent thirteen-month notes. These terms were not especially attractive in view of prevailing market conditions and the Federal Reserve found it necessary to support the prices of Treasury obligations and also to buy an appreciable amount of the June and July maturities in order to prevent an undue amount of these issues being presented for cash redemption. (See Table 7.)

Thus the clash between the Federal Reserve and the Treasury had its origins prior to the Korean invasion. The rapid expansion of bank credit subsequent to the outbreak of fighting, however, and the severe refunding problem faced by the Treasury rapidly widened their differences. Under the strain of political pressures it became impossible to gloss over the basic issue.

TABLE 7

REDEMPTION EXPERIENCE IN REFUNDINGS,
SELECTED DATES, 1950

(Dollar Amounts in Millions)

	Refunding		
Item	March and April	June and July	September and October
Issues being retired			
Total outstanding	$9,444	$10,620	$13,570
Federal Reserve holdings			
At time of announcement	1,040	2,812	2,370
Purchased after announcement	—	1,384[a]	8,030
Exchanged			
By Federal Reserve	1,040	4,196[b]	10,400
By others	7,954	5,973[b]	794
Redeemed for cash	450	451	2,376
Percentages of total			
Exchanged by Federal Reserve			
Total	11.0	39.5	76.7
Original holdings	11.0	26.5	17.5
Purchased	—	13.0	59.2
Exchanged by others	84.2	56.2	5.8
Redeemed for cash	4.8	4.3	17.5

Source: General Credit Control, Debt Management, and Economic Mobilization, Joint Committee Print, printed for the use of the Joint Committee on the Economic Report, 82d Cong., 1st sess., 1951, p. 5.

a. Includes Federal Reserve purchases through June of the new notes issued in exchange for the certificates maturing June 1, 1950.

b. Purchases by the Federal Reserve during June of the new notes issued on June 1, 1950, are considered as exchanged by the Federal Reserve.

The August 18 Announcements

The events immediately leading up to the open break of August 18 are not a matter of public record, although the general positions taken by the two parties were well known. No doubt a number of communications passed between the Treasury and the Federal Reserve. On July 17, Secretary Snyder wrote the Chairman of the Board of Governors regarding the government debt and the public's confidence in the government's credit, saying, in part:

I know you will agree with me that it is of the utmost importance at the present time to maintain that confidence and, in addition, to do everything possible to strengthen it. This involves, first of all, avoiding any course which would give rise to a belief that significant changes in the pattern of rates were under consideration. The operations of the Open Market Committee since the beginning of the crisis have been well adapted to this end.

As I have studied the situation, I have become convinced that present circumstances call for one further precaution, which is, perhaps, of even greater importance than maintaining a good balance in current market operations. In my view, we must take extreme care to avoid introducing any factor which would run the risk of producing unsettlement in the broad market for federal securities represented by investors throughout the nation. It is my belief, in particular, that no new financing program should be undertaken at the present time without maximum assurance that it will be well received and can be carried through to a successful conclusion. . . .

As you know, developments in the government bond market have repercussions which fan out through the entire economy. Both the size and the wide distribution of the federal debt are unprecedented in comparison with the situation which faced us at the start of other periods of crisis. Under these circumstances, we have an obligation of the highest order not only to maintain the finances of the government in the soundest possible condition but also to fulfill our responsibilities to the millions of federal security holders throughout the nation.[2]

In any event, on Friday, August 18, the Secretary of the Treasury announced that, in exchange for the 2 per cent and 2½ per cent bonds called for redemption on September 15 and the 1⅛ per cent certificates maturing on that date and on October 1, which together totaled slightly more than $13.5 billion, he would offer 1¼ per cent thirteen-month notes. Notwithstanding the very large size of the offering these terms were identical with those of June and July, when the refunding achieved success only through the intervention of the Federal Reserve.

On the same day the Board of Governors of the Reserve System announced that it had approved an increase in the discount rate of the New York Reserve Bank, effective Monday, August 21, from 1½ per cent to 1¾ per cent. This increase, as was customary, was presently followed by similar action in the case of the other Reserve Banks. Even more important, the August 18 announcement stated that "the Board of Governors of the Federal Reserve System and the Federal Open Market Committee are prepared to use all the means at their command to restrain further expansion of bank credit consistent with the policy of maintaining orderly conditions in the Government securities market."

Thus the astonishing situation arose in which one of the chief

2. *Monetary Policy and the Management of the Public Debt,* Replies to Questions and Other Material for the Use of the Subcommittee on General Credit Control and Debt Management [Reply by the Secretary of the Treasury], Joint Committee on the Economic Report, 82d Cong., 2d sess., Joint Committee Print, 1952, Part I, p. 67.

federal fiscal authorities was endeavoring to adhere to the existing level of interest rates—or perhaps more accurately, in view of existing market conditions, to enforce a slightly lower rate—while the other principal authority announced that it would use every means at its command—including, quite evidently, an increase in rates—to restrict credit expansion. Not unnaturally the market was greatly confused as to what portended. The immediate question was how the Treasury could successfully consummate its financing if the Reserve Board adhered to its announced policy and allowed rates to rise above those attached to the new Treasury offerings.

The Outcome

The answer was not long in coming. The Reserve Banks began a series of spectacular and unprecedented open-market operations. In essence, they bought in the maturing issues, while selling other Treasury obligations, at relatively lower prices. These actions were designed, on the one hand, to lower the prices and raise rates of Treasury obligations other than the four issues coming due in September and October and, on the other hand, to put within the Reserve Banks' own portfolio a major portion of the maturing issues. These could then be offered by the Reserve Banks to the Treasury in exchange for the new 1¼ per cent notes, whereas if the public continued to hold the maturing obligations, it seemed clear that the public would ask that these securities be redeemed for cash.

The Reserve Banks, while bidding par or better for the maturing issues, sold very large amounts of other obligations, sometimes at price concessions in order to move them. Thus the rate on thirteen-month federal obligations went to approximately 1⅜ per cent, as compared with the 1¼ per cent rate for the new notes offered by the Treasury. These sales served two purposes. They raised the level of interest rates and they checked the growth of the Reserve Banks' own portfolio. As an additional means of restricting the expansion of its holdings and the volume of Reserve credit, the Reserve Banks each week permitted some of their bill holdings to run off without replacement. During this period, from the middle of August to the beginning of October, total Federal Reserve holdings of governments increased by a little less than one billion dollars, nothwithstanding the system's enormous purchases of $8 billion.

As shown in Table 7, after the terms of the new notes were announced on August 13, the Reserve Banks acquired more than $8 billion of the maturing issues. These purchases, together with the $2.4 billion already held, amounted to 76.7 per cent of the total. Aside from the securities owned by the Reserve System, only some $56 million of obligations were offered the Treasury for exchange in September and October, and $2,376 million of the four issues were redeemed for cash. Thus about 17.5 per cent of the four maturities were paid off, as compared with a "normal" figure of five to ten per cent. If the Reserve System, while it was permitting rates to rise, had not acquired so large a portion of the September and October maturities, the volume of redemptions would have been very much greater. Nevertheless, the redemptions were unusually large and, together with the securities presented for payment in the March and April and the June and July refundings, "cost" the Treasury $3,277 million in cash.

The Conclusion to be Drawn

What conclusions can be drawn from this episode? 67584

First, the issuance of so large a volume of securities at so low a rate probably could not have been consummated smoothly, even if the Board of Governors had concurred with the Treasury's terms. As it was, with the Board of Governors taking an independent line, very large aid from the Reserve System was necessary to prevent a complete fiasco. At the completion of the financing the Reserve Banks owned approximately three fourths of the new issue.

Second, even with the aid of the Reserve System, the Treasury suffered a considerable loss of cash, and this was an unwelcome development.

Third, the employment of so short a maturity ensured that the Treasury would again be faced with severe refunding problems a year later.

Fourth, while the Reserve System in its fight against inflation had achieved a change in the interest rate structure, the change had entailed an appreciable expansion in the volume of Federal Reserve credit outstanding, and *that* was inflationary, not deflationary. On the other hand, had the open market operations of the Reserve System been conducted less skillfully, the increase in the volume of Reserve credit might easily have been much larger than in fact it was.

Fifth, the incident underlined the fact that when investors have ample and attractive uses for funds outside the government securities market an attempt by the Treasury to issue obligations on unattractive terms must almost inevitably lead to an expansion in the credit base. That is, failure to adapt the terms of new issues to the wishes and needs of debt holders will convert the instability inherent in the pattern of ownership into actual large-scale transfers of obligations.

Finally, while the outcome of the incident must have been unsatisfactory to both parties, and while the incident itself provided no basis for reconciling the differences between the two fiscal authorities, it strongly emphasized the necessity for cooperation between them.

The Next Phase

In November the Treasury reverted to the policy of refunding maturing debt into securities with a longer maturity than twelve or thirteen months, which it had abandoned in August, and offered a 1¾ five-year note in exchange for $2,635 million of bonds maturing on December 15 and $5,373 million of certificates coming due on the first of January. This offering was generally regarded as well designed to meet the conditions of the market then existing and was reasonably well received. The market, however, was still disturbed and nearly 15 per cent of the maturing issues were redeemed for cash rather than exchanged for the new issue. On December 29 the Board of Governors, pursuant to its policy of restraining credit, raised reserve requirements of member banks—effective as of varying dates in January and February—virtually to the permissible legal limit. On January 17 they amended Regulations T and U and raised margin requirements of brokers and banks from 50 to 75 per cent.

It might have been thought that the events of the autumn of 1950 —commonly referred to as a "fiasco"— would have put sufficient pressure on the Treasury and the Board of Governors so that they would have been compelled to heal their differences and reach at least a working agreement, particularly since the course of events could not have been pleasing to either side. Such was not the case, however, at least immediately. Before considering the next stage in the argument, however, we should note the reintroduction of direct credit controls in the autumn of 1950.

The Renewal of Direct Controls

On September 8 the Defense Production Act of 1950 was signed. This act, among other things, restored to the Board of Governors power to regulate the extension of consumer credit and gave it authority to restrict the use of private credit in new real estate construction. Accordingly, the Board reissued Regulation W, effective September 18. This required minimum down payments when automobiles and certain other durable goods were bought, and limited the period during which the balance could be paid. On October 10 the Board issued Regulation X, which set minimum down payments and amortization schedules in connection with the purchase of privately financed new housing.

These measures reflected the belief that, whatever the general effect of indirect credit regulations, in some areas of the economy specific controls might appropriately be applied to supplement them. Indeed, much of the argument about general controls centered on the question whether an extensive set of specific controls—the word "harness" was sometimes used—designed to achieve particular goals in particular economic fields, might not be an effective substitute for over-all, indirect measures, notably changes in discount rates, member bank reserve requirements, and prices of government securities. As the Secretary of the Treasury later said:

> In this situation [after Korea] the Treasury felt that major reliance in controlling inflationary pressures should not be placed on traditional methods of general credit control. As already stated, the Treasury felt that higher taxes, restraint in nondefense Government expenditures, greater savings, and various *selective measures suitable to the defense situation* were called for.[3]

And again:

> It should be noted that the widespread use of physical controls [allocations, price controls, etc.] in wartime adds greatly to our arsenal of anti-inflationary weapons and tends to reduce the need for reliance upon general credit controls. Selective credit controls likewise may be employed to supplement direct controls.[4]

The Spring of 1951

After the refundings of December and January were completed no further Treasury issues matured or moved within the first call date until June 15. Thus there was an interval of five and one half

3. *Ibid.,* pp. 69-70. Italics supplied.
4. *Ibid.,* p. 101.

months within which the situation could be reappraised, a policy of credit control could be re-established and new procedures of debt management, if these seemed desirable, could be developed. Careful consideration of the matter was essential, for during the second half of 1951 some $28.5 billion of bonds and notes matured, and another $10.4 billion moved within the first call date. In addition, about $14 billion of bills had to be rolled over continuously and, during the latter part of 1950, redemptions of savings bonds showed a persistent tendency to run ahead of sales, except at times when special offerings boosted purchases. Finally, there was the common expectation that the Treasury would need to go to the market for new money some time during the second six months of the year, perhaps for large amounts. All in all it seemed likely that for refunding and new money purposes something like $60 billion of securities might have to be sold during the latter part of the year.

The Controversy Is Renewed

On January 18 in a speech in New York, Secretary Snyder voiced sentiments suggesting that the Treasury had not changed its position of the preceding summer.

While adequate revenues are an essential safeguard against the development of inflationary tendencies, they cannot do the job alone. Measures for allocating essential materials have been adopted in order to assure priority for our military needs without increasing the strain on the price structure. Selective credit controls such as those embodied in the Defense Production Act passed by the Congress last September are also of definite help. Other measures of demonstrated effectiveness in curbing inflationary tendencies, such as price and wage controls, are under consideration and will assuredly be adopted soon.

You will note that I have not included the use of fractional increases in interest rates on Government securities as one of the measures of effectively controlling inflation. The Treasury is convinced that there is no tangible evidence that a policy of credit rationing by means of small increases in the interest rates on Government borrowed funds has had a real or genuine effect in cutting down the volume of private borrowing and in retarding inflationary pressures. The delusion that fractional changes in interest rates can be effective in fighting inflation must be dispelled from our minds. . . .

Now let us go on to the subject of interest rates. It is my view that a 2½ per cent rate of interest on long-term Treasury bonds is a fair and equitable rate—to our Government which is borrowing the money, to the purchaser of Government bonds who is lending the money, and to the taxpayer who has to pay the interest on the money borrowed.

The 2½ per cent rate of interest on long-term Government securities is an integral part of the financial structure of our country. During the past ten years—a period in which we fought our most costly war and made a most extensive reconversion to peacetime activities—the 2½ per cent rate has become a most important influencing factor in financial policy in the country. It dominates the bond markets—Government, corporate, and municipal. Moreover, it dominates the operations of financial institutions. Most of these have already adjusted themselves to the 2½ per cent rate—and after so doing, have become more prosperous than ever before. . . .

Any increase in the 2½ per cent rate would, I am firmly convinced, seriously upset existing security markets—Government, corporate and municipal.[5]

This was an unequivocal statement. It reiterated and made explicit the position of the Treasury. Whatever might have happened in recent months to short- and intermediate-term rates, this speech made the long-term 2½ per cent rate the keystone of Treasury policy and a symbol in men's minds.

The Situation Becomes Acute

The reaction by those groups who disagreed with the Treasury's policy was immediate and violent. A storm of protest broke out in the press and various members of Congress expressed strong disapproval and threatened Congressional intervention in the dispute. Within a few days both Governor Eccles of the Reserve Board and President Sproul of the New York Reserve Bank publicly disagreed with the Treasury views. Indicative of the depth of feeling was a statement in the *New York Times:*

In the opinion of this writer, last Thursday constituted the first occasion in history on which the head of the Exchequer of a great nation had either the effrontery or the ineptitude, or both, to deliver a public address in which he so far usurped the function of the central bank as to tell the country what kind of a monetary policy it was going to be subjected to.[6]

By the end of the month President Truman found it necessary to intervene, and the Federal Reserve Open Market Committee was invited to the White House for a conference on January 31. On the same day, in the words of the *New York Times,* Secretary Snyder "broke his silence" in the dispute and "struck out" at critics

. . . who would have the Government make it possible for the banks to make even bigger profits at a time when industry, business and labor is asked to forego part of the profits they would realize from the defense mobilization.

5. Address by Secretary Snyder before the New York Board of Trade, January 18, 1951.
6. Edward H. Collins in the *New York Times,* January 22, 1951.

And we are asked to do this just to support a theory that higher interest rates might have a retarding influence on inflation when actual experience shows that the effect, if any, would be negligible.

The Secretary of the Treasury has got to be a lot more practical than that. The Congress has given me the responsibility of protecting the government credit, of issuing government securities, fixing their maturities and the rate of interest they shall bear. The discharging of that responsibility does not leave much room for playing around with other people's theories.[7]

On the next day three successive reports of the White House conference appeared on the news ticker. The first, in effect, stated that the President "backed" the Secretary of the Treasury; the second quoted a White House report that the Federal Reserve had given a pledge to maintain stability in the market for government securities; the third contained the Treasury's interpretation of the pledge, namely that it meant a freezing of the whole pattern of yields on government securities for the duration of the emergency. But it was only after the third report appeared that government securities showed strength.[8] On February 2 in a public letter President Truman thanked Chairman McCabe of the Board of Governors for

. . . your assurance that you would fully support the Treasury defense financing program, both as to refunding and new issues. . . . As I understand it, I have your assurance that the market on Government securities will be stabilized and maintained at present levels in order to assure the successful financing requirements and to establish in the minds of the people confidence concerning Government credit.[9]

Misunderstandings Become Public

This seemed, however, not to be the understanding of the Reserve officials. The *New York Times* reported that it would be "difficult to exaggerate" their "shocked surprise" and that "They called it, among other things, a complete misrepresentation of both the tenor and substance"[10] of the meeting. The next day, February 3, Governor and former Chairman Eccles of the Reserve Board released to the press the text of the Reserve Board's own memorandum concerning the meeting with the President, which he stated had been approved by all the members of the Open Market Committee. This memorandum did not contain a pledge to support the interest rate pattern.

7. As reported in the *New York Times,* February 1, 1951.
8. *Ibid.,* February 2, 1951.
9. *Ibid.,* February 3, 1951.
10. *Loc. cit.*

Vigorous agitation continued in the press as the financial world strove to understand the implications of the several statements. Sales of government securities continued heavy. In the six weeks ending February 28 the Federal Reserve found it necessary to acquire over $1 billion worth. On February 22 Senator Douglas attacked the Treasury policy in a strong speech on the floor of the Senate. It was against this background that President Truman called his famous meeting of February 26.

The Meeting of February 26

On that day it was announced that the President had met with the Chairman of the Board of Governors of the Federal Reserve System, the Director of the Office of Defense Mobilization, representatives of the Treasury including the Undersecretary,[11] the three members of the Council of Economic Advisers, the Vice Chairman of the Federal Open Market Committee and the Chairman of the Securities and Exchange Commission. The President read the group a statement and requested the Secretary of the Treasury, the Chairman of the Federal Reserve Board, the Director of Defense Mobilization and the Chairman of the Council of Economic Advisers—the so-called "Wilson Committee"—"to study ways and means to provide the necessary restraint on private credit expansion and at the same time make it possible to maintain stability in the market for Government securities."[12] The President also said he hoped that while the study was under way no attempt would be made to change the interest rate pattern, and Mr. Wilson, Chairman of Defense Mobilization and head of the four-man committee, expressed the hope that a report could be made to the President within ten days or two weeks.

In his statement the President said, in part:

One outstanding problem which has thus far not been solved to our complete satisfaction is that of reconciling the policies concerning public debt management and private credit control. Considering the difficulty of this problem, we should not be discouraged because an ideal solution has not yet been found. The essence of this problem is to reconcile two important objectives, neither of which can be sacrificed.

On the one hand, we must maintain stability in the Government security market and confidence in the public credit of the United States. . . .

11. The Secretary was at that time in the hospital and unable to attend the meeting.
12. White House Press Release, February 26, 1951.

On the other hand, we must curb the expansion of private loans, not only by the banking system but also by financial institutions of all types, which would add to inflationary pressures. . . .

The maintenance of stability in the Government securities market necessarily limits substantially the extent to which changes in the interest rate can be used in an attempt to curb private credit expansion. Because of this fact, much of the discussion of this problem has centered around the question of which is to be sacrificed—stability in the Government securities market or control of private credit expansion. I am firmly convinced that this is an erroneous statement of the problem. We need not sacrifice either.

Changing the interest rate is only one of several methods to be considered for curbing credit expansion. . . .

Among other things, I ask that you consider specifically the desirability of measures: (1) to limit private lending through voluntary actions by private groups, through Government-sponsored voluntary actions such as was done in a narrow field by the Capital Issues Committee of World War I, and through direct Government controls; and (2) to provide the Federal Reserve System with powers to impose additional reserve requirements on banks.

I should like you to consider also the establishment of a committee similar to the Capital Issues Committee of World War I, but operating in a broader area. . . . The activities of this committee could be correlated with those of the defense agencies under Mr. Wilson with the objective of curtailing unnecessary uses of essential materials.

Furthermore, I should like you to consider the necessity and feasibility of using the powers provided in the Emergency Banking Act of 1933 to curtail lending by member banks of the Federal Reserve System. These powers are vested in the Secretary of the Treasury subject to my approval. . . . The program could be extended to institutions other than the member banks, if desired, by using the powers provided by the Trading with the Enemy Act.[13]

This statement was notable in several respects. It brought into the Treasury-Federal Reserve controversy executive agencies of the government other than the two directly involved and made the Director of Defense Mobilization responsible for a report on this highly technical subject. It supported the Treasury's position as regards interest policy and also the position taken by the Reserve System as early as 1945 in respect to the desirability of additional powers for the System, although implementation of this suggestion required new legislation of a type that could not be enacted quickly, if at all. It brought to public notice voluntary credit control, a matter already being explored by the Federal Reserve under Section 708 of the Defense Production Act of 1950. For the first time in the controversy public mention was made of the ex-

13. *Ibid.*

treme powers in the Emergency Banking Act of 1933[14] and the Trading with the Enemy Act of 1917.[15] In effect, these powers would permit the executive branch in time of emergency to regulate the lending operations of all financial institutions of all kinds. Finally, the statement included the suggestion that, in the interest of effective mobilization, it might be necessary to correlate the extension of credit with some system of materials allocation. This drastic approach was far removed indeed from the traditional thinking regarding the function of a central bank or the responsibilities of the Treasury in financing the needs of the government and managing its outstanding obligations.

The Accord of March 4

Before the President's Committee appointed on February 26 could report, however, events took a new turn. On March 4—significantly, a Sunday—the Secretary of the Treasury and the Chairman of the Board of Governors released for publication the following announcement:

> The Treasury and the Federal Reserve System have reached full accord with respect to debt-management and monetary policies to be pursued in furthering their common purpose to assure the successful financing of the Government's requirements and, at the same time, to minimize monetization of the public debt.

At the same time the Treasury initiated a change in its offering policy. It announced that late in March and early in April it would offer in exchange, not for any maturing issues but for the bank-restricted 2½ per cent issues of June and December 1967-1972 which had been pressing on the market, a long-term nonmarketable 2¾ per cent obligation. On Monday, March 5, it became evident that the Reserve System was withdrawing its support of Treasury obligations, and prices of government securities worked to lower levels. The decline continued and by the middle of the month the prices of all bank-restricted issues except one had dropped below par. On March 19 the Treasury announced the details of the new type of security it was offering. It was to be a 2¾ per cent nonmarketable obligation, dated April 1, 1951, redeemable by the government on and after April 1, 1975, and maturing April 1, 1980. Although these

14. Sec. 4, 48 Stat. 2; 12 U.S.C. 95.
15. Sec. 5b, 12 U.S.C. 95a; 50 U.S.C. App. 5.

bonds were nonmarketable, holders could at their option exchange them into *marketable* five-year 1½ per cent notes, which they would then be able to sell if in need of cash. The prices at which these notes might sell, however, was clearly not being guaranteed. From the point of view of fiscal authority, concerned with debt management and price stability for marketable issues, this security had the advantage of nonmarketability and at the same time precluded the possibility, inherent in redeemable issues, of large and uncertain demands on the Treasury for funds. From the point of view of the owner, it had the advantage of providing ready conversion into cash.

Subscriptions for this optional exchange were permitted during the period March 26–April 6, and during the conversion period the Federal Reserve provided support at 99¹⁄₁₆ for the two issues that could be exchanged. On April 12 the Treasury announced that $13,576 million of the new bonds had been issued in exchange for the two issues of 1967-1972. Of the amount exchanged, $5,584 million was converted by the Reserve Banks and the Treasury investment accounts; of this amount a substantial portion had been acquired in support operations during and prior to the conversion period.

Summation

How shall we sum up this unprecedented operation which was vibrant with drama and unquestionably one of the great turning points in recent American financial history? Assurance was removed that holders of long-term governments could sell them at any time at par value. The threat that the Reserve Banks, in supporting par, might have to buy in very large amounts of the long-term 2½s, and thereby calamitously expand Reserve credit, was eliminated, for the two issues exchanged had been the focal point of liquidation. Federal Reserve credit was no longer freely available, without a penalty, to all who had government obligations to sell. The Treasury's long-continued practice of offering only short- and intermediate-term securities had been sharply broken through the employment of a new type of security. The entire interest structure for all types of financing had been stiffened. A signal had been given that, for the time being at least, the money market was freed from some of the rigidities which had bound it for so many months and, more important, from the threat that the rigidity might be increased. While the argument between the Treasury and the Federal Reserve was not settled, at least the government's financing problems of the second half of 1951 could now be faced without the confusing rancor that had clouded the issues during the preceding year.

Conclusion

The Korean crisis forced a reorientation of the debt management policies pursued since the end of the war. The pressure for such a redirection came from two sources: from the expectation of large-scale expenditure for armament and from the spurt in private spending precipitated by the crisis.

In view of the large refundings in 1950 and, especially, 1951 the need to remake policy came at an unfortunate time. Indeed, the prospect of these refundings, and the problems inherent in them, was one of the factors that contributed importantly to the crisis. Had the Treasury pursued a different course after 1945 in refunding maturing issues or in setting the level of interest rates, the acute situation of the winter of 1950-1951 probably would not have developed. At the least, its character would have been very different. But the Treasury repeatedly failed to take advantage of excellent opportunities to refund short- into long-term debt, and new policies had finally to be adopted practically as a matter of compulsion, not of choice. Likewise, the Federal Reserve lost opportunities to alter its support policy, when such a change would not have had the semblance of being forced by necessity. Had it acted earlier at least some of the unfortunate occurrences of the winter of 1950-1951 could, presumably, have been averted.

As events worked out, the dispute between the two agencies reached an intense stage before policy was reformulated, and the procedures which the two agencies had been employing since the end of World War II had the appearance of breaking down under the strains imposed by the Korean crisis. The changes made in debt management and credit operations in early March—or at least the "accord" between the Treasury and the Federal Reserve—were an essential preliminary for the successful solution of the government's financial problems in the second half of 1951. They laid a foundation for a new departure in financial management once that period was passed.

The argument between the Treasury and the Federal Reserve was, of course, extremely technical. The public could not have been expected to comprehend and did not fully understand the somewhat abstruse points of monetary theory on which the dispute turned. But the disagreement was not exclusively theoretical. At least two other elements were involved. One was the fact that the prerogatives, indeed the statutory responsibilities, of each of the agencies was at stake. The other was the less tangible consideration of prestige within the governmental framework. These currents and crosscurrents largely explained the extreme acrimony that developed.

Perhaps the most significant lesson to be drawn from the experience is that even the potent deflationary factors of a cash surplus in the federal budget, a huge tax increase, and the expectation of further tax increases could not prevent a spurt in private spending and in investment, and a sharp rise in the money supply, so long as the government securities market was supported and interest rates thereby stabilized. These deflationary tools of fiscal management were unable to preserve unscathed the cheap money policy when a substantial demand for financing appeared and attractive avenues of investment, outside the government securities market, opened up. The cheap money policy could of course have been maintained, but only at the expense of an increase in deposits that, under prevailing conditions, would have been grossly inflationary. Once the public chose to spend its money and a strong demand for funds developed, the instability inherent in the debt structure compelled a change in debt policy. The reduction in the Reserve System's support prices for Treasury obligations is to be regarded as a determined effort to increase stability in debt ownership by exacting a penalty from the seller of these obligations.

It seems probable that the lowering of the support prices of government securities below par during the first part of March 1951 will come to be regarded as the most important decision made in monetary management during the postwar period. There is even a possibility that it will ultimately be looked on as the most important decision made subsequent to 1933. The effect of Korea, in short, was to force, against great opposition, a most significant redirection of debt and monetary policy.

PART II

ANALYSIS OF THE PROBLEM

Chapter 7

DEBT COMPOSITION AND MATURITIES

BETWEEN DECEMBER 1945 and December 1950 the total gross federal debt declined from $278.1 billion to $256.7 billion. This was not, of course, a steady reduction, for the debt reached its peak of $279.8 billion in February 1946, its postwar low point of $251.6 billion in April 1949, and then rose again. Movements of the several kinds of issues of which it was made up, however, did not parallel movements of the total.

THE COMPOSITION OF THE DEBT

During this five-year period the composition of the debt changed significantly. At the end of 1945, public marketable issues were $198.8 billion, some 71.5 per cent of the total, as shown in Table 8.

TABLE 8

COMPOSITION OF THE TOTAL GROSS FEDERAL DEBT,
AS OF DECEMBER 31, 1945 AND 1950

(Dollar Amounts in Millions)

Type of Security	1945		1950	
	Amount	Percentage of Total Debt	Amount	Percentage of Total Debt
Total gross debt	$278,115	100.0	$256,731	100.0
Interest-bearing public marketable securities	198,778	71.5	152,450	59.4
Interest-bearing nonmarketable issues U.S. savings bonds (current redemption value)	48,183	17.3	58,019	22.6
Other[a]	8,732	3.1	10,106	3.9
Special issues to government agencies and trust funds	20,000	7.2	33,707	13.2
Matured issues, debt bearing no interest and guaranteed issues[b]	2,421	.9	2,449	.9

Source: Treasury Bulletin, February 1946, p. 28 and February 1951, p. 20.

a. Includes Treasury tax and savings notes, depository bonds, armed forces leave bonds, Treasury bonds investment series.

b. Guaranteed issues not included in the 1945 figures.

Nonmarketable issues amounted to $76.9 billion, about 28 per cent of the gross debt. Of this amount nearly two thirds were savings bonds, and about one fourth special issues held by government agencies and trust funds. The remaining $2.4 billion of the gross debt was made up of matured issues and miscellaneous types of debt bearing no interest.

By the end of 1950, this pattern was very different. The new arrangement reflected Treasury policy and was the result of tendencies that operated continually during these five years. By December 1950 marketable issues had fallen to $152.5 billion, a decline of about $46 billion, more than double the shrinkage in the gross debt. These securities were now less than 60 per cent of the total. Nonmarketable issues, however, had increased $25 billion, more than half the advance taking the form of special issues held by government agencies and trust funds. In other words, while the gross debt fell about $21 billion approximately $25 billion of marketable issues were replaced with nonmarketables.

The Nonmarketable Issues

Some of the nonmarketable issues, such as the tax notes, the depository bonds and even part of the savings bonds were issued in response to demands which reflected new uses that had been developed for Treasury obligations. Presumably the issuance of these debt forms, since they reduced the outstanding volume of marketable issues, somewhat simplified the handling of the marketable debt.

The savings bonds, however, and part of the special issues were demand obligations of the government. This rise in the outstanding volume of nonmarketable demand obligations in a sense made the Treasury's position more precarious, since the amount of cash that could be demanded from it at a moment's notice was thereby increased. Yet so long as new sales of the nonmarketable issues equalled or exceeded redemptions, cash demands from this direction would be nil, and it could be argued that under these conditions this portion of the debt was "placed" as securely as the outstanding marketable obligations.

As the proportions of the marketable, nonmarketable and other types of issues shifted during these years other changes, equally significant, took place in the maturity schedule of the marketable portion of the debt.

THE MATURITY SCHEDULE

Table 9 shows, as of the end of 1945 and of 1950, the maturity schedule of the public marketable issues. The securities are arranged according to the due dates of fixed maturity issues and the first call dates of callable issues.[1] Several points in this table merit notice.

TABLE 9

MATURITY SCHEDULE OF INTEREST-BEARING PUBLIC MARKETABLE
SECURITIES OF THE U.S. TREASURY, AS OF
DECEMBER 31, 1945 AND 1950

(Dollar Amounts in Millions)

Due or First Becoming Callable	December 31, 1945		December 31, 1950	
	Amount	*Per Cent*	*Amount*	*Per Cent*
Total	$198,663[a]	100.0	$152,342[a]	100.0
Within 1 year	70,430	35.3	57,904	38.0
1-5 years	35,392	17.8	33,379	21.9
5-10 years	33,025	17.0	17,411	11.5
10-15 years	17,239	8.6	12,598	8.2
15-20 years	17,796	8.9	31,050	20.4
Over 20 years	24,781	12.4	—	—

Source: Treasury Bulletin, February 1946, pp. 29-32, and February 1951, pp. 21-22.
a. The total does not reconcile with comparable figures in Table 8 because of adjustment made for Postal Savings and Panama Canal Bonds.

During this period the total marketable debt fell from $198.6 billion to $152.3, a shrinkage of $46.3 billion. Issues due or first callable within one year, however, declined only $12.5 billion, notwithstanding the fact that most of the obligations paid off were those currently maturing. Thus the one-year debt was a higher percentage of marketable issues at the end of this period than at the beginning. The explanation of this seeming paradox was two-fold: the passage of time steadily moved longer-dated debt into the one-year category and the Treasury refunded very large amounts of the maturing obligations that were not repaid into short-term obligations, although many of these issues had originally been issued for longer terms.

The volume of issues outstanding in the five- to ten-year maturity bracket was almost cut in two. The dollar amount of debt with a

1. An alternative arrangement would be to group the securities according to final maturity date, but in view of the fact that the Treasury since 1945 has generally chosen to call issues at the first opportunity, the arrangement based on the first call date has been used here.

maturity or call date in excess of ten years fell sharply, from $59.8 to $43.6 billion (although the proportion of marketable issues represented by these maturity brackets stayed about the same) and the debt with a maturity or call date in excess of twenty years disappeared. Thus the average maturity of the marketable debt shortened substantially.

There was ample opportunity, had the Treasury wished, to maintain the maturity pattern existing in 1945, or even to lengthen it. It chose the policy of mainly refunding on the short end, and while this procedure lowered the interest and furthered the Treasury's "cheap money" policy, it also enhanced the refunding problems. Whether the maintenance of so large a volume of one-year floating debt fulfilled a real economic need appears doubtful, and there is at least a possibility that the sharp reduction in the volume of debt in the six- to ten-year bracket and the elimination of obligations with more than a twenty-year maturity left unsatisfied a legitimate demand for certain types of government issues. Whether either the 1945 or the 1950 maturity pattern was the result of a conscious plan and was designed to fit the needs of actual or potential owners of federal obligations is unknown. Certainly it was never explained or defended in those terms.

The mechanics of the maturity schedule, however, and the implications of changes made in it, deserve further consideration.

Forces Affecting the Maturity Schedule

Three forces determine the maturity schedule of the federal debt: the length of maturity of issues offered by the Treasury, the passage of time, and the amount of debt retired periodically from budgetary surpluses, through a reduction in the Treasury's cash balance or in other ways. The types of securities offered by the Treasury, either for refunding purposes or to raise new money, are the only one of these three forces that it can control, aside from reductions in its cash balance used for debt reduction. Budgetary policy and the creation of a surplus or a deficit does not lie within its authority nor does, of course, the passage of time.

The importance of time derives from the fact that its passage steadily moves all issues closer to maturity and constantly shortens the average maturity of the debt. This effect can in part be offset by the offering policy of the Treasury.

Budgetary surpluses used to retire debt of course reduce the total amount of debt outstanding. In recent years virtually all of the debt retired has been maturing debt. Thus the effect of budgetary surpluses has been not only to reduce the total of obligations outstanding but also to reduce the amount of short-term, floating debt, thereby affecting the maturity schedule. But the volume of short-term debt outstanding is also influenced by the offering policy of the Treasury. That is, if the Treasury pursues a policy of refunding the maturing debt into intermediate- or long-term securities, such a policy tends to reduce the short-term, floating debt and to lengthen the average maturity of the total. On the other hand, if the Treasury refunds maturing obligations into short-term securities, such a procedure sustains, or even increases, the volume of short-term obligations that will presently have to be dealt with again, either by repayment or by a new refunding.

What the Treasury Offered

From the end of the eighth war loan in December 1945 until December 1949 the Treasury's offerings of securities were, with minor exceptions, confined to three basic types: nonmarketable issues sold to the public which were redeemable on demand (chiefly the E, F and G bonds); special issues sold to the trust funds, some of which were redeemable on demand and some of which had a longer maturity; and marketable issues with maturities not longer than twelve months, save in one or two instances of minor importance. That is, during the four-year period December 1945— December 1949 the Treasury's offerings of securities to the public were all either short-term or demand obligations. In December 1949 the Treasury sold a fifty-one-month note issue and in 1950 two issues of certificates—respectively of twenty-month and sixteen-month maturity—and two issues of five-year notes. In the spring of 1951, as noted in Chapter 6, came the major change of policy when it issued some $13.5 billion of long-term, nonmarketable bonds in exchange for the outstanding marketable bonds of 1967-1972.

But to return to the four years December 1945—December 1949. Since this was, for the most part, a period of debt retirement in which there was no need to raise new money, the Treasury's offering policy was in effect a refunding policy also. Maturing obligations, if not redeemed, were consistently refunded "on the short end" of the maturity schedule. The result was to lower the average maturity of the debt and to maintain the volume of short-dated obligations at a higher level than would have been the case if intermediate- or long-term marketable securities had been issued.

A Specific Case

Let us examine a specific instance, the period from September 1945 to December 1948. During this interval about $140.5 billion of bonds, notes and certificates matured or were called. Of this amount, $40 billion were retired for cash, and the remainder, $100.5 billion, were exchanged for new securities. During these months virtually all newly issued Treasury issues were securities with a maturity of twelve months or less.[2]

As these issues came due a year later they of course had to be dealt with again, through repayment or refunding. For example, on February 1, 1946, $5,043 million of certificates matured, of which $89 million were retired for cash and $4,954 million were exchanged for a new issue of one-year certificates. A year later this issue of $4,954 million fell due, and $1,007 million were repaid; the remainder, $3,947 million, again being exchanged for another issue of one-year certificates, which in turn matured on February 1, 1948. At this time $1,758 million were redeemed and the rest exchanged for another issue of one-year paper.

Of the $140.5 billion of bonds, notes and certificates that were retired during this period, $39.6 billion were in the form of bonds and notes, which when first issued had had maturities in the general range of five to twenty years. Of this $39.6 billion, $14.3 billion were retired for cash, and the remainder, $25.29 billion, were refunded into twelve-month paper, not into obligations with maturities comparable to those of the called or maturing obligations. Three results followed: the interest charge on the budget was lowered, since the interest rate on the certificates was less than that paid on the obligations retired or refunded; the short-term debt, and consequently the Treasury's refunding problem, was maintained, if not augmented, by the continual issue of twelve-month paper; investors were not given the opportunity to keep the volume of intermediate- or long-term

2. Exceptions were: the twelve-and-one-half-month note issued in September 1947 and the thirteen-month note issued in December of that year, at a time when the certificate rate was being advanced, and the eighteen-and-one-half-month note issued in September 1948.

securities they had previously held, and the maturity patterns of their portfolios were altered, indirectly if not directly, by Treasury policy.

Summation

During the five years ending December 31, 1950, the gross federal debt declined $21.4 billion. The fall in marketable issues, however, was much sharper and amounted to $46.3 billion. The difference was largely accounted for by the rise in nonmarketable issues, which grew by $25 billion. The major part of these nonmarketable issues were demand obligations.

Although marketable issues fell by almost one fourth, the shrinkage was not spread evenly among all maturity brackets and the average maturity of the marketable debt declined appreciably. The shrinkage in the one-year floating debt, for example, was only $12.5 billion, as compared with the over-all fall of $46.5 billion, whereas obligations with a maturity or first call date in excess of twenty years disappeared.

In December 1950 nonmarketable issues (mostly demand debt) and one-year floating debt together were nearly 63 per cent of the gross debt, as compared with 53 per cent five years earlier. In its operations the Treasury clearly relied heavily on the continuance of a strong market for its securities, a continuance of conditions that would permit it to refund maturing obligations easily and cheaply, and the continuance of a situation in which new sales of nonmarketables would exceed redemptions.

Chapter 8

THE PATTERN OF OWNERSHIP

SALES OF TREASURY SECURITIES by one class of owner—unless at that time the debt is being reduced by repayment of the same amount—result in increased debt holdings by another class or classes. Thus the pattern of ownership is similar to a balloon—compress it at one point and it expands at another. At all times a sufficient amount of society's resources must be devoted to the purpose of debt ownership so that the debt is accommodated within the framework of available assets.[1] While this statement of the necessity for ownership is a truism, some of its implications are only too often ignored.

DEBT OWNERSHIP AND RESOURCES

Resources Available for Debt Ownership

Funds available in the economy for the ownership of debt, other than those so employed at any given time, consist of three types: inactive cash balances, currently accruing savings, and deposits newly created by the banking system. During World War II the rate of debt expansion was so rapid that it outran the amount of cash balances and new savings available for the purchase and retention of federal obligations. As a result, the money supply expanded rapidly, in order that there should be a sufficient volume of resources available to absorb the debt. In the event of renewed large-scale deficits, whether occasioned by war or some other cause, it seems probable this experience would be repeated.

Means of Allocating Resources

Resources can be allocated for the purpose of debt ownership in two ways. They can be contributed voluntarily, as is done when persons or corporations willingly utilize idle cash or newly accruing savings in the acquisition of Treasury securities. Or they can be

1. This generalization needs only minor qualification to allow for the small amount of debt owned outside the country.

compulsorily assigned, as is the case with government trust accounts which are required by law to invest only in Treasury obligations. Compulsory ownership would also result if commercial banks were required to hold a stated portion of their assets in the form of federal obligations or if the government instituted a compulsory savings program which necessitated that savings be invested in Treasury issues. It could also come about if the government directly regulated the way in which various types of institutions, not only banks, employed their assets, and thereby made the ownership of Treasury issues obligatory.

Were heavy deficits to reappear as a result of military necessity it is at least possible that efforts would be made to compel various segments of the population and of the business world to buy and hold government securities, aside from what amounts might be purchased voluntarily. Indeed, proposals of this nature have already been made by private persons. These measures would be advocated as a means of partially offsetting the rise in purchasing power generated by deficit financing. Were mechanisms of this nature employed, such arrangements would, of course, directly affect the way in which the debt was distributed. Indeed, they could—and presumably would—be used to "plan" and regulate its distribution.

Basic Analytical Questions

Basic analytical questions, then, in studying debt management are: What are the sources of the assets used for debt ownership? Why are they employed in this way?

These questions are pertinent to virtually every facet of debt policy and management procedure. For example, one of the aspects of World War I financing that subsequently was much criticized, perhaps unjustly, was the use by persons and corporations of borrowed money for the purchase of Liberty Bonds. This was alleged to have increased inflationary pressures, caused considerable hardship, and to have had other undesirable consequences. Again, debt retirement policy certainly must consider whose securities are to be retired, for the results of the redemption of bank-held securities differ from those which follow the repayment of obligations held by persons. The Treasury recognized this in the retirement policy pursued in the years 1946-1948. Finally, the terms of new issues emitted for refunding purposes must be set with an eye to the wishes of existing holders, otherwise the old holders will simply turn in their obligations and take their money, and other owners must be found for the newly issued securities.

INSTABILITY IN THE PATTERN OF OWNERSHIP

If debt owners never increased or decreased their holdings, debt management would be much more simple than typically is the case. One called or matured issue would simply be replaced with another of like amount, held by the same owners. The Treasury would not suffer a loss of cash when issues were called or redeemed. Transfers of debt among owners would be negligible in amount and debt management would interfere little if any with credit regulation, so long as the debt did not expand or contract. As Seltzer pointed out when discussing the relation of interest, credit and debt policy:

> The authorities will be able to maintain a high degree of marketability in long-term government securities—meaning a quick, close market—without making their credit policy subordinate to this purpose, *only if relatively small amounts of long-term governments are bought and sold in any short period*.[2]

Transfers of debt from one class of owner to another will, of course, take place in a free market economy, and many such transactions are legitimate and desirable from any point of view. Indeed, were the transactions prohibited, we would no longer have a free market economy. Nevertheless, if these shifts and exchanges are small, many of the problems of debt management will be easier to solve.

Forces Producing Instability

Among the many forces that affect the amount and type of Treasury securities that a particular owner or class of owners possesses at a given time, two, in the light of our experience during and since the war, appear to be of paramount importance. The first is the total amount of assets, or in some cases the amount of liquid assets, at the command of the debt holder. The other is the complex of economic needs that the debt owner currently is experiencing or, when these needs are translated into action, the purposes that he wishes to accomplish or must accomplish through his choice of assets.

The wartime behavior of the assets of financial institutions, dis-

2. Lawrence H. Seltzer, "Notes on Managing the Public Debt," *Review of Economics and Statistics,* February 1949, p. 20. Italics supplied.

cussed in Chapter 2, shows the importance of the first of these two forces. The expansion of the money supply caused by an unbalanced budget furnished the resources which absorbed a large part of the growing debt. The increase in the total of federal obligations outstanding was closely paralleled by a rise in the assets of financial institutions and of other classes of debt owners.

The second force may be illustrated by the postwar behavior of the life insurance companies' portfolio of government securities. The reduction that occurred in these holdings did not take place because the assets of these institutions diminished—on the contrary, assets increased. The reduction in holdings of governments took place because there was a demand for financing on the part of private borrowers, and such loans yielded a higher return than government securities. Consequently, insurance companies shifted their assets from one to another and more remunerative form.

Types of Instability

From an analytical point of view government portfolios of particular debt holders exhibit three types of instability. The first is illustrated by increases or decreases in the total volume of resources of an owner, while the proportion of resources invested in government securities remains the same. The second shows up in the form of significant changes in the proportion of assets invested in governments. During World War II both the volume of resources of financial institutions and the proportion of resources invested in Treasury obligations grew. Thus their portfolios reflected both these types of change. During the postwar period the proportionate amount of resources of life insurance companies invested in federal obligations fell. Thus during this period their holdings were characterized by the second type of change.

The third kind of instability is manifested by substantial shifts in the relative amounts of different types of Treasury obligations held—for example, short-, intermediate- and long-term issues—without accompanying changes of appreciable amount in the total dollar amount of government securities carried. This type of action is exemplified by the large proportional increase in late 1947 and early 1948 in the volume of Treasury bills in the portfolios of commercial banks and the substantial advance in 1948 in the amount of long-term obligations held by Reserve Banks. Even though such shifts in the portfolio pattern of one particular class of owner do not appreciably change the dollar volume of governments held, the buying and selling precipitated by such rearrangements of investments may nevertheless have repercussions on the position of the central bank and on the money supply.

In actuality, these kinds of instability are often combined in the portfolio behavior of a particular class of owner and may be difficult to distinguish. In studying types of portfolio behavior, however, their distinction can often be helpful.

The Significance of Changes of Ownership

The chief importance of instability in the pattern of ownership lies in the fact that transfers of debt have a radically different significance, depending upon which classes of owners are buyers and which sellers. Sales by individuals to insurance companies, for example, do not affect the money supply, whereas sales to Reserve Banks do. Purchases of securities from the commercial banks by persons, savings banks or insurance companies do not affect importantly the reserve position of the commercial banking system as a whole, whereas purchases by the Reserve Banks do, since such acquisitions supply the banks with reserve funds. Liquidation of savings bonds by persons are likely to result in an increase in the volume of money used for consumption purposes, whereas sales of governments by insurance companies or savings banks are likely to signify an increase in the flow of funds going into capital formation. Thus changes in the pattern of debt ownership produce important economic consequences of themselves, independently of whether the debt itself is increasing or decreasing.

From what has been said it is clear that as instability in debt ownership increases and the volume of transactions in federal securities grows, the problems of management become more complex. Particularly is this the case if transfers of government obligations lead to a rise in the portfolio of the central bank, an expansion in the credit base and an increase in the money supply. Consequently, authorities responsible for debt management naturally favor policies directed at producing stability in the pattern of ownership, except, perhaps, in times of business recession when an expansion in the money supply is desired as a recovery measure. The procedures used to achieve such stability, however, may partake of the character of compulsion or may be of the nature of inducements. Herein lies a basic policy decision, and herein lies one of the major differences between those persons who do not trust the free market process and those who favor it.

THE DISTRIBUTION OF THE DEBT

Notwithstanding the importance of the forces of instability, their action since the termination of hostilities has not served to upset certain underlying logics in the pattern of ownership. On the contrary, the record since V-J Day suggests the presence of fundamental relationships in the economy, upon which the distribution of the debt is necessarily based, that are not easily disturbed. What support is there for this statement? While numerous pieces of evidence could be cited, only four will be mentioned here.

A Basic Inertia

In the first place, the relative magnitudes of the portions of the marketable debt held by the several classes of owners did not change during the five and one half years following the termination of hostilities. This in itself suggests an over-all stability, a basic inertia in the pattern of ownership.

Constant Characteristics

In the second place, the portfolios of some individual classes of owners exhibited certain well-defined and reasonably constant characteristics. For example, the portfolios of fire, marine and casualty insurance companies and so-called "personal holdings" of government securities, which include private trust funds, showed a steady and persistent tendency to grow. The holdings of mutual savings banks were, consistently, comparatively stable. On the other hand, holdings of life insurance companies were volatile. In other words, the portfolio action of one class of owner was, in a behavioristic sense, often significantly different from the action of another class of debt owner, and these different types of behavior persisted throughout the period of time here surveyed.

These characteristics of the pattern of ownership are generally delineated in Table 10. This table shows the maximum and minimum holdings of marketable Treasury securities of the chief classes of owners during the period October 1945—December 1950, arranged

TABLE 10

MAXIMUM AND MINIMUM HOLDINGS OF MARKETABLE FEDERAL SECURITIES OF MAJOR CLASSES OF OWNERS, OCTOBER 1945–DECEMBER 1950

(Dollar Amounts in Billions)

Class of Owner	Maximum Holding				Minimum Holding				Difference Between Maximum and Minimum Holdings	
	Amount	Date Held	% of Total Gross Debt	% of Marketable Public Issues	Amount	Date Held	% of Total Gross Debt	% of Marketable Public Issues	Amount	% of Maximum Holding
Commercial banks	$84.7	Feb. '46	30.3	42.3	$53.2	Mar. '49	21.1	34.1	$31.5	37.1
"All other investors" (excludes banks, insurance companies and U.S. government agencies and trust funds)	51.0	Dec. '45	18.3	25.6	41.8	Dec. '49	16.2	26.9	9.2	18.0
U.S. government agencies and trust funds, including Federal Reserve Banks	31.3	Dec. '45	11.2	15.7	22.7	Oct. '49	8.8	14.6	8.6	27.4
Federal Reserve Banks	23.8	{ Dec. '46 and Feb. '47	9.1	13.6	17.4	Sept. '49	6.8	11.2	6.4	23.9
Life insurance companies	21.6	July '46	8.0	11.5	12.7	Dec. '50	4.9	8.3	8.9	41.2
Mutual savings banks	11.9	Aug. '47	4.5	7.0	9.6	Nov. '45	3.6	5.1	2.3	19.3
Fire, casualty and marine insurance companies	4.1	Aug. '50	1.5	2.6	2.5	Nov. '45	0.9	1.3	1.6	39.0
Stock savings banks	0.5	Sept. '46	0.2	0.2	0.4	June '49ᵃ	0.1	0.2	0.1	20.0

Sources: Treasury Survey data, Appendix Tables 16–29, except for Federal Reserve Banks; for Federal Reserve Banks, *Federal Reserve Bulletin*, November 1946—March 1951.

a. Data not available after June 1949.

by order of magnitude, and the differences between the maximum and minimum holdings.[3] This table should, of course, be read in the light of the sharp reduction in the marketable debt that was commented on in Chapter 7. It will be noted that commercial banks held the largest volume of marketable obligations, followed by "All other investors," a category that includes persons, business concerns other than banks and insurance companies, private trust funds, municipalities and other miscellaneous types of owners. Following these in order of size were: United States government agencies and trust funds, together with Reserve Banks; life insurance companies; mutual savings banks; fire, casualty and marine insurance companies; and stock savings banks.

Possible Minimal Levels

In the third place, the failure of the portfolio of all classes of owners, with the possible exception of life insurance companies, to drop below certain levels appears of consequence. It suggests that, with a given volume of assets in the economy as a whole, there may be certain minimal holdings of Treasury securities for particular classes of owners that are not likely to be violated unless economic conditions and relationships are greatly upset. If this presumption is correct, the problem of instability of debt ownership will, under ordinary circumstances, chiefly center on holdings in excess of these minima. Interest policy, or any other policy of debt management, will have its primary effect on those holdings that are in excess of these "minimal" levels.

Reserve System a "Stabilizer"

Finally, so long as the position of the Reserve Banks continues to be that of "stabilizer" it is clear that, given the fiscal policies prevailing during this period, the size and character of the Reserve System's portfolio will, in substantial degree, be determined by the actions of other classes of holders.

CONCLUSIONS

In short, we reach the following conclusions. The portfolio behavior of particular classes of owners has been much affected by

3. This table is based upon the statistics and upon the classes of ownership used in the Treasury Survey of Ownership.

Treasury policy in such matters as the types of securities offered, the interest rates attaching to them, and the relative amounts of different kinds of securities available, including the quantities of short-, intermediate- and long-term obligations. But portfolio behavior has also been much influenced by the investment needs and desires of particular types of owners. In turn, these needs and desires have in part been shaped by business and economic conditions. While the margin of instability in the pattern of ownership, the amount of securities the several classes did sell at one time or another, was not large when compared with the total debt, the effect of this margin on the money supply could have been very serious if the Reserve Banks had absorbed all of the selling. Fiscal authority, when formulating debt management policies, must inevitably consider carefully whether a particular procedure will widen or narrow this margin of instability.

A Possible Approach

These considerations in turn suggest that study of this problem of ownership can, perhaps, be approached by asking the following questions: What has been the general nature of the pattern of ownership? What shifts have taken place in it since V-J Day? What lessons can be learned from studying the experience of the last five years that may be helpful in formulating programs in the future? Will the pattern of ownership behave differently if the political prospect is for peace, for war, or for a continuance of the armed-camp economy?

Precise answers to all of these questions obviously cannot be attained. Nevertheless, the questions themselves provide in some measure a frame of reference for studying the problem. And even answers that are, in reality, little more than informed guesses may be helpful in dealing with these matters.

Let us take first the last question, the effect of war on debt ownership. The experience of the last period of hostilities is illuminating. War means large deficits. Deficits increased the money supply, and the dollars thus created provided the resources necessary for absorption of the growing volume of Treasury securities. One can say either that this expansion of resources allowed holdings of governments by persons and corporations to grow as the total volume of Treasury securities grew, or that the increase in the debt caused their resources, and their portfolios of Treasury obligations, to expand.

Presumably the pattern of debt ownership of World War II would not be exactly repeated in the event of new large deficits resulting from military expenditure. Nevertheless, an increase in federal debt necessarily means increased holdings of federal securities by at least some of the several classes of debt owners. Either savings or newly created money will supply the wherewithal for absorbing the obligations. If the rise in the debt brings an increase in the money supply (as it must if the debt increase is rapid) then the assets at the disposal of potential security purchasers will also expand, and as this occurs they will engross an increasing amount of federal obligations. Which groups of potential security owners will acquire the new issues, and in what amounts, will depend on a variety of factors. Three of the determinants will be the inducements to purchase offered each group as exemplified by the terms attached to the new offerings, the currently existing alternative uses of funds, and the degree of compulsion applied, one way or another, to each type of buyer to acquire governments.

In short, in the event of large deficits the basic policies that will determine the behavior of the pattern of ownership will be: first, the extent to which the money supply is inflated in order to provide the resources for debt absorption; and, second, the combination of force and persuasion that is employed in selling obligations to each segment of the economy.

If, however, the prospect is for peace, or at least for a continuance of a heavily armed economy, and if there is a reasonable chance that the federal budget will be close to a balance or even show a surplus now and then, how will that affect the behavior of the pattern of ownership? Here we may draw on our experience since 1945. The conduct of the Treasury portfolio of the several classes of debt owners since that date will perhaps afford some clue as to how the pattern may act in the future under these conditions.

Chapter 9

PORTFOLIO BEHAVIOR: I

COMMERCIAL BANKS

THE TREASURY MARKETABLE PORTFOLIO held by commercial banks, while the largest of any class of owner, has also been one of the most volatile. From its high point of $84.7 billion in February 1946, also the high month for the total debt, it fluctuated downward to a low of $53.2 billion in March 1949, a reduction of over 37 per cent.[1] Thereafter it rose sharply, reaching $60.5 billion in January 1950. By December of that year, however, it had fallen once more to $54.9 billion. At the peak the banks held roughly 30 per cent of the gross debt and slightly more than 42 per cent of the public marketable issues. At the low point the banks still held approximately 21 per cent of the gross debt and 34 per cent of the marketable securities outstanding.

Volatility Misleading

The picture presented by these over-all figures, however, is misleading unless carefully analyzed. Actually, bank holdings of government securities have been more stable than would at first appear. During 1946 and 1947, when the debt was being reduced, the banks' government portfolio declined rapidly, most of the fall coming in the earlier year. By December of 1947 their holdings amounted to $60.9 billion. Since that time they have been relatively constant. In fact, if we omit two months (January 1948 and March 1949), commercial bank holdings during the three years 1948-1950 stayed within the range of $54.5-$60.5 billion. That is, the magnitude of fluctuation was about $6 billion, roughly 10 per cent of the maximum amount. A similar picture is presented when marketable issues are compared with deposits. At the end of 1945 these issues were about half of total deposits, but since the middle of 1946 they have consistently been some 40-46 per cent of the deposit figure.

1. Unless otherwise indicated, the figures used in this and succeeding chapters are those of the Treasury Survey of Ownership.

Forces Influencing Banks' Holdings

A wide variety of forces combine to determine both the total amount of commercial banks' holdings of federal securities and the quantities of short-, intermediate- and long-term obligations. Important among these are such considerations as the size of the debt, whether the federal government is operating with a surplus or a deficit, the policies pursued by the Treasury regarding debt retirement and offerings of new securities, the volume of legal reserves required to be held by banks against deposits, the amount of liquid assets that banks believe they should have, the level of interest rates and the demand for loans.

Figure 10 shows, for all commercial banks, the course of total deposits and of holdings of Treasury obligations, semiannually, for the period June 1945—December 1950. Through June 1947 these roughly paralleled each other, but subsequently there was little similarity. The rise of both total deposits and holdings of governments in 1945, and their fall in 1946 and the first part of 1947 seem attributable to the rise and decline in the total debt during this period, and to the Treasury's policy of reducing the volume of bank-held obligations. The new pattern that emerged in the latter part of 1947 apparently was the result of uncertainty engendered by changes in the interest structure at that time and the lowering of the support prices of governments on Christmas Eve 1947, the increase of reserve requirements in 1948 and perhaps the Treasury's policy in 1947 and 1948 of reducing the volume of bills outstanding. The rise in banks' holdings of governments in the latter half of 1949 presumably represented the reinvestment of funds released by the lowering of reserve requirements in the summer of that year. The rapid rise in deposits in the latter part of 1950 reflects the sharp demand for loans precipitated by the outbreak of fighting in Korea, a demand that was, in part, accommodated by a further reduction in the government portfolio.

In the light of this and other material dealt with earlier, three conclusions are warranted. First, during periods when deficits are large, bank holdings of federal securities are likely to rise as the banks—either the commercial banks, the Reserve Banks, or both—create the deposits necessary for the purchase of securities not taken by other types of investors. Second, during the period February 1946—April 1947 the reduction in the total debt and the Treasury policy of reducing the amount of bank-held debt exerted a dominant influence on the magnitude of the government portfolio of the commercial banking system, and did decrease it. Third, following the spring of 1947 other factors played a large part in shaping the behavior of the banks' portfolio of Treasury obligations.

The Maturity Pattern

Table 11 compares the maturity distribution of commercial banks' holdings on three dates: February 1946, when their portfolios were at their maximum; March 1949, when they were at their minimum; and December 1950, the last month covered by this survey. This

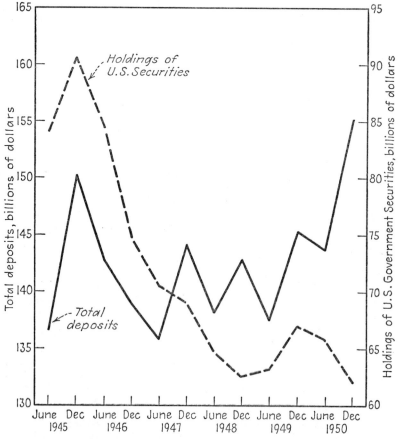

FIGURE 10. ALL COMMERCIAL BANKS: TOTAL DEPOSITS AND HOLDINGS OF U.S. GOVERNMENT SECURITIES, SEMIANNUALLY, JUNE 1945—DECEMBER 1950

Source: Appendix Table 10.

TABLE 11

COMPARISON OF MATURITY DISTRIBUTION OF COMMERCIAL BANK
MARKETABLE GOVERNMENT PORTFOLIOS IN FEBRUARY 1946,
MARCH 1949 AND DECEMBER 1950

(Dollar Amounts in Millions)

Due or First Becoming Callable	Maximum Holding, February 1946		Minimum Holding, March 1949		Holdings as of December 1950	
	Amount	Per Cent	Amount	Per Cent	Amount	Per Cent
Total	$84,727	100.0	$53,247	100.0	$54,893	100.0
Within 1 year	31,876	37.7	16,152	30.3	20,088	36.6
1-5 years	25,339	29.9	26,812	50.4	24,534	44.7
5-10 years	21,394	25.3	6,658	12.5	7,329	13.4
10-15 years	3,566	4.2	1,406	2.6	181	0.3
15-20 years	66	—	2,216	4.2	2,753	5.0
Over 20 years	2,474	2.9	—	—	—	—
Various years	12	—	4	—	9	—

Source: Based on Appendix Tables 18, 19.

table reveals four pronounced characteristics of the portfolio behavior of commercial banks during the postwar period—characteristics that are generally confirmed by study of the sixty-three-month pattern given in Appendix Tables 18 and 19.

First, during the period covered by this analysis, obligations due or first callable within ten years consistently accounted for 90 per cent or more of total holdings. Longer maturities accounted for 10 per cent or less. This division in the banks' list was in part caused by Treasury offering policy, which limited the volume of securities with more than ten years' maturity that were available for purchase by commercial banks. It also in some measure reflected the investment preferences of the banks themselves. Within this rigid framework of 90 per cent of holdings due or first callable within ten years and 10 per cent with longer maturities, however, appreciable changes took place.

Second, the dollar volume of securities due or first callable in one to five years remained remarkably constant. In fact, during the period covered by this survey, the dollar amount of these holdings stayed steadier than did the amount of securities due or callable within one year.

Third, the dollar amount of the longest-term securities held by the banks also stayed comparatively steady, in the range of $2.2-$2.7 billion. While these securities in 1946 were in the "over 20 years" bracket the passage of time had by 1949 moved them into the 15-20-year classification.

Fourth, notwithstanding the stability in the longest-term holdings of the banks, there was a very sharp decline in the volume of securities in the 5-10- and 10-15-year maturity brackets. The fall was pronounced, whether measured in terms of dollars or in percentages. This change was chiefly occasioned by Treasury offering policy. Except in small degree it was not initiated by the banks themselves and did not reflect a change in their investment policies and behavior.

Explanation of this pattern of behavior is to be found in the investment and liquidity needs of the banks themselves, in the offering policy pursued by the Treasury, in the government's interest policy and in the demand for loans experienced by banks. As we consider the meaning of this behavior for future problems of debt management, however, the critical questions, perhaps, are these: If during the period covered by this survey the Treasury had in its refunding operations offered commercial banks the opportunity to purchase securities due or callable in five to fifteen years, yielding returns compatible with the interest structure currently prevailing, would the banks have bought these securities? If they had absorbed such investments would these acquisitions have been net additions to their holdings or would absorption of these obligations have been at the expense of holdings in other maturity brackets, leaving total holdings substantially unchanged? Would such acquisitions have increased or diminished the range of fluctuation in their total holdings which, subsequent to 1946, was in the neighborhood of $6 billion?

Answers to these questions are not susceptible of proof, statistical or otherwise. It is the author's belief that if Treasury policy had permitted the banks to purchase such securities the banks would have bought them, and that the purchases would not have added appreciably to their total holdings but would, in large measure, have been accompanied by a reduction in the volume of securities due or first callable within one year. Securities of so short a term are chiefly held by banks to satisfy their needs for liquidity, and these needs, during the period surveyed, could hardly have required the banks to hold so large a volume of twelve-month paper as they at times carried. Thus the banks seemingly were in a position to reduce their short-term holdings and increase their intermediate- and longer-term holdings. If the banks had held a relatively larger amount of longer-term securities and a relatively smaller volume of short-dated issues, the wide swings in their holdings of twelve-month obligations would probably have been reduced and, consequently, their total holdings would also have been more stable.

Conclusion

The experience of the years 1947-1950 suggests, with the size and type of deposit structure then prevailing, that commercial banks had a fairly constant demand for approximately $54 billion of government securities.[2] This "minimum" demand was little affected by Treasury interest or offering policy. It was the fluctuating volume of holdings above this "minimum" that was influenced by Treasury policy, as well as by the demand for loans and the level of reserve requirements.

If stability in the pattern of ownership is accepted as a proper objective of debt management, in order that shifts in holdings should not affect the money supply, then management policies should be so directed as to ensure that this "floor" is not violated. Indeed, a real question exists as to whether efforts should not be made to raise it.

So long as commercial banks continue their practice of holding some 90 per cent of their portfolios in securities with maturities of ten years or less, the major part of their portfolio adjustments must take place in this section of their list. Thus it may be assumed that the unstable portion of the banks' holdings is largely concentrated in this type of paper. This presumption is supported by other evidence. There is even a possibility that the whole portfolio of the banks would be inherently somewhat more stable if so large a portion were not in the form of very short-term obligations.

Should large-scale deficit financing be renewed and the deposit structure thereby expanded, commercial bank holdings of Treasury securities will almost certainly increase, probably at a more rapid rate than deposits. Indeed, it is quite conceivable that they might rise to the point reached during World War II when they were something more than 50 per cent of deposits, or even to higher proportions.

2. This figure applies to the commercial banks covered by the Treasury Survey of Ownership. The figure applicable for *all* commercial banks should be increased by something like 10 per cent.

TABLE 12

COMPARISON OF TOTAL GROSS FEDERAL DEBT WITH TOTAL GOVERNMENT SECURITY HOLDINGS OF OWNERS OTHER THAN BANKS, INSURANCE COMPANIES AND GOVERNMENT AGENCIES AND TRUST FUNDS, AS OF DECEMBER 1945–1950

(Dollar Amounts in Billions)

Item	1945		1946		1947		1948		1949		1950	
	Amount	Percentage of Total Debt	Amount	Percentage of Total Debt	Amount	Percentage of Total Debt	Amount	Percentage of Total Debt	Amount	Percentage of Total Debt	Amount	Percentage of Total Debt
Total gross federal debt	$278.7	100.0	$259.5	100.0	$257.0	100.0	$252.9	100.0	$257.2	100.0	$256.7	100.0
Treasury estimate[a]	101.9	36.6	89.0	34.3	95.5	37.1	97.1	38.4	100.6	39.1	105.4	41.1
Federal Reserve estimate[b]	86.9	31.2	79.8	30.7	80.6	31.4	82.1	32.5	85.4	33.2	89.7	34.9

Sources: "Treasury Estimate," *Treasury Bulletin*, September 1951, p. 33. "Federal Reserve Estimate," *Federal Reserve Bulletin*, July 1951, p. 808.

a. Includes: Individuals, partnerships, personal trust accounts, corporations (other than banks and insurance companies), state and local governments, savings and loan associations, nonprofit institutions, corporate pension trust funds, dealers and brokers, investments of foreign balances and international accounts in this country; beginning with December 1946 includes investments by the International Bank for Reconstruction and Development and the International Monetary Fund; beginning with June 1947 includes Federal Land Banks.

b. Includes: Nonfinancial business corporations, real estate companies, finance and credit companies, insurance agencies (not carriers), investment trusts, security brokers and dealers, holding companies not otherwise classified, unincorporated business and persons, including farmers, professional persons and trust funds administered by corporate trustees.

"ALL OTHER INVESTORS"

The category "All other investors" as employed in the Treasury Survey of Ownership is a catchall that includes such subgroups as persons, business concerns and private trust and pension funds, state and local governments, farmers and other unincorporated businesses and financial corporations other than banks and insurance companies. The aggregate holdings of this catchall category have also been one of the more stable types of ownership.

The reduction in the government portfolio of this group, from the high point in December 1945 to the low point in December 1949, was only 18 per cent, as shown in Table 10—the smallest decline shown by any class of debt holder. At both times this category of ownership held very nearly the same percentage of gross debt—18.3 per cent and 16.2 per cent—and virtually identical proportions of the public marketable debt—25.6 per cent in December 1945 and 26.9 per cent in December 1949. Another way of indicating the general stability in this part of the pattern of ownership is by pointing out that after a decline in the first part of 1946 these holdings remained within the limits of $46.1-$41.8 billion throughout the rest of the period covered by this survey, a fluctuation of only about 10 per cent.

The Relation of Marketable and Nonmarketable Debt

Another characteristic that distinguishes this from other classes of ownership is the large proportion of its *total* holdings that are in the form of *nonmarketable* issues.

Table 12 traces changes in the magnitude of the total gross federal debt for the five years 1945-1950 and compares the gross debt with two estimates[3] of the *total* government holdings of classes of owners that roughly correspond to those in the category "All other investors." Table 13 shows for the same period the portion of total marketable public issues held by "All other investors." Study of these data suggests the following conclusions.

First, during this period "All other investors" have consistently

3. While the ownership groups included in these two estimates (one made by the Treasury and one by the Federal Reserve), are not precisely the same as those grouped in the category "All other investors," they are roughly comparable. Thus these estimates furnish an indication of the size of the *total* holdings of "All other investors," and by deducting marketable holdings from the total we can get an approximation of the magnitude of nonmarketable holdings.

TABLE 13

COMPARISON OF TOTAL MARKETABLE PUBLIC ISSUES OF TREASURY SECURITIES WITH MARKETABLE GOVERNMENT SECURITIES HELD BY "ALL OTHER INVESTORS," AS OF DECEMBER 1945–1950

(Dollar Amounts in Billions)

Type of Security	1945		1946		1947		1948		1949		1950	
	Amount	Percentage of Total Debt	Amount	Percentage of Total Debt	Amount	Percentage of Total Debt	Amount	Percentage of Total Debt	Amount	Percentage of Total Debt	Amount	Percentage of Total Debt
Total marketable public issues	$198.8	100.0	$176.6	100.0	$165.8	100.0	$157.5	100.0	$155.1	100.0	$152.5	100.0
Marketable issues held by "All other investors"	51.0	25.6	44.2	25.0	42.2	25.4	42.6	27.1	41.8	26.9	44.4	29.1

Sources: Appendix Tables 28, 29 and *Federal Reserve Bulletin*, July 1951, p. 847.

held approximately one third of the gross debt and one fourth (or a little more) of total marketable public issues. Second, the portions held have remained remarkably steady, although during the latter part of this period this type of ownership has exhibited a tendency to absorb a growing percentage of both the total and the marketable debt. For example, in December 1950 "All other investors" held 29.1 per cent of marketable public issues, as compared with 25.0 per cent in December 1946. Third, marketable holdings of this group are about half of their total holdings, but marketable issues declined slightly as a percentage of the total during these years.

How has the marketable portion of the government portfolio of this type of ownership behaved? Following a moderate decline in the spring of 1946, the volume of marketable issues owned remained within the range of $41.7-$46.0 billion through December 1950. That is, the maximum fluctuation of $4.3 billion was less than 10 per cent of the largest amount held, notwithstanding steady shortening in the average maturity of the portfolio.

The Subgroups

Was the degree of stability that characterized the portfolio of "All other investors" also characteristic of holdings of the several subdivisions within this class, or was it produced by portfolio changes on the part of one group that were offset by changes on the part of others?

Some light is shed on this question by Table 14. Here is shown the portfolio behavior of several subgroups within the over-all classification. The data are as of December for the years 1945-1950 and cover total holdings, not simply marketable debt.[4]

Here we see clearly the behavior of the portfolios of various types of owners. Financial corporations (excluding banks and insurance companies) and nonfinancial corporations had a fluctuating demand. Their combined holdings dropped from $21.3 billion in December 1945 to $14.2 billion at the end of 1947 and then recovered nearly to the 1945 level. Unincorporated business, on the other hand, steadily liquidated its portfolio. Private trust funds steadily absorbed Treasury obligations. Indeed, these latter holdings at the end of 1950 were 70 per cent higher than they had been five years earlier.

4. Note that the material in Table 14 is a breakdown by subgroups of the Federal Reserve estimate in Table 12.

TABLE 14

GOVERNMENT SECURITY HOLDINGS OF INDIVIDUALS AND BUSINESSES,
AS OF DECEMBER 1945-1950

(In Billions)

Class of Owner	1945	1946	1947	1948	1949	1950[a]
Total	$86.9	$79.8	$80.6	$82.1	$85.4	$89.7
Financial corporations[b]	2.7	2.2	2.0	2.2	2.8	2.7
Nonfinancial corporations	18.6	13.1	12.2	12.1	13.5	16.6
Unincorporated businesses	10.0	8.9	8.0	7.5	7.1	6.5
Trust funds[c]	14.0	17.2	19.5	20.6	21.7	23.8
Other personal[d]	41.6	38.4	38.9	39.7	40.3	40.1

Source: Federal Reserve Bulletin, July 1951, p. 808.

a. Preliminary.

b. Real estate companies, finance and credit companies, insurance agencies (not carriers), investment trusts, security brokers and dealers, holding companies not otherwise classified, etc.

c. Includes only amounts administered by corporate trustees.

d. Includes holdings of farmers and professional persons.

"Other personal," which in this breakdown amounts to nearly half the total, remained relatively constant, ranging from $38.4 to $41.6 billion.

Factors Influencing Portfolio Behavior

Among the numerous influences that affect the volume of Treasury securities held by the subgroups included in "All other investors" are such matters as the wish of the public to build up, or to spend, liquid assets; the steady accumulation of resources in the hands of private trust funds; the need of business to hold, in liquid form, reserves for taxes and for other purposes; and the availability of materials and durable goods. Furthermore, the fact that nonmarketable government securities constitute a large part of the total holdings of many subgroups within this general classification makes the behavior of the marketable portion of the portfolio especially difficult to interpret. Nevertheless, one tentative conclusion may be warranted. Perhaps the very heterogeneity of the subdivisions within this category is a source of stability for the portfolio of the entire class. That is, very often when one subgroup is selling another may be buying, so that the two operations tend to counteract each other.

The variety of subgroups which make up the category "All other investors," and the diversity of their motivations in investing in

Treasury obligations, lends special interest to such fragmentary data as we have regarding the portfolio behavior of the constituent parts. Fortunately we have estimates of the *total* holdings of governments of persons and private trust funds and of business corporations other than banks and insurance companies. Collectively these classes account for something like two thirds, or perhaps a little more, of the total holdings of "All other investors."

Personal Holdings

Figure 11 compares the Federal Reserve estimates of liquid asset holdings of persons, including trust funds, and the portion of these

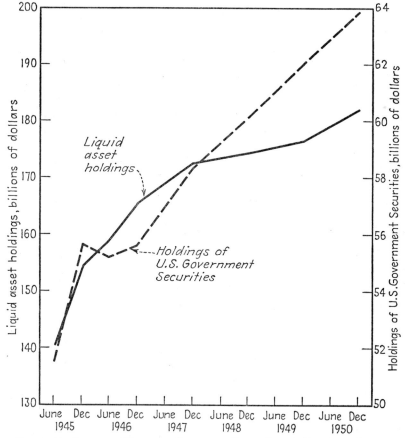

FIGURE 11. PERSONAL HOLDINGS, INCLUDING TRUST FUNDS: ESTIMATED LIQUID ASSET HOLDINGS AND HOLDINGS OF U.S. GOVERNMENT SECURITIES, SEMIANNUALLY, 1945-1946, ANNUALLY, 1947-1950

Source: Appendix Table 11.

holdings represented by federal obligations for the period June 1945—December 1950. The picture here is one of steady accumulation, and it should be noted that this class of ownership is one of the few in which the Treasury portfolio has shown a persistent tendency to grow.

After V-J Day, just as during the war, the steady growth of liquid assets in the hands of persons and trust funds was accompanied by a steady accumulation of federal securities. The postwar experience, however, differed from that of the war period in two important respects. During the war, between December 1941 and June 1945, personal holdings of governments increased $39.4 billion—more than four times. This rate of expansion was nearly double that exhibited by total liquid assets, which in June 1945 were approximately two and one half times what they had been at the time of Pearl Harbor. In the postwar period both the dollar growth and the rate of increase for personal holdings of governments were much smaller, respectively about $12.4 billion and about 24 per cent, for the five and one half years ending December 1950. Furthermore, reversing the wartime relationship, this 24 per cent rate of growth was *below* that exhibited by total liquid asset holdings. These increased almost 30 per cent during the same interval, so that Treasury securities lost ground to other types of liquid assets.

The ending of the war and the disappearance of large deficits in the postwar period largely explain why persons absorbed government securities at a much lower rate after V-J Day than before. These factors, however, do not explain why government securities proved less popular during the five-and-one-half-year period, when liquid assets were advancing, than did other forms of investment. Apparently the rates and other terms attached to the securities were not sufficiently attractive in the eyes of potential buyers for the obligations to retain the popularity they held at the beginning of the period relative to other types of assets.

United States Corporations

Following the end of the war the volume of Treasury securities held by corporations other than banks and insurance companies declined rapidly, as shown in Figure 12. Then, beginning in the latter part of 1948, the amount rose again, but at the end of 1950 had not regained the mid-1945 level.

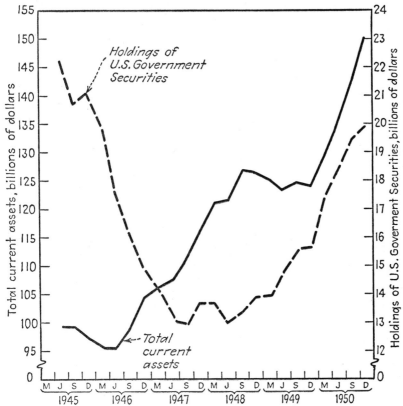

FIGURE 12. U.S. CORPORATIONS, EXCLUDING BANKS AND INSURANCE COMPANIES:
TOTAL CURRENT ASSETS AND HOLDINGS OF U.S. GOVERNMENT SECURITIES,
QUARTERLY, JUNE 1945—DECEMBER 1950

Source: Appendix Table 12.

The fall in 1945 and 1946 presumably in part reflected the reduction in the tax liability of business and in part represented the conversion of security holdings into cash that was used to meet the expenses incurred in changing from a war to a peace footing—the rehabilitation of plants, the restocking of inventories and the financing of sales to private rather than to governmental buyers. The stabilization of these holdings in 1947 and 1948, however, and their later rise, require a different explanation.

Since December 1946 these holdings of Treasury securities by business corporations have stayed remarkably constant as a percentage of current assets. During the four years 1947-1950 they remained within a range of approximately 10.5-13.5 per cent of total current assets. This consistent relationship suggests that during the postwar period forces inherent in the economy virtually required the business world to hold this proportion of current assets in the form of federal obligations. Probably these forces pertain to liquidity needs of business and to requirements for reserves, particularly tax reserves. In the event of war, and perhaps of severe depression, this relationship would almost certainly change. In the absence of such crises, however, the record suggests that it is likely to be maintained and that, were there a way to forecast the behavior of the total current assets of the business world we would, by the same token, have a method of guessing with moderate accuracy the volume of federal debt likely to be carried by business concerns.

The Maturity Pattern

Table 15 shows the maturity distribution of the marketable hold-

TABLE 15

COMPARISON OF MATURITY DISTRIBUTION OF MARKETABLE GOVERNMENT
SECURITIES HELD BY "ALL OTHER INVESTORS" IN DECEMBER 1945,
JANUARY 1950 AND DECEMBER 1950

(Dollar Amounts in Millions)

Due or First Becoming Callable	Maximum Holding, December 1945		Minimum Holding, January 1950		Holdings as of December 1950	
	Amount	Per Cent	Amount	Per Cent	Amount	Per Cent
Total	$51,046	100.0	$41,767	100.0	$44,430	100.0
Within 1 year	15,778	30.9	18,912	45.5	20,117	45.4
1-5 years	6,685	13.1	5,150	12.1	5,661	12.7
5-10 years	6,064	11.9	4,677	11.2	4,615	10.4
10-15 years	6,982	13.7	3,120	7.5	4,329	9.7
15-20 years	4,972	9.7	9,905	23.7	9,706	21.8
Over 20 years	10,559	20.7	—	—	—	—
Various years	6	—	3	—	2	—

Source: Appendix Tables 28, 29.

ings of "All other investors" as of three dates: December 1945, when they were at their maximum; January 1950, when they were at their minimum; and December 1950, the last month covered by this survey. Examination of these data indicates that the major increase in holdings, both in dollars and in percentages, was in the maturity bracket due or first callable within one year; that the holdings in the 1-5-year and the 5-10-year brackets taken as a unit were surprisingly stable, both in dollar terms and in percentages, and that the big reductions in the portfolio were in the brackets with a maturity or call date beyond ten years. Generally speaking, these findings are confirmed by examination of the monthly figures for the entire period.

The question then arises whether the substantial fall in the long-term securities signifies that an important change took place in investment habits or whether it indicates the presence of some sort of unsatisfied demand, since such securities were not made available by new Treasury offerings during this period. An answer to this question must in part be a matter of opinion. Even admitting that a substantial fraction of the government securities held by these ownership groups were carried for some sort of liquidity purpose, such as tax reserves, it is the author's belief that had long-term securities been made available by the Treasury the long-term holdings of "All other investors" would not have declined as much as they did. Consequently, he believes that either the $10 billion fluctuation in their total marketable holdings would have been narrowed or that, possibly, the volume of federal issues owned by "All other investors" would have risen, had long-term securities been available.

Summary and Conclusion

During the five and one half years ending in December 1950 those elements in society called "All other investors" held approximately one third of the total gross debt. Securities held by this block of ownership were divided more or less half and half between marketable and nonmarketable issues. The marketable issues amounted to roughly one fourth of all marketable securities outstanding. After 1946 the portion held, both of gross debt and of marketable public issues, showed a slight tendency to rise.

This stability in holdings was maintained in the face of a steady fall in the average maturity of the marketable debt owned and concealed the diversity of portfolio behavior that existed among the subgroups that make up "All other investors."

A large part, though not all of the holdings of these subgroups, probably represented the satisfaction of a variety of investment "needs" for liquidity, for tax reserves or for high-quality investments. Yet this fact does not diminish the importance of those "marginal" holdings that were responsive to the rate of return.

Furthermore, it is doubtful—at least in the author's eyes—if the stability in these holdings characteristic of the years 1945-1950 will be indefinitely maintained if the average maturity of the marketable portfolio continually shortens, notwithstanding the fact that the ownership of short-term obligations satisfies admirably certain "needs," such as those for liquidity.

The behavior of the portfolio of "All other investors" during the years 1945-1950 leaves unanswered the question whether this segment of the economy might have absorbed a somewhat larger portion of the federal debt if securities—particularly intermediate- and long-term securities—had been available on a higher-yield basis. That is, was there an unsatisfied demand for this type of obligation? If there was, and if the Treasury had issued such obligations, some of the subgroups within the over-all classification, notably trust funds and "other personal" would presumably have moderately increased their holdings. While the dollar amount of such increases might not have been great when compared with the total debt, their significance would have been larger when compared with that part of the debt the ownership of which appears unstable.

Chapter 10

PORTFOLIO BEHAVIOR: II

FEDERAL RESERVE BANKS AND UNITED STATES GOVERNMENT AGENCIES AND TRUST FUNDS

THE TREASURY SURVEY OF OWNERSHIP of marketable government issues groups together the Reserve Banks, and government agencies and trust funds. Collectively these two constitute the third largest category of debt owners. Marketable government debt held by the Reserve Banks typically amounted to about 75 per cent of the marketable debt held by the two classifications. The marketable obligations carried by the trust funds, nevertheless, have been appreciable during the period of this study—in the general range of $5-$8 billion—even though the great bulk of trust fund holdings have been in the form of nonmarketable, special issues. Fluctuations in the portfolio held by the Reserve Banks, however, have been the dominant factor in the category "United States government agencies and trust funds, including Federal Reserve Banks." Reserve Bank holdings have in turn been the controlling element determining the volume of Federal Reserve credit outstanding. (See Figure 7.)

Similarities and Dissimilarities

From some points of view it is logical to consider together the Reserve Banks and the government trust funds. Both are public agencies, notwithstanding the fact that the Reserve Banks are owned by the member banks. Furthermore, during the period covered by this study, virtually all of the resources of each of these classes of owners was invested in federal securities. Finally, these two classes of owners are in the position of being the ultimate and residual purchasers of government obligations that private owners do not wish to carry. Insofar as sales of any issue of Treasury securities by one class of private holder, such as savings banks, are not absorbed by some other private category, such as insurance companies or commercial banks, these securities pass into the hands of one of the classes of public purchasers. Thus these two public types of holders, and particularly the Reserve Banks, are in the position of "stand-by" owners of the federal debt. This generalization applies both to the size of the portfolios carried by these public holders and to the make-up or maturity pattern of the holdings, subject to the legal limitations that affect the purchase of marketable issues by the trust funds.

Yet in some respects the grouping of the trust funds with the Reserve Banks is misleading. In the first place, the sources of funds that these two classes of owners use to purchase federal securities are radically different. Within the limits imposed by the legal requirements for reserves the Reserve Banks in case of need can create the funds with which to purchase Treasury obligations. This limitation, under the conditions that have existed since the war, has, in effect, been no limitation. The trust funds, on the other hand, have at their disposal only the moneys paid into them, in accordance with the various laws governing contributions to the funds, less payments made from the funds. The volume of moneys paid into or withdrawn from the funds varies with changing economic conditions, but during the period covered by this survey the annual increases in holdings of Treasury securities were very large, running as high as $3.9 billion in 1946. (See Table 16.)

TABLE 16

U.S. GOVERNMENT SECURITIES HELD BY U.S. GOVERNMENT AGENCIES AND TRUST FUNDS, QUARTERLY, JUNE 1945–DECEMBER 1950

(In Billions)

Month	1945			1946			1947		
	Special Issues	Public Issues	Total Issues	Special Issues	Public Issues	Total Issues	Special Issues	Public Issues	Total Issues
March				$21.1	$7.0	$28.1	$25.2	$6.4	$31.6
June	$18.8	$6.1	$24.9	22.3	6.8	29.1	27.4	5.4	32.8
Sept.	20.5	6.1	26.6	23.9	6.6	30.5	29.5	4.4	33.9
Dec.	20.0	7.0	27.0	24.6	6.3	30.9	29.0	5.4	34.0

Month	1948			1949			1950		
	Special Issues	Public Issues	Total Issues	Special Issues	Public Issues	Total Issues	Special Issues	Public Issues	Total Issues
March	$29.3	$5.7	$35.0	$31.9	$5.7	$37.6	$32.0	$5.5	$37.5
June	30.2	5.5	35.7	32.8	5.5	38.3	32.4	5.5	37.9
Sept.	31.2	5.6	36.8	33.9	5.5	39.4	33.4	5.5	38.9
Dec.	31.7	5.6	37.3	33.9	5.5	39.4	33.7	5.5	39.2

Source: Federal Reserve Bulletin, September 1945—March 1951.

In the second place, whereas all the securities held by the Reserve Banks have been public marketable issues, the bulk of the securities owned by the trust funds have been special issues that were nonmarketable but redeemable at the Treasury. Only a minor portion of their holdings have been in the form of marketable issues. Thus the make-up of their respective portfolios has been radically different.

Finally, the motives governing the investment policies of these two classes of owners are quite unlike. The considerations which have actuated the Reserve authorities have already been discussed and are commented on further below. By way of contrast, the major influences affecting the government portfolios of the trust funds have been the rate of growth of the funds, the debt retirement policy of the Treasury and the volume of marketable issues that the managers of the trust funds, operating within the latitude permissible under the law, chose to hold.

In view of these differences it will be desirable to discuss these two classifications of ownership separately.

Federal Reserve Banks

During the period covered by this study the Reserve Banks' government portfolio was dominated by two considerations: the control of credit conditions and, in cooperation with the Treasury, the stabilization of the government securities market. At times these policies required the purchase of securities by the Banks, at times their sale. One other factor also influenced the Banks' position in governments in the immediate postwar years—namely, the debt retirement policy of the Treasury. So far as possible, this policy was designed to redeem maturing obligations in the hands of the banks, particularly Reserve Banks. Since at this time by far the larger portion of the Banks' portfolio was in short-dated debt, this circumstance facilitated Treasury policy and, at the same time, permitted its operations to influence directly a substantial portion of the Banks' holdings. These factors, as they affected the Reserve Banks' position, produced wide variations both in the total amount and in the make-up of the portfolio.

Figure 13 shows the major movements in the System's portfolio from June 1945 through December 1950. At the peak in December 1946 the Bank's holdings amounted to $23.8 billion; at the low point, in September 1949, they were no more than $17.4 billion, a

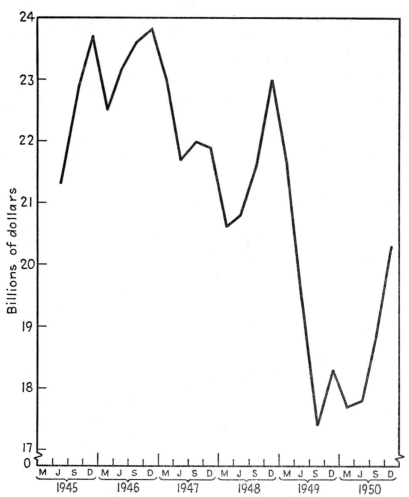

FIGURE 13. FEDERAL RESERVE BANK HOLDINGS OF U.S. GOVERNMENT SECURITIES,
QUARTERLY, JUNE 1945—DECEMBER 1950
Source: Appendix Table 13.

shrinkage of more than one fourth. By December 1950, however, the
last month covered by this study, they had risen again to $20.3 billion.

Large changes in the composition of the portfolio also took place.
In February 1947, the Reserve's holdings of Treasury bills were at
their maximum, $15.7 billion. At that time these bills were approxi-
mately 92 per cent of all bills outstanding. These bill holdings,
together with other obligations due or callable within one year,
amounted to some 95 per cent of the entire portfolio of the Reserve

System. By way of contrast, in November 1948 obligations due or callable beyond one year accounted for only about half of the Banks' portfolio, and securities in the ten-to-twenty-year maturity bracket were nearly one third of the total. Changes such as these illustrate the magnitude of the adjustments made by the Reserve authorities in adapting their position to changing conditions.

Conclusions Regarding Reserve Banks

The influences that dominated Reserve Bank portfolio policy in this period placed the Banks in a difficult position for at least two separate, though related, reasons. First, the policies continually threatened to become antithetical and at times, as at the end of 1947 when the support prices were lowered, it became impossible to conceal that fact. Thus the Banks were periodically faced with difficult decisions as to which policy should have preference. Second, insofar as the Banks pursued a policy of stabilizing the prices of the different kinds and maturities of government securities, not only was the *size* of their portfolio in large measure determined by the *volume* of sales that other classes of owners wished to make, but the *make-up* of the portfolio was also greatly influenced by the *types* of securities other holders wished to liquidate. Certainly at times during the postwar period a "lack of ammunition"—a shortage of securities in the longer-maturity brackets in the Reserve System's portfolio—handicapped its stabilization operations. Thus the acquisition and maintenance of a portfolio diversified and spaced according to the needs of the System was not always easy of achievement.

If the position of the Reserve System continues to be that of "stabilizer" both for the economy as a whole (insofar as that can be done by credit regulation) and for the government securities market, as presumably in some measure will be the case, even if prices are not meticulously supported, then the Reserve Banks' portfolio will continue to be more or less shaped by the action of other classes of debt holders. That is, the Reserve System, as the residual purchaser, will continue to be in the position of having the size and make-up of its holdings directly affected by the purchases and sales of other classes of owners, subject to such limitations as the needs of credit regulation may impose. In short, the System's portfolio will exhibit changes in size and composition similar to those we have noted, notwithstanding the fact that its purchases and sales will in turn be influenced by the general fiscal and financial policies of the government, in which the Reserve System will have some voice.

Since the Reserve's portfolio is, roughly, three times as large as the marketable securities held by the government trust accounts, and since these trust accounts will be much affected by the same influences shaping Reserve Bank action, it is reasonable to assume that these two portfolios taken together will continue to fluctuate more or less as they have in the past.

Should the federal debt be increased or decreased substantially, or should the Board of Governors be forced to give relatively much more weight to credit control than has been the case since V-J Day, or should the government trust accounts increase the proportion of marketable securities acquired by them (diminishing proportionately the volume of special issues) these expectations would be altered. In the absence of any of these changes, however, the most reasonable anticipation is for an extension of the same general pattern of behavior that has existed since the end of the war. In this respect the outlook for these holdings differs from the outlook for some of the other classes considered in this study.

United States Government Agencies and Trust Funds

Table 16 shows that in June 1945 government agencies and trust funds held $24.9 billion of federal securities, or nearly 10 per cent of the gross debt. By December 1949 their portfolio had risen $14.5 billion, to $39.4 billion, or nearly 15 per cent of the gross debt. In 1950, however, their holdings declined slightly. Taking the period as a whole, however, this advance was the largest dollar accretion shown by any type of ownership.

Their holdings of public marketable issues, however, which have consisted almost entirely of long-term obligations, did not follow the pattern of total holdings and were not a constant percentage of the entire portfolio. In June 1945 marketables were a little less than one fourth of total holdings; by the end of 1950 the proportion had dropped to about one seventh.

Conclusions Regarding Government Agencies and Trust Funds

During periods when these funds grow, their increase is a most important element in managing the debt. In periods when the government has a deficit, increments to the funds serve to reduce the

Treasury's demands for financing. In periods when the government's debt is staying constant or declining, the accretions can serve to reduce the volume of government obligations in the hands of the public, particularly marketable issues. This reduction may take place either through direct purchase of marketable issues or through the refunding of maturing marketable obligations into special issues.

The extent to which marketable obligations can be directly absorbed by these funds depends on a number of factors, of which the chief appear to be: the rate at which the funds' resources increase; the yield bases on which marketable issues at any given time can be bought;[1] the volume of marketable debt which the managers of these funds, for one reason or another, consider it practicable to hold. If the funds continue to grow, and were the legal and other circumstances under which they can acquire marketable obligations more flexible than they appear to be, their portfolios seemingly could be operated in such a way as substantially to diminish the effect on the money supply of liquidations by the private segment of the economy. That is, purchases could be made by these funds, rather than by the Reserve Banks, with less effect on the credit base.

In a period when these funds disburse greater sums than they receive, they have the option—assuming they hold both marketable and nonmarketable obligations—of selling marketable securities in the market or presenting nonmarketables to the Treasury for redemption. If securities were presented for redemption during a period of deficit financing, the Treasury would be compelled to increase the volume of new money that it was raising by borrowing. The effect of this increase on the money supply would largely depend on the way in which the Treasury borrowed, whether it tapped funds in the hands of banks or of "nonbanks." Thus accumulation of federal securities in the trust funds may be looked on as a sort of contingent liability of the government (even though the securities are actual liabilities) that may become "real liabilities" and inflate the money supply. When and as portions of these contingent liabilities are transformed into actual demands for cash the inflationary consequences may or may not be socially desirable, depending on prevailing economic conditions.

1. In general these funds are required by statute so to invest their assets as to earn a stated average return. If marketable debt is selling so as to yield less than is required, presumably the funds will not find it practical to invest in any large amount of such securities.

LIFE INSURANCE COMPANIES

Life insurance companies, while not one of the largest categories of debt owners, are nevertheless quantitatively an important group, particularly as regards the longest-term marketable issues. During the first two or three years after the war they were the largest owners of this type, though they relinquished their position later. Their portfolios have also, in recent years, been the most volatile of any group.

In July 1946 government holdings reached their peak of $21.6 billion and during 1946 and the first five months of 1947 were very steady, remaining above $21.0 billion. Thereafter they declined persistently, falling approximately $1.5 billion in the second half of 1947, $3.0 billion in 1948, $1.4 billion in 1949 and $1.8 billion in 1950. In December 1950 they amounted to $12.7 billion, the lowest level reached in the period covered by this survey and about 41 per cent below the high point of July 1946. During this decline the percentage of the gross debt accounted for by life insurance company holdings dropped from 8 per cent to less than 5 per cent, and the portion of marketable issues from over 11 per cent to a little more than 8 per cent.

As with other types of debt holders, the behavior of the insurance companies' government portfolio is subject to a number of influences. Chief among these are the volume of insurance company resources, the rate of return obtainable on governments, the availability and yields of other kinds of investments and the desire of the companies that their assets be characterized by a diversification of risk.

Government Portfolio Compared with Resources

Figure 14 compares the growth of the admitted assets of life insurance companies with the behavior of their portfolios of governments. It shows that during the first year following the termination of hostilities the volume of Treasury securities owned continued the wartime growth, a growth more rapid than the increase in admitted assets. Thereafter the holdings of life companies began a swift and virtually uninterrupted decline, one that, apparently, had not come to an end by December 1950. This fall took place notwithstanding a growth in total admitted assets. The magnitude of the change that took place during this period is emphasized by the fact that during the first part of 1946 governments accounted for nearly half of total

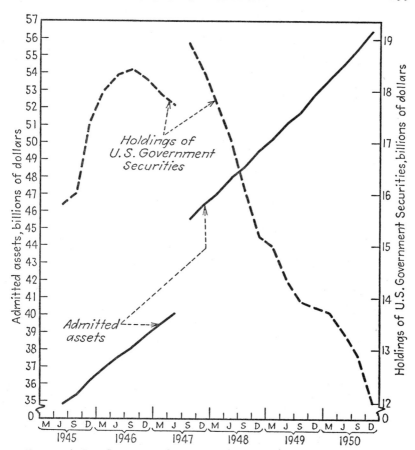

FIGURE 14. LIFE INSURANCE COMPANIES: ADMITTED ASSETS AND HOLDINGS OF
U.S. GOVERNMENT SECURITIES, QUARTERLY, JUNE 1945—DECEMBER 1950
Source: Appendix Table 14.

admitted assets, whereas in December 1950 they were about one
fifth.

It appears probable that the growth of the insurance companies'
portfolio in the immediate postwar period was chiefly caused by two
factors: the continued rise of the gross federal debt and the absence
of other attractive outlets for funds sufficient to absorb their available resources. The federal debt reached its peak in February 1946,
however, roughly six months before the peak of the insurance companies' holdings. Thus it seems likely that it was the second influence that was operative during the spring of 1946, a time when the
total of federal obligations outstanding was declining.

As postwar investment opportunities opened up, however, the picture quickly changed and life insurance companies became heavy sellers of governments. This selling was stimulated by three types of motives: a belief that sound policy required satisfaction of at least a part of the demand from business for financing which the insurance companies were experiencing; a feeling on the part of many insurance company executives that the rate of return obtainable on federal obligations was inadequate for their needs, in view of the companies' commitments to policyholders; and a wish of many company officials to achieve a wider distribution of risk in their investments. Whether, had the Treasury pursued different policies, this selling would have been smaller and the instability in this section of the pattern of ownership less, will be considered further on.

The Maturity Pattern

Table 17 compares the maturity distribution of life insurance company portfolios at their high point in July 1946 and their low point in December 1950.

The salient fact is the constancy in the proportion of obligations maturing or becoming callable in ten years or less to those of longer date. In July 1946, when insurance company portfolios of Treasury obligations were at their peak, roughly 82 per cent of their holdings, about $17.6 billion, had maturities of ten years or longer. In December 1950, securities with maturities of ten years or more had risen

TABLE 17

COMPARISON OF THE MATURITY DISTRIBUTION OF LIFE INSURANCE COMPANY GOVERNMENT PORTFOLIOS IN JULY 1946 AND DECEMBER 1950

(Dollar Amounts in Millions)

Due or First Becoming Callable	Maximum Holding, July 1946		Minimum Holding, December 1950	
	Amount	Per Cent	Amount	Per Cent
Total	$21,569	100.00	$12,746	100.00
Within 1 year	844	3.91	655	5.14
1-5 years	938	4.35	398	3.13
5-10 years	2,162	10.03	906	7.10
10-15 years	1,876	8.69	5,947	46.66
15-20 years	9,706	45.00	4,832	37.90
Over 20 years	6,031	27.96	—	—
Various years	13	.06	9	.07

Source: Appendix Tables 22, 23.

slightly to about 85 per cent of the total, although the dollar amount held, $10.8 billion, was less than two thirds of what it had been in July 1946.

What do these facts mean? In the first place, they show clearly that insurance companies, because of the character of their operations and investment needs, are primarily interested in owning long-term securities as distinguished from short- or intermediate-term obligations.

In the second place, the facts strongly suggest that insurance companies have a continuing demand for a moderate amount of short- and intermediate-term issues with maturity or call dates of less than ten years. Presumably such holdings serve as a source of ready cash and as an aid in adjusting their investment position. This demand appears, under the circumstances that have been prevailing since the end of the war, to be of the general magnitude of $2 to $4 billion.

In the third place, the data indicate that as time passed and as the longer-term securities held by insurance companies in 1946 became shorter dated, these holdings were reduced. Although Table 17 shows that reductions took place in all maturity brackets except the 10-15-year bracket, the great bulk of the fall in insurance company holdings took place in the maturity classes of 15 years and up. The question logically arises, why did this happen? Why did not insurance companies, if they were interested in long-term issues, replace with longer-term obligations those that, with the passage of time, became of shorter duration?

The answer is twofold. First, as was indicated in Chapter 3, the Treasury did not offer any intermediate- or long-term marketable issues. If insurance companies had wished to replace obligations that were growing shorter with those of longer terms, they would have had to buy these in the open market and they would have had to buy them on yield bases which insurance executives generally considered unsatisfactory in view of their companies' needs. Second, there was a very large demand for financing on the part of business, and thus the insurance companies had attractive alternative uses for their funds. While it cannot be proven, there is a presumption that if insurance companies had been able during this period to acquire long-term governments on yield bases deemed satisfactory, the shrinkage in their government portfolios would not have been so great. That is, as the passage of time reduced the maturity of their portfolios, some of the issues with a shorter period to run would have been replaced with longer-dated ones. Had that occurred, the instability in the pattern of ownership represented by the decline in insurance company portfolios from $21.6 billion in July 1946 to $12.7 billion in December 1950 would have been reduced.

Conclusions as to Life Insurance Companies

From the point of view of future debt management policy, this postwar experience presents a number of interesting questions. Barring the contingency of extreme economic dislocation, is there some minimum amount of government securities that life insurance companies are likely to continue to hold, some minimum percentage of admitted assets they are likely to keep invested in this way, virtually irrespective of the return earned and of Treasury policy? For example, is the decline in their holdings likely to continue to the point where $2-$4 billions of short-term governments, carried for purposes of liquidity, are all that they hold? Or are the insurance companies likely to do as they did during the early 1920's, after World War I, and liquidate virtually their entire government portfolio? If we assume that such is not likely to be the case and that the life insurance industry will probably not permit its government holdings to fall below a certain level, then how close are we to that level and how much more selling can be anticipated from this quarter? Or, if Treasury policy were to change and a larger volume of long-term securities were to be made available at yields which insurance executives thought commensurate with their needs, what effect—if any—would that have on insurance company investment policies and the portion of their assets employed in owning federal securities?

Exact answers to these questions cannot be given. Admittedly a variety of factors, not all of which can be foreseen, will influence the future behavior of insurance company portfolio holdings. One or another of these might prevent much further liquidation. Should the demand for financing on the part of private business decline, so that the possibility of employing insurance company resources in that area were reduced, the companies might, in a sense, be compelled to build up their Treasury portfolios. Or if, for any one of a number of reasons, insurance company executives concluded they did not wish their holdings of governments to drop below some approximate dollar figure or below some percentage of admitted assets, further decreases in these holdings might be checked. Or if large-scale deficit financing, stemming from defense requirements, were renewed, insurance company portfolios of governments presumably would rapidly expand, as they did in each of the two world wars.

Until the course of future events is clearer and knowledge of these matters more definite, perhaps the safest conclusion is that postwar experience indicates a minimum continued holding of short-term Treasury securities by life insurance companies of some $2-$4 billion, and that the volume in excess of this amount they hold in the future will primarily be determined by the terms the Treasury offers and the demand for financing on the part of the private economy.

SAVINGS BANKS

Unlike life insurance companies, savings banks,[2] the other principal type of savings institution, showed no pronounced tendency during the period of this study either to absorb or disgorge Treasury obligations. In January 1946 the holdings of mutual savings banks reached $10.7 billion. Thereafter, until the last few months of 1950 the savings banks' portfolio was never below this figure nor above $11.9 billion, the peak reached in August 1947. In other words, for four and a half years it stayed within the comparatively narrow range of $10.7-$11.9 billion, a magnitude roughly equal to 4 per cent of the gross debt. Although the portfolio fell below this range in the latter part of 1950 it was still, in December, above $10 billion. The holdings of governments of stock savings banks, while much smaller, were almost equally stable.

Influences Affecting Portfolios

The amount of Treasury securities owned by these savings institutions is chiefly influenced by the size of their total resources, the alternative uses of funds available to them, the rates of return yielded by these other uses, the volume and character of securities available for purchase by banks and the need for liquid assets felt by them. Most if not all of these factors changed appreciably during the period under inspection. For example, total deposits of all

2. This discussion is based on the data for mutual savings banks. Data for stock savings banks are available only through June 1949. At no time did they hold as much as $500 million of Treasury securities. The conclusions regarding mutual savings banks would not have been affected by inclusion of the holdings of stock savings banks.

mutual savings banks increased roughly one fourth between December 1945 and December 1950. The mortgage market opened up and the banks were able to place very large sums in it. Rates on mortgages and on other investments also rose slightly, particularly after 1946. In view of the postwar experience it would appear that these various developments on the whole tended to offset each other so that the net result was to keep the banks' government holdings comparatively stable.

Comparison with Resources

Figure 15 compares the course of time deposits of all mutual savings banks with their holdings of government securities. As in

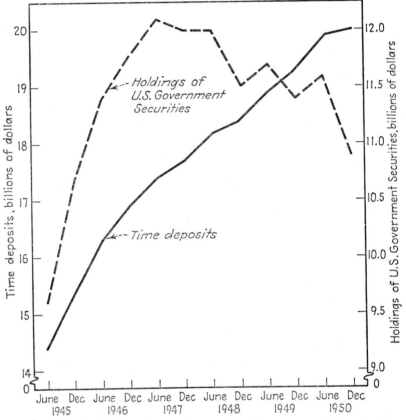

FIGURE 15. ALL MUTUAL SAVINGS BANKS: TIME DEPOSITS AND HOLDINGS OF U.S. GOVERNMENT SECURITIES, SEMIANNUALLY, JUNE 1945—DECEMBER 1950

Source: Appendix Table 15.

the case of commercial banks, from June 1945 through June 1947 the two series roughly paralleled each other, and the rise of deposits permitted, if it did not cause, the expansion in the banks' holdings of governments. After June 1947 the government portfolio tended downward, whereas time deposits continued to advance. From June 1945 through December 1947, the governments held by the banks were equal to roughly two thirds of time deposits; as of December 1950, however, they were only about one half the deposit figure.

From the evidence presented here, as well as that in Table 11, it appears that during the first two years of peace, as during the war, the volume of resources at the disposal of the banks was the chief influence affecting the size of their portfolios. Thereafter their government holdings failed to keep pace with the increase in deposits and, indeed, began to fall in the latter part of 1948 as outlets for savings banks' funds more attractive than federal securities began to appear. Notwithstanding this changing pattern, however, some stability characterized the banks' portfolios during this period.

Maturity Distribution

Consistently the banks held approximately $200-$500 million of Treasury obligations—some 2 to 5 per cent of their portfolio—with a maturity or first call date of less than one year. This block of investments presumably was carried as a ready source of cash. Beyond this liquidity reserve the banks' portfolios were typically divided fairly evenly among the several maturity brackets, the larger part of their holdings consistently being in the longer-term maturities with a maturity or call date in excess of ten years. This general pattern was maintained in the face of the decrease in the average maturity of the debt as a whole that took place, and notwithstanding the fact that after 1947 there were no obligations available with a maturity or call date in excess of twenty years, since the bonds of 1967-1972 had by then moved within a shorter maturity bracket. From time to time, however, substantial changes took place in the amounts of securities held in particular maturity brackets, as the passage of time forced a reclassification of the obligations carried and as the banks adjusted their portfolio position.

Conclusions Regarding Savings Banks

The savings banks have represented a very steady demand for roughly $10-$11 billion of Treasury obligations. The demand of the banks for these issues has not, since early 1947, been closely geared to the volume of their resources, for their holdings have not increased with the increase in their deposits. This may be a change in investment habits of some significance. On the other hand, they have not liquidated appreciable portions of their portfolios as alternative outlets for funds have appeared.

In view of the investment needs of savings banks the presumption is that a large part of their demand for governments is for long-term securities, and this presumption is borne out by the behavior of their portfolios during the five years following the end of the war. Conceivably, part of the explanation of the failure of their portfolios to grow as resources expanded lay in their inability to replace longer-term obligations as these moved into shorter-maturity brackets. In any event, the record strongly suggests that if in the future the banks are unable to obtain the longer-term securities necessary to maintain a spaced maturity pattern their willingness to retain the volume of securities held since the war may be diminished. This tendency may be enhanced if rates of return obtainable from other investments rise relative to the yield of Treasury obligations.

An important question for future debt management—assuming deficit financing is not renewed on a large scale—is whether the banks' holdings are likely to stay at about the level they have maintained or to continue the decline that began in the latter part of 1950. If it is assumed that present holdings are not much more than adequate for the liquidity needs of the banks, particularly if deposits continue to advance, then it is perhaps reasonable to believe that this category of assets will not shrink much more, even if the demand for mortgage money continues strong. On the other hand, if it is thought that government holdings are more than sufficient for the banks' needs, and if attractive investments giving a higher return than governments continue in plentiful supply, then the presumption must be that further liquidation is to be expected.

FIRE, CASUALTY AND MARINE INSURANCE COMPANIES

Fire, casualty and marine insurance companies hold the smallest amount of government securities of any of the classes of ownership here identified, only some one to 2 per cent of the gross debt. These companies, however, absorbed Treasury issues virtually without interruption during the five and one half years under observation.

Marketable holdings, at $2.6 billion in October 1945, advanced to $4.1 billion by December 1950, a rise of 58 per cent or approximately 10 per cent per year. This rise increased by two thirds the portion of the gross debt which they held and doubled the percentage of marketable public issues. As holdings increased the maturity pattern remained reasonably constant, with roughly two thirds of holdings consistently falling in the classification of ten years or less to maturity or first call date.

This investment behavior was one of the most consistent exhibited by any class of ownership. The portfolio of no other private group of owners showed so persistent an increase during this period or, proportionately, so great a one. Presumably the explanation for these steady acquisitions lay in the growing volume of resources of fire, casualty and marine insurance companies.

While the dollar volume of securities represented by these insurance companies' portfolios is not large, the significance of this type of behavior should not be underestimated. The steady accumulation of Treasury issues by government agencies and trust funds, by private trust funds and other types of personal holdings, and by these companies offset in some measure the liquidations of other classes of owners and eased the task of debt management. Since sales of government obligations—necessary and desirable as they are in a free market economy—are one of the roots of instability in the pattern of ownership, and since these sales—if not offset by private buying—may affect the money supply, this type of portfolio behavior is of great aid in cushioning the inflationary effects of a large debt. Steady buying, of a type that does not require an increase in the money supply, diminishes the dangers inherent in necessary portfolio adjustments. As we look to the future, one of the important tasks of debt management is to cultivate new and additional classes of private purchasers that can be relied upon to absorb government securities liquidated by one or another of the classes of debt owners. "Marginal" purchases are necessary if "marginal" sales are not to affect the money supply.

LESSONS AND SUMMARY

The foregoing detailed analysis permits us to draw conclusions regarding portfolio behavior that have validity not only for the past but, it would seem, for future problems of debt management as well.

Forces Determining the Distribution of the Debt

Treasury obligations issued during World War II were absorbed partly through the use of existing cash balances and of newly accruing savings, partly through the expansion of bank deposits. The new deposits, spread throughout society by the economic processes entailed in the production and distribution of goods and services, increased the assets, particularly the current assets, of the several classes of debt owners. Such increases, together with the investment needs, desires and habits of these various classes, produced by the end of the war the pattern of ownership that has been discussed.

In this distribution there was a certain underlying logic and stability. The termination of hostilities, however, brought new forces into play, such as a modest amount of debt retirement in 1946 and 1947, the Treasury policy of refunding into short-term obligations, the financial needs of business in converting to peacetime production and, later, in expanding productive capacity. These occasioned some redistribution of the debt. But the relative amounts held by the several classes of owners on V-J Day were not upset and the basic pattern was not greatly changed. Unless economic relationships are greatly distorted, as presumably would be the case in the event of war, depression, severe inflation or renewed large-scale deficit financing, it seems probable that this pattern is likely to prevail in its essential form.

The Changing Situation

On the other hand, with the passage of time the factors affecting the distribution of the debt changed little by little. During the war the increase of resources at the command of the several segments of the economy, caused by the expansion of the debt and of the money supply, was the dominating force affecting portfolio behavior. For a short time after the war the volume of resources at the disposal of the several categories of debt owners continued to exert great influence. This situation, however, came to an end in the case of life insurance companies in mid-1946, and in mid-1947 in the case of commercial banks and savings banks, although it continued to be important for other types of debt owners. In short, as the heavy wartime deficits receded further and further in time, their effect on the pattern of ownership was increasingly superseded by other influences. Some of these new influences worked in the direction of maintaining stability in the pattern of ownership, whereas others had the reverse tendency. Were large deficits to recur it seems virtually certain that we would see a recurrence of the wartime relationship of rising debt, expanding money, increasing assets and growing government portfolios.

Types of Portfolio Behavior

As the new situation developed several passably well-defined types of portfolio behavior appeared. The ability to distinguish these kinds of behavior aids appreciably in isolating some of the crucial problems of debt management.

For much the larger portion of the five and one half years following the end of hostilities the government security holdings of commercial banks and of savings banks fluctuated within comparatively narrow ranges—narrow in the sense that the extent of fluctuation was roughly 10 per cent of the maximum held. In the case of commercial banks this "margin of instability" was roughly $6 billion; in the case of savings banks about $1 billion. Likewise the marketable security holdings of "All other investors" had a similar range of fluctuation —one of about 10 per cent, or something more than $4 billion. This behavior, however, concealed the widely differing action of the portfolios of the subgroups that compose "All other investors." In particular it obscured the steady accumulation of Treasury issues by private trust funds. This tendency to acquire federal obligations was also exhibited by fire, marine and casualty insurance companies. Life insurance companies, on the other hand, after the middle of 1946 steadily liquidated their government portfolios. Federal Reserve Banks, and in some measure government trust funds and agencies, were in the position of "stabilizers," cushioning the effect on the market of the buying and selling that took place among the private categories of debt owners.

Three points should be made plain. First, the acquisitions of government obligations by private trust funds and by fire, marine and casualty insurance companies, while useful in absorbing the sales of other classes of investors, were not large relative to such sales and, particularly, were not large relative to the potential selling represented by the "margin of instability" in the portfolios of other classes. Second, generally speaking, the potential selling represented by the "margin of instability" in the holdings of the various classes did not *all* materialize at the same times. In other words, while some classes of debt holders were selling, typically, other classes were building up their positions. Had all the potential selling come into the market at any given time the situation of the Reserve System as "stabilizer" would have been much more difficult than was the case, and its task would probably have been impossible. Third, the Treasury obligations acquired by the Reserve Banks supplied the commercial banking system with reserve funds and thus, potentially, increased inflationary pressures. In other words, their stabilizing operations were conducted only at the expense of enhancing inflationary dangers.

Instability in the Pattern of Ownership

Thus we see that when sales, or potential sales, by some private classes of owners are greater than purchases, or potential purchases, by other classes, these sales can take place only if the Reserve System, directly or indirectly, furnishes the funds—unless the debt is currently being reduced. Such action by the Reserve Banks, of course, enhances the danger of inflation. Further, these sales and potential sales substantially augment the operational problems of the Treasury in managing the debt, such as refunding maturing issues without suffering an undue loss of cash and adapting the terms of new issues to the requirements of the market.

What are the causes of these sales, actual or potential, by private classes of owners? Roughly speaking, they are of two sorts, although the two are not completely unrelated. On the one hand, they reflect changing investment needs and desires of debt owners, the necessity for cash, the wish to acquire other types of investments and all the other elements that lead to rearrangements and reallocations of assets by persons or institutions. On the other hand, they stem in part from Treasury policy as evidenced by the terms attaching to new securities, such as interest rates, lengths of maturity, tax privileges, marketability, and so forth. Each of these sets of forces, of course, reacts on the other.

It may appear that the dollar amount of securities which have been described as being "potentially unstable" during the immediate postwar period was not large, at least when compared with the magnitude of the entire debt. This is the case, but it is a misleading view. Their principal significance lay not in their absolute amount but in the effects their transfer could produce on the money supply and on the management problems of the Treasury.

What are the mechanisms by which these potential transfers, this possible market activity, can be checked or, if the situation calls for it, stimulated? Interest policy is one of the principal methods for damping down potential selling by one or another of the classes of debt owners or for quickening purchases by others. Changes in the level or structure of rates, however, will not—except over a long period—bring a radical change in the over-all distribution of the debt and thus in a large sense may seem of little consequence. Yet changes in rates, up or down depending upon circumstances, markedly affect *marginal* shifts in the portfolio position of the several classes of debt owners and stimulate or depress the extent to which potential sales or purchases take place within the margin of instability. This is the case, even though it is not possible without considering the elements of each particular situation to make a reasonable estimate of the probable consequences of a stated increase or decrease in rates. Thus interest policy, as a part of debt management, has a great deal to do with the way in which potential transfers of Treasury obligations may influence the money supply.

If it is accepted that instability in the pattern of ownership occasions difficulties for fiscal managers, then it follows that stability must ordinarily be one of the chief objectives sought in debt management. From this point of view the types of obligations issued by the Treasury, their terms and the other procedures of debt management should be chosen with a view to offsetting the instability that arises from the needs and desires of actual or potential debt owners. If this is not done the risk is that instability stemming from one group of causes may be augmented by instability originating in the other group.

Perhaps what this amounts to is an argument that, in the long run, even the Treasury can disregard only at its peril the needs of the market and the wishes of its customers. For if these needs are not met in some fashion moderately satisfactory to those who buy and keep government securities, the natural wish of debt owners to liquidate their holdings will create very serious problems.

There is another reason also for respecting, in some degree, the wishes and requirements of the market. Funds for debt ownership can be allocated in only two ways, voluntarily and compulsorily. If sufficient funds are not allocated voluntarily, fiscal authority must resort to compulsion. That is its last recourse. And if its policies have departed too far and too long from the wishes of the market and the needs of the actual or potential buyers, it is in the position of having itself created the conditions that require compulsion. Unwillingness on the part of fiscal authority to make its obligations competitively attractive when compared with alternative uses for funds, notwithstanding the very great powers which it has for influencing the number and character of these alternatives, leads ultimately to the use of force—the final mandate of the state—the possession of which distinguishes it from all other elements in the economy.

Chapter 11

DEBT REPAYMENT AND REDUCTION

IN VIEW OF THE PRESENT and prospective commitments of the United States at home and abroad—commitments which are moral and political as well as legal—it may seem unrealistic to devote much attention to the economic effects and methods of debt retirement. Yet there are substantial reasons for so doing, two in particular. One is to explore some of the aspects of an operation that, in many quarters, is considered "desirable in itself," at least during periods other than those of business depression or acute international crisis. The other is that some aspects of debt reduction possess implications almost if not quite as far-reaching as do some aspects of debt expansion.

There may also be a question why reduction of the total marketable issues outstanding should be made a separate topic in a discussion of debt repayment. The most obvious answer is that total marketable issues and the gross debt do not necessarily rise and fall together. For example, during periods when the gross debt remains constant or, even when it is increasing, marketable issues may be redeemed through a reduction of the Treasury's general cash balance or from the proceeds of sales of nonmarketable issues. But there are other reasons for calling particular attention to the behavior of marketable issues. First, some of the major problems of debt management, particularly those involving the relation of the debt to the money supply, center on the behavior of the marketable issues rather than on the behavior of the total. Second, such debt reduction as has taken place since the end of World War II has been concentrated in the marketable part. Indeed, the fall of public marketable issues that took place during the period of this survey, roughly $47 billion, was nearly double the $28 billion decline in gross debt that took place between early 1946 and mid-1948. Thus it would be highly unrealistic to discuss debt repayment without consideration of this fact. We should not forget, however, that the marketable debt is the major part of the whole. Consequently the two magnitudes are not likely to move independently of each other, let alone in opposite directions, to any large degree or for any extended period of time.

REASONS FOR DEBT REDUCTION

Generally speaking, four kinds of reasons are advanced to support the desirability of debt reduction. The first involves the effects of a large debt on the position of the government itself. The second has to do with the potential repercussions of a large debt on the money supply and with the implications that the existence of a large debt has for the locus of fiscal authority. The third concerns the budgetary consequences of debt. The fourth relates to the influence exerted by a large debt, and by debt repayment, on economic activity and the expansion of the economy.

Debt and Government

Whatever the dangers and disadvantages inherent in a large debt, these will be reduced by debt reduction. Big debt has contributed to the growth of "big government," and debt repayment will reduce the role that government plays in the life of the nation. If, as the preceding analysis has suggested, the ownership of a substantial part of the debt was inherently unstable under conditions existing during the five and one half years following the end of World War II, because there were no self-evident, long-term owners of a substantial amount of Treasury securities other than the Reserve Banks and the government agencies and trust funds, the repayment of some or all of this amount would increase the stability of the pattern of ownership. Moreover, insofar as the freedom of action of fiscal authority in credit policy and interest policy is restricted by the existence of a large debt, debt repayment tends to make the position of fiscal authority less confined and thereby reduces not only the likelihood of conflict between public financial agencies but also pressure for the grant of additional powers.

The Debt and the Money Supply

The large size of the debt and the fact that portions of it can readily be shifted into the Reserve Banks create an inflationary potential. Under by no means impossible conditions the money supply could be greatly inflated through the sale of federal obligations to the Reserve System. In such a situation the money supply might become uncontrollable—or the only possible ways to control it, which would not necessarily be successful, would be through governmental measures inherently repugnant to a free market economy. As Professor Ratchford has phrased it:

> Debt instruments may move into or out of the banks, and thus vary the money supply at the option of the banks and their customers and the government has no direct part in the operation. Thus in this way it is possible that the debt could act as a time bomb and cause an explosive inflation years after it was originally incurred and while the total amount of debt was not changing.[1]

In other words, a shifting in the ownership of the debt, if fiscal authority were the only buyer, might lead to an expansion of assets in the hands of particular classes of debt owners (that is, an increase in the money supply) that was not justified by the level of productivity or the prevailing economic conditions. If such a shift took place at a time when federal deficits were expanding the debt, the possibility of severe inflationary pressures would be all the greater.

The Interest Burden of the Debt

Some of the implications, particularly the political implications, of a budgetary interest burden in excess of $5 billion have been discussed. This sum is a fixed charge. In a financial and moral, though not in a legal sense, it is a prior claim on the public revenues, not subject to congressional control, not available for other purposes, reducible only through a lowering of the average interest charge or through debt repayment. Its existence means that an important portion of tax receipts must, during an indefinitely long future, be earmarked for debt service. In short, "the larger the debt and interest load currently, the less room there will be for the Government to finance readily and soundly some future emergency, such as war or depression."[2]

This situation in itself might not be cause for concern. Yet it is quite clear, in the fifth decade of the twentieth century, that the government of the United States is certain to spend in excess of its

1. B. U. Ratchford, "The Monetary Effects of Public Debts," *Public Finance,* Extract of No. 1, 1949, N. Samsom, Alphen-on-the-Rhine, p. 10.
2. *Our National Debt and the Budget* (National Debt Series No. 4), Committee on Public Debt Policy, New York, 1948, p. 7.

income periodically, to combat business recessions, to expand various types of services and benefits offered its people, to support its foreign policy or—if its efforts to preserve peace fail—to prosecute war. Such spending will certainly result in an increase in the debt and may very likely result in a rise in the debt burden more rapid than the ability of the country to carry it easily, unless federal obligations are paid down during good times.

This statement does not deny that an increase in federal spending may, under some circumstances, increase the country's ability to carry a higher tax load. The statement does point to the fact that there is no necessary and inviolable relationship between an increase in debt and an increase in taxable capacity, however taxable capacity may be computed. History affords many examples in which the rate of advance in the one has exceeded the rate of advance in the other. In view of possible future contingencies, some of which will certainly be realized, it is foresighted to reduce the debt in the intervals between the spending crises. If there is truth in the old maxim that it is prudent for a private company to raise capital when it can, it is equally true that it is prudent for government to reduce debt when *it* can.

ECONOMIC EFFECTS OF DEBT REPAYMENT

Whether debt repayment may have a repressive or a stimulative effect on the economy is a question that students of the subject will answer differently, depending both on their economic philosophy and on time and circumstance. The issue may be phrased as follows: Will the taxes necessary for debt retirement be so repressive as to more than offset the stimulation that may be expected from increasing the supply of funds in the hands of the paid-off debt owner which will be available for consumption or for investment?[3] Will the process of transferring funds from those who pay taxes to those

3. On this point compare the dictum of Bastable:

"Debt redemption must also be affected by the position of taxation. Where inconvenient and oppressive duties are levied it may be wiser, even with a view to ultimate repayment of loans, to relieve industry and trade from their burdens and trust to the increased productiveness of the reformed system for compensation. A thorough reform in fiscal policy may prove the best sinking fund, or at least its best feeder. Between the remission of very bad taxes and their retention for the redemption of debt, there is often ground for deliberation. . . . [On the other hand] if we hesitate to redeem debt on account of the badness of the necessary taxes, we must remember that we are thereby retaining worse taxes in the future than would otherwise be required." C. F. Bastable, *Public Finance*, Macmillan, New York, 1892, p. 615.

who receive the proceeds of redeemed obligations tend to expand or to contract economic activity?

The answers to these questions will depend, among other things, on the effect produced on the money supply; on the level of taxation and the nature of the tax structure in the situation being examined; on the nature and economic position of those persons and institutions paying the bulk of the taxes, as well as the nature and position of those holding the bulk of the redeemed obligations; on the current level of economic activity; on the view held regarding the stimulative effects of increases in the volume of funds used for consumption purposes compared with increases in the volume of funds seeking productive investments; on the number and character of investment opportunities present, and the psychological effects of taxation. Nor can the consequences of debt repayment realistically be considered independently of the results to be expected from the long-continued payment of a large volume of interest, not reduced through debt retirement.

Dangers of a Rentier Class

The older view of this question was that a public debt provided a basis for the existence of a rentier class. The funds transferred from the taxpayer to the bondholder in servicing the debt were generally regarded as representing the transfer of funds from the more energetic and ambitious elements in society to those less eager to undertake the risks of business. Consequently such transfers were on the whole deemed repressive, in that the more enterprising elements in the economy were deprived of resources, while the less enterprising received them. Typical of this view were certain statements of Henry C. Adams:

> In this manner [through the creation of public debts] there is established within the community a class living out of the proceeds of taxes, who are yet not of necessity actively engaged in current production. They were originally constant producers and taxpayers; they are now at liberty to become idlers and tax-receivers.[4]

> And when we remember that industrial leisure, rendered possible by proprietorship in fixed investments of any sort, is a habit easily acquired, we may discern how the funding system readily lends its influence to the permanency of class relations.[5]

4. Henry C. Adams, *Public Debts*, Appleton, New York, 1893, p. 72.
5. *Ibid.*, p. 42.

The tendency of private trust funds during the whole postwar period to absorb Treasury securities is the kind of development on which this view was based. How will this type of thinking be affected if government agencies and trust funds, particularly the old-age and survivors and the unemployment funds, continue their recent growth and come to hold much of the debt, so that a large part of the interest burden goes to the servicing of the obligations owned by them? This question opens up an interesting avenue of speculation as to whether persons living on the income from private and public pension funds may not be the modern equivalent of the old rentiers, but the question is not one that can be explored here.

In any event, under many conditions there is a good deal of validity in this older line of reasoning. If the bulk of the taxes are paid directly or indirectly by the bulk of the people, and interest payments are received by a minority of the population, the transfers of funds are repressive in their effect. As Professor Ratchford puts it:

A large national debt not only transfers funds from one group to another but at the same time it also causes a change in the use to which the funds are put. Although our federal tax system is progressive, small income receivers still pay a substantial amount of federal taxes either indirectly as excise taxes or directly as income taxes. It is a fairly safe assumption that a large majority of these funds would be spent for consumer goods if they were not paid as taxes. The part of those funds which is paid out as interest on the debt goes, on the average, to financial institutions or to individuals who are higher in the income scale. . . . Those bondholders who receive the interest will spend some part of it for consumer goods, but the proportion so spent will be smaller than if the funds had remained in the hands of the taxpayers. More of those funds will be saved, directly or indirectly, and hence the total amount of savings will be increased by the transfer. The net effect, therefore, is to reduce consumer buying and to increase savings.[6]

In passing, we should note that this reasoning is not entirely valid with respect to a period of deficit financing, particularly if the increase in debt is sold to the banking system. Under these conditions money is borrowed and the money supply increases, in part, at least, in order to pay interest on money previously borrowed.

Is Debt Repayment Like Interest Payment?

Whether, under all circumstances, "The economic effects of the

6. B. U. Ratchford, "The Economics of Public Debts," *Public Finance,* Extract of No. 4, 1948, N. Samsom, Alphen-on-the-Rhine, p. 306.

repayment of public debts are much the same as the effects of interest payments except that they are more intense,"[7] as Professor Ratchford says, is not so clear.

It may be true, under some conditions, that debt repayment has an even more repressive effect on the economy than does the payment of interest, since debt repayment enhances the tax burden, and there can be little doubt as to the constrictive effects of heavy taxation. Yet this burden may be the price necessary to pay in the short run if the interest charge, and the tax burden, is to be lowered in the long run. Furthermore, a considerable part of the sums received through debt repayment are likely to be viewed by the recipients as capital, and if debt repayment so increases the volume of funds seeking investment as to permit undertakings that would not otherwise be initiated, the greater productivity and flow of income that ultimately result from these investments must be looked on as an offset to the repressive consequences of the taxes necessary for debt repayment. This is true even if the tax receipts used for debt repayment are at the expense of consumption. Certainly situations are known in which it is necessary or desirable for consumption to be restrained in order to increase the rate of capital formation.

Perhaps there was too rapid a rate of capital formation in this country during the 1920's, and that circumstance may have contributed to the collapse of the 1930's. Conceivably the amount of capital formation was stimulated by the repayment of Treasury obligations that then took place. An examination of the financial history of the United States from 1920 to 1930 strongly suggests that some of the funds released by the reduction of the federal debt found their way into the capital markets and swelled the volume of investment.

It also seems permissible, assuming the tax burden and the volume of tax receipts held constant, to consider whether the consequences to the economy will be the same if 10 per cent of the tax receipts are used for wasteful or unnecessary government expenditure, as contrasted with the employment of 10 per cent of the tax receipts for debt repayment. The repressive effects of taxation will be the same in the two situations, since the tax burden is assumed to be constant. Most government expenditures feed the stream of funds used for consumption purposes rather than that which provides for capital formation, and we may assume that the 10 per cent of un-

7. *Ibid.,* p. 309.

necessary government expenditure is likely to be so employed. However, unless one is greatly dazzled by the virtues of maintaining the stream of purchasing power, irrespective of all ancillary consequences, it seems difficult to contend that wasteful or useless government expenditure for operating purposes—even if consumption is thereby temporarily enhanced—is less repressive, except under the most unusual circumstances, than would be the employment of the same funds for debt retirement.

Fundamentally what this line of argument suggests is that it is not realistic to appraise the consequences of debt retirement solely in terms of the global statistical effects that may be produced on the pattern of consumer buying and the flow of savings and of funds for investment purposes. Attention must also be directed to the character of consumer purchasing that is checked because of the tax payments used for debt repayment, and to the type of investments made with funds released by debt reduction. In short, the qualitative effects—the moral consequences, if you like—of economic policies must be studied in appraising their influence on human affairs, not simply their over-all quantitative results.

WHOSE SECURITIES SHOULD BE RETIRED?

Under the conditions prevailing in this country at present, when the debt is held by several classes of owners, it is necessary to consider the differing economic consequences that may be expected depending on *whose* securities are retired—whether obligations held by Reserve Banks, by commercial banks or by nonbank owners. Probably the results that follow from the retirement of debt held by one or another type of owner differ most importantly in the effect produced on the money supply. As Ritter points out, "The effects of debt retirement depend upon both the source of the funds used for the redemption and the unit of decision from whom the obligations are redeemed."[8] The key to an understanding of these events is the effect of debt reduction on the reserve position of the commercial banks.

First consider the results of repaying Treasury obligations held by Federal Reserve Banks. The effect is deflationary, since the funds

---

8. Lawrence S. Ritter, "A Note on the Retirement of Public Debt During Inflation," *The Journal of Finance,* March 1951, p. 67. The analysis of the succeeding paragraphs generally corresponds with Ritter's, though it differs in some important respects.

transferred by the taxpayer from his account in the commercial bank to the Treasury are not restored to the banking system. Assuming that after this transfer the legal reserves of the banks are deficient, there may be an additional deflationary effect if the banks permit or induce a contraction of deposits sufficient to restore their legal reserve ratios, and this contraction may be a multiple of the deficiency.[9] On the other hand, if the banks' reserve position was not deficient in the first instance (because the banks held sufficient excess reserves before the tax payment), or if the banks restore their reserve position by selling governments to the Reserve Banks, this additional contraction of deposits will not take place.

When debt held by commercial banks is repaid, the funds transferred to the Treasury by the taxpayer from his account in the commercial bank[10] are restored to the bank in payment for the securities surrendered. Since the bank's deposits declined because of the tax payments, a portion of the restored funds is likely to result in excess reserves. The bank may then do one of three things, or a combination of all three. It may continue to hold the excess reserves, and the deposit structure will not increase. It may use the excess funds for the purchase of Treasury securities from the Reserve Banks, and in this case the deposit structure will not increase. Or it may use the excess reserves as a basis for an expansion of loans (or the purchase of governments from nonbank holders), and the volume of deposits will increase. Thus the effect on the deposit structure and the money supply will primarily depend on the action of the banks, and the effect may or may not be deflationary.[11] Of equal significance, perhaps, is the fact that the diminution in the volume of debt held by the banks reduces the amount of Treasury securities they are able to sell to the Reserve Banks—thereby creating reserve funds—and consequently the "inflationary potential" of bank-owned debt is cut.

The retirement of nonbank-held debt—debt owned by savings institutions, business corporations, persons, etc.—does not affect the

9. The extent of the contraction will depend on the level of the legal reserve ratio as well as on the steps taken by the banks to restore their reserve position.

10. To simplify the exposition a single commercial bank is here spoken of rather than the commercial banking system as a whole.

11. Whether the funds restored to the money supply by the creation of new deposits will be more actively used—and hence have greater inflationary consequences—than would the deposits transferred to the Treasury if the tax payments had not been made, need not concern us here.

money supply, since the funds transferred by the taxpayer to the Treasury are returned to the paid-off debt owner and redeposited in the banking system. The chief consequences of this type of debt repayment are to be found in the uses to which the funds received in exchange for government securities are put, as compared with the uses to which the funds would have been put if the tax payment had not been made. For example, if we conceive that during some time period tax payments are mainly at the expense of consumption, and if we also assume in this same time period that the debt retired is chiefly obligations in the hands of insurance companies and trust funds—who will reinvest the proceeds of the redeemed obligations— clearly debt repayment in these circumstances will reduce the stream of consumer purchasing power and enhance the flow of funds seeking investment.

Net Effects of Repayment Policy

Redemption of securities held by Federal Reserve Banks is the most deflationary type of debt reduction. How deflationary it will be depends on the action taken by commercial banks to restore their reserve position. Payment of debt held by commercial banks is likely to be deflationary, though in lesser degree, depending on the uses to which the banks put the excess reserves created by debt repayment. Repayment of debt held outside the banking system will not affect the money supply; it will, however, have a repressive or stimulative effect depending on the way it influences the pattern of consumption and of capital formation, and the need of the economy at the time for consumption or investment to be stimulated.

Changes occasioned in the money supply by debt repayment are, of course, reflected in the volume and character of the assets held by the several classes of debt owners. But debt repayment does not necessarily have the exact reverse of the effects of debt expansion noted in Chapter 2, namely, a reduction in the total assets held by the several elements in the economy and, particularly, a reduction in the volume of liquid assets held by each element. For example, repayment of obligations held by the Reserve Banks reduces the money supply and thus shrinks the volume of assets held by each element in the economy, as well as tending to make all elements (except perhaps the Reserve Banks) less liquid, particularly the commercial banks. On the other hand, insofar as reserve funds made available to commercial banks through redemption of governments held by them are kept in the form of cash, the banks tend to become more liquid; insofar as these funds are employed as a basis for loans and deposits, the reverse is the case, and governments as a percentage of bank assets decline. The effect produced on the assets of non-bank investors by the retirement of Treasury securities held by them depends, of course, on the uses made of the funds received.

With each class of holder the immediate effect of repaying maturing or demand debt is to lengthen the average maturity of the remaining government portfolio; whether this is the consequence in the longer run depends on the character of the portfolio held and the rate at which short-term or demand debt is lost from the portfolio, as compared with the rate at which intermediate-term securities move into the short-term category. From September 1945 to December 1950, for most debt holders, the second rate exceeded the first, and the average maturity of the government portfolio shortened perceptibly, notwithstanding the debt reduction, with a consequent increase in the portfolio's liquidity.

The Use of Nonmarketable Securities

A striking feature of debt management during the period of this study was the continous decline in the amount of public marketable securities and the rise in the volume of nonmarketable obligations outstanding, including special issues sold to government trust accounts.[12] To understand the significance of this development we should first consider the effect of the growing quantity of non-marketables outstanding when these are viewed in the aggregate, disregarding the fact that they are, actually, composed of different types.

Marketables and Nonmarketables

As nonmarketable issues replace marketables the difficulties involved in supporting the prices of marketable obligations and in maintaining stability in the pattern of ownership are in some measure lessened, simply because the outstanding dollar volume of this type of debt is reduced. Likewise, the possibility that the money

---

12. In the tabulation of "Nonmarketable interest-bearing securities" in the *Treasury Bulletin* special issues are not included. For purposes of this analysis, however, it is proper to include them with the types covered in the *Bulletin's* classification.

supply may be inflated by transfers of marketable issues to the Reserve Banks is, in some ways, reduced.

In a sense, the effect of the substitution of nonmarketables for marketables is similar to that which would be produced by a sinking fund which withdrew marketable issues from the hands of the public but which held the obligations, uncancelled, within the sinking fund. Particularly is this the case with those government trust funds that receive tax payments and which exchange these moneys for Treasury obligations.

The Treasury's Cash Position

So long as the volume of nonmarketable obligations outstanding increases, the growth supplies the Treasury with cash. This is the case whether the Treasury has a budgetary surplus or a deficit. If the Treasury has a surplus, these funds can be used to retire some of the marketable obligations in the hands of the public. If the Treasury has a deficit, the funds reduce the demands of the Treasury on the market for financing. Thus a continuing growth in the volume of nonmarketable securities is of great importance in the management of the Treasury's general cash balance.

But if the volume of nonmarketable securities outstanding begins to fall, either because maturing issues are not replaced by their owners or because issues are presented to the Treasury for redemption prior to maturity, the situation is reversed, and the Treasury is confronted with a demand for cash. If the government's cash inflow and outgo were previously balanced, they then become unbalanced. If the Treasury were already in the position of raising new money through borrowing it would then have to borrow additional funds. The question is: Where and in what form?

Since we have assumed that nonmarketable issues in the aggregate were being liquidated, the presumption must be that the new, additional borrowing will be in the form of marketable obligations, unless the Treasury suddenly puts on sale some new type of nonmarketable security, proceeds from the sale of which offset the cash required by redemptions. Sales of "new money" issues can be made only to banks or to "nonbanks." If to nonbanks, the money supply will not be affected. But if sales are made to banks, the effect will be directly inflationary.

Thus the existence of nonmarketable obligations represents a possibility that the money supply may be inflated, not by the action of the government but by the action of the debt owners. In effect, the nonmarketables represent a contingent liability of the government to pay out cash—though such payments would not be a result of ordinary expenditures—even though the obligations themselves are actual liabilities of the Treasury. The larger the volume of these issues outstanding, the greater the potential payments that may be required and the greater the potential inflation. Consequently, instability in the ownership of nonmarketable issues signifies, potentially, an increase in the money supply, just as does instability in the ownership of marketable obligations. Such an increase may or may not be socially desirable, depending upon prevailing economic conditions.

Types of Nonmarketables

During the period of this study the government has made use of several kinds of nonmarketable obligations: United States savings bonds, Treasury savings notes, depository bonds, armed forces leave bonds, certain guaranteed securities and Treasury bonds investment series, as well as the special issues sold to government trust funds. The relative amounts outstanding on December 31, 1950, are shown in order of magnitude in Table 18. Savings bonds were the largest category, some 57 per cent of the total, and special issues, the second largest group, approximated one third of the entire amount outstanding.

The forces that will lead to an increase or decrease in the amounts outstanding of each of these types will be extremely diverse. Many

TABLE 18

NONMARKETABLE AND SPECIAL ISSUES OF THE U.S. GOVERNMENT
OUTSTANDING, AS OF DECEMBER 31, 1950

(*In Millions*)

Issue	Amount
Total	$101,832
U. S. savings bonds (current redemption value)	58,019
Special issues to government agencies and trust funds	33,707
Treasury savings notes	8,640
Treasury bonds, investment series	953
Depository bonds	292
Armed forces leave bonds	221

Source: Treasury Bulletin, February 1951, p. 20

of them have already been discussed in connection with the portfolio behavior of the marketable issues held by the several classes of debt owner. Of particular significance are the factors that influence personal holdings, since the great bulk of nonmarketable issues, particularly the savings bonds and the armed forces leave bonds, are in the hands of individuals.

Special Issues

The special issues are in some ways to be distinguished from the other types of nonmarketable obligations. These are sold directly to various government trust funds. The trust funds, of course, are able within limits to buy marketable issues, but the great bulk of their holdings are special issues.

While these trust funds grow their increase can be most helpful either in reducing the marketable debt in the hands of the public or in preventing its increase. This may take place in either of two ways —through the direct purchase of outstanding marketable obligations or through the acquisition of special issues. In the latter event the special issues either preclude the necessity of issuing more marketable obligations or replace some already outstanding. Since the end of World War II these funds have annually absorbed some $2-$4 billion of Treasury obligations.

The effect of the funds' growth is not unlike that of a sinking fund, particularly since the resources of the funds are supplied by tax receipts. Yet since the securities acquired by the funds are not retired, but only removed from the market, there is no guarantee that at some future date some of the obligations they have accumulated may not come back into the market. This could take place either through sales of marketable obligations by the funds themselves or by presentation of special issues to the Treasury for redemption, which in turn might cause the Treasury to increase its offerings of marketable securities.

The situation may be described another way. As a matter of public policy the Congress has provided various kinds of pensions, social insurance and old-age assistance. An incidental effect of these actions has been to create a mechanism that, with a high-level economy, may furnish the Treasury either with a market for $2 to $4 billion of new securities annually or permit an annual reduction of that magnitude in the outstanding marketable debt.

One fortuitous result of these broad social policies may be to reduce the volume of outstanding marketable debt, even though what we have called the contingent liabilities of the government for cash payments thereby steadily increase. Indeed, the government may have a contingent liability for the welfare of its citizens, whether or not the liability is "acknowledged" by the existence of these funds; but that question need not be discussed here.

A situation in some measure similar existed during the half century following the Civil War. The great reduction in the federal debt that then took place was viewed, particularly by European eyes, as one of the marvels of the age. Contemporary observers, however, generally agreed that the debt was repaid not so much because of fiscal orthodoxy as because the country at that time embraced a high tariff policy—again, for broad reasons of policy. The customs duties received, which increased with the growth of the economy, were sufficient to permit the reduction of the debt. Thus debt retirement was in large part an incidental result of other policies that were adopted for reasons almost entirely foreign to fiscal considerations. Admittedly, high protective tariffs and social welfare policies do not have much in common; but the possibility that they may produce somewhat similar effects on the outstanding marketable debt, assuming a balanced budget, provides an interesting avenue of speculation.

WHAT PAST POLICIES PORTEND

If we project into the future the debt retirement or refunding policies pursued since August 1945, the logical expectations seem to be approximately as follows.

Any excess Treasury cash, whether arising from a surplus in the cash budget or in other ways, will be used to reduce the debt,[13] pro-

---

13. As Langum points out:
". . . leaving aside changes in the General Fund balance . . . Net cash borrowing or *repayment of borrowing* is the net result of five types of transactions: (1) cash issuance or retirement of marketable issues; (2) cash issuance or retirement of certain nonmarketable issues, such as depository bonds, savings bonds, savings notes, and Treasury bonds, investment series; (3) net borrowing through the Postal Savings System, that is, the net increase in total government securities held by the Postal Savings System; (4) net market sale or purchase of marketable United States securities for Treasury investment accounts, including trust accounts, government corporations, and the Postal Savings System; and (5) the net change in other miscellaneous types of debt, such as certain matured obligations and debt bearing no interest and obligations of government corporations not guaranteed by the United States." (Italics supplied.) John K. Langum, "Monetary and Public Debt Aspects of Budget Policy," reprinted from the *Proceedings* of the Forty-first National Tax Conference held at Denver, Colorado, October 4-7, 1948, p. 3.

vided the Treasury general balance is thought large enough. But there will be no clear, identifiable plan or program for debt retirement.[14]

Excess cash may, of course, be used to build up the Treasury's balance, rather than to reduce debt, and the concept of "excess cash" and the desired size of the general balance will be influenced by many considerations, political as well as economic. If a reduction in the balance is thought expedient, the volume of debt redeemed during a given period may exceed the accumulation of cash. Indeed, it is conceivable that debt might be repaid through a reduction in the general balance, even though no cash was currently being accumulated.

Even if there should be a series of budgetary surpluses, the amount of debt retired during any given period will be virtually fortuitous, for three distinct reasons. First, the size of the Treasury cash surplus during any fiscal year or part thereof is unpredictable, at least with any degree of accuracy. Second, not the least of the forces that determine the amount of excess cash on hand at any particular time is the Treasury's decision as to the level of the general balance that is desirable. Third, the behavior of the nonmarketable debt may be such as to offset the effect of a surplus.

Granted the existence of excess cash, under conditions and policies that have prevailed in recent years, much the larger portion of any debt retired during a given period will be maturing marketable debt —most of which will be bank-held debt.

There will not, however, be any direct, immediate or predictable relationship between the reduction, if any, in the total debt during a year and the volume of maturing, short-term debt redeemed during this same period, the amounts of short-term debt outstanding at the beginning and end of such period, or the volume of bank deposits. The behavior of the total debt will be influenced by increases and decreases in the nonmarketable debt and in special issues as well

14. In his discussion of the various types of sinking funds, Ross points out that the use of "casual" surpluses, while the simplest form of debt reduction, is not likely to lead to substantial results.

"As the simplest reduction of a debt takes place by casual appropriations, so the simplest sinking fund is the permanent appropriation of casual, budgetary surpluses. If these surpluses are really casual, there is no guarantee that they will more than cover, in the long run, casual deficits." [Ed. note: In other words, there is no guarantee that the use of casual or fortuitous surpluses will lead to any real debt reduction.] Edward A. Ross, "Sinking Funds," Publications of the American Economic Association, VII, 4 and 5, July and September 1892, p. 89.

as by changes in the volume of marketable obligations outstanding. The amount of marketable debt due within twelve months will be affected by the passage of time as well as by the amounts of such obligations sold and redeemed, since with the passage of time intermediate-term issues continually move into the twelve-month category. The level of bank deposits will be influenced by a wide variety of forces, of which debt management is only one.

Under the offering policies pursued during the period of this study the amount of intermediate-term marketable issues outstanding will steadily decline, as such issues turn into debt due within twelve months, irrespective of whether there is a Treasury surplus or not, and regardless of the behavior of the total debt, the marketable and the nonmarketable debt.

Nonmarketable debt, including special issues, will increase—at least so long as efforts to keep sales of savings bonds at a higher level than redemptions are successful and so long as resources in the hands of the various government agencies and trust funds increase.

By and large the increase in the various types of nonmarketable obligations signify the assumption by the federal government of contingent liabilities for money outlays, in that these issues represent potential demands for cash. Savings bonds and special issues redeemable on demand can legitimately be regarded as "long-term" only so long as new sales continue to exceed redemptions.[15]

The amounts of short-, intermediate- and long-term debt outstanding at a given time are likely to be almost accidentally determined by the interplay of forces previously mentioned, rather than by decisions based directly on consideration of the type of balance in the maturity schedule that is desirable or the legitimate needs and desires of the several classes of debt holders who own or might own the obligations.

Although debt retirement is likely to be concentrated in the bank-held debt, the degree of deflationary effect thereby produced is difficult, if not impossible, to predict with any degree of accuracy.

15. In this connection the underlying implications of Musgrave's comment, made in a different connection, are interesting. "A sound debt structure . . . is one where some direct control over bank holdings [of government securities] exists, where the bulk of the long-term debt has been converted into non-marketable issues, and where the remaining sector of marketable debt is largely in short-term form." Richard A. Musgrave, "Credit Controls, Interest Rates, and Management of Public Debt," in *Income, Employment, and Public Policy,* essays in honor of Alvin H. Hansen, Norton, New York, 1948, p. 244.

These expectations regarding the effects of debt retirement are generally valid only on the assumption that the policies pursued by the Treasury during the five and one half years ending in December 1950 continue in the future. Relatively minor shifts in Treasury policy, or a return to deficit financing, would affect substantially the prospect here outlined.

Chapter 12

CONCLUSIONS

WHEN, IN THE REALM of practical affairs, some element greatly expands or contracts, the problems and issues inherent in it commonly change not only in *size* but also in *kind*. Often the significance of the qualitative change outweighs that of the quantitative. This was the case with the federal debt between 1939 and 1945. The problems presented by debt management in August 1945 were not the same as those of 1939 multiplied by seven. New factors, new considerations, were present in the postwar situation. Many lines of thinking that before 1939 had been useful in managing the federal debt, and much of the pre-Pearl Harbor frame of reference, were no longer valid when applied to postwar conditions. The new situation required new approaches, new methods of analysis. It was this fact that made the wartime growth of the debt a turning point in the financial history of the United States and at the same time made understanding and resolution of the postwar situation so difficult.

Generally speaking, postwar problems were of two kinds, though the line of demarcation was by no means always clear. On the one hand were those questions chiefly important because of their dollar magnitude. In this category fall such parts of the debt problem as its size, especially when compared with national income or with the total of all other kinds of debt, the interest burden placed on the federal budget and the fact that something like half the resources of financial institutions on V-J Day was composed of Treasury obligations. On the other hand were issues of far-reaching economic and political consequence; questions which in many instances the country had not hitherto faced and which were now forced to the fore by a variety of circumstances, including the size of the debt. Fundamentally, these issues were of far greater importance than the problems which centered on the amounts of dollars involved. Indeed, the way in which these underlying questions are finally settled will largely determine the way in which the problems of dollar magnitudes are solved.

To point to federal deficit spending as the root cause of the difficulties does not appreciably aid in the discovery of a solution. The consequences of past spending are now inescapable, and the probability of large future expenditures, in view of the temper of public psychology, is likewise one of the conditions under which debt management must be conducted.

The Basic Question

Opinions, of course, will differ as to which of the several issues involved in postwar debt management is of the most consequence. In the author's mind the basic question is the future of the quasi-regulated market that in the United States has commonly been described as the free market process. The problem may be stated in several ways. Is a politically controlled money market compatible with the free market process? Or, if this phraseology seems too pointed, what kinds of monetary controls are practical if an economy is not to lose its free market character? This question has a particular cogency, partly because the debt may have become so large as to make it impractical any longer to think of it in the context of a market, partly because of the likelihood of its further increase in the future.

In view of our postwar experience, a different set of questions appears when these matters are translated into operating problems. How much discretion in administering a price should a governmental administrator have? How far, and for how long, can he force a price against the will of the market without creating at least the semblance of a black market? And at what social costs in other areas are his results achieved? To what extent should he be permitted to employ compulsion, a noneconomic measure, to achieve economic goals, instead of utilizing inducements? And if he is permitted to use compulsion, will the ultimate results be better and socially more acceptable than would have been the case if determination of the market's course had from the outset been left in the hands of the people? Certainly compulsion, if carried any appreciable distance, will seriously disturb the investment habits of persons and institutions, upon which many debt management procedures in the past have been based.

Treasury versus Federal Reserve

In the postwar period these questions of debt management precipitated a contest between the Treasury and the Federal Reserve System. The growth of the debt gave a new and much greater significance to the traditional administrative discretion of the Treasury regarding the types of debt forms issued, the terms attached to them, the size and handling of its cash account and the Treasury's relation to the government's own investment accounts. The enhanced financial power in the hands of the executive branch brought the Treasury's interest in debt management into conflict with the Reserve System's statutory responsibility for credit regulation. The immediate point at issue was interest policy since it became evident that the ownership of the debt could not be kept stable within the price structure desired by the Treasury. Support and enforcement of that price structure by the Reserve Banks led, or threatened to lead, to an expansion of the credit base that the Federal Reserve authorities thought unjustified in view of prevailing economic conditions in the country and which they feared would violate their statutory responsibilities.

Thus two further issues developed: To what degree should the central bank be able to pursue an independent policy, free from the dictates of the executive branch of the government? How could transfers of federal obligations among the several classes of debt owners—a necessary concomitant of a free economy—be prevented from affecting the money supply in random, irrational and economically undesirable ways, particularly if the central bank were not at least moderately independent?

As a consequence of these developments, interest policy, an extremely complex problem that had hitherto been of interest primarily to economists, moved into the arena of political debate. And the argument was further confused by the fact that the United States would clearly resume deficit financing in the near future, with all that that implied as regards an augmentation of various economic pressures, including the prospect of further inflation.

As the country's postwar experience is surveyed it is fair to say that the policies pursued by the Treasury and the Reserve System did not solve the problems inherent in the situation that existed in August 1945. There is even doubt that the procedures employed pointed a way toward a solution.

Treasury Policy

The Treasury, for its part, showed little disposition to depart from the mechanisms and techniques developed during the war, notwithstanding the return of peace. It showed a commendable interest in spreading the ownership of the debt, and developed a number of new types of debt forms to meet special needs. It continued to rely heavily on various types of nonmarketable issues which, broadly, caused additional growth in the volume of securities redeemable on demand. This use of nonmarketables meant that the volume of public marketable issues outstanding shrank almost continuously.

The obligations that were redeemed were almost entirely short-term, maturing issues, and an effort was made to repay bank-held obligations. No systematic plan of debt repayment, however, was set up. Because of a variety of circumstances, principally the Treasury's offering policy, the effect of debt redemption on the volume of short-term, floating debt outstanding and on the quantity of bank-held securities was less than might have been anticipated. Lip service was paid to the importance of tailoring the debt to the needs of the market. But some scepticism of these protestations is warranted in view of the Treasury's offering policy and its virtual failure, until the very end of the period studied, to issue any kind of marketable security with a due date in excess of twelve months, notwithstanding the opportunities to sell longer-term issues that presented themselves.

The Treasury's most dubious policy, however, was its insistence on the continuance of "cheap money"—irrespective of war, peace or cold war, irrespective of whether the federal government had a surplus or a deficit, irrespective of the changes that took place in business conditions. Official Treasury spokesmen were insistent that their views regarding interest policy should prevail, but their unwillingness to consider what the consequences were to other segments of the economy, or how they affected the availability of credit, suggested that they themselves were not cognizant of all the responsibilities inherent in the position they assumed.

Federal Reserve Policy

For its part, the Federal Reserve System pursued a cautious and in some respects orthodox central banking policy. In attempting to stabilize various areas of the economy it made use of a wide variety

of measures—open market operations, changes in reserve requirements of banks, direct regulation of particular kinds of credit and
changes in discount rates. Paradoxically, however, its very caution
led to radical results. Unclear as to what its position should be, in
peacetime, in the face of the tremendous debt and the Treasury's
need for a stable securities market, flanked on the one side by the
growth of governmental lending agencies not susceptible to its influence and on the other side by government investment accounts
whose activities could largely duplicate its own open market operations, it continued after the return of peace many of its wartime
policies. The growth of Reserve credit that had taken place during
the war, however, was checked, and an evident effort was made to
keep the amount outstanding reasonably stable. Nevertheless, the
policy of supporting the prices of Treasury securities meant that
interest rates in all other areas of the economy—in business, in agriculture, in housing, in consumer financing—were also held both low
and stable, irrespective of the merits of individual borrowers and, in
some instances, irrespective of whether increases in private debt were
socially desirable.

This stability of interest rates signified that the central bank lost,
or was likely to lose, control of the money supply. An incidental
result of the situation was the radical change that took place in the
composition of the System's own portfolio. There were occasions
when the prices of government obligations were above the Federal's
support levels, but the System did not seize these opportunities to
change its objectives and procedures. Ultimately, when the situation
became acute, the support policy broke down under pressure. The
comparative stability in the volume of Reserve credit outstanding
might have been superficially interpreted as indicating that the Reserve System was not attempting, at least through its open market
operations, to influence the reserve position of the commercial banking system or to offset the consequences of gold imports and other
developments that tended to ease the position of the commercial
banks. In actuality, the System's interest in stabilizing the prices of
Treasury securities meant that changes in its portfolio were chiefly
used for this purpose, rather than for influencing the reserve position
of the commercial banks. Consequently, changes in bank reserve
requirements became the principal instrument for regulating the
credit base.

The Basic Issues Are Political

As a whole, the postwar policies and procedures of the Treasury and the Reserve System do not reveal the outline of a broad, long-range, statesmanlike program that gave promise of settling the basic questions. They did not ensure allocation of sufficient assets in the hands of the private segments of the economy to debt ownership, so that transfers of federal obligations would not affect the money supply in random and unpredictable fashion. These policies did not indicate the respective responsibilities of the Treasury and the Federal Reserve System in the financial management of the country, or suggest how further deficits might be accommodated without imposing undue strains on the economy or accentuating existing problems. Nor did these policies face up to the issue of what inducements and what types of compulsion might be necessary to ensure continued ownership of federal securities. Perhaps some of the responsibility for this situation rested with the Congress, since it did not deal with these questions during the immediate postwar years, nor give any appreciable guidance regarding the principles of debt management and fiscal supervision which it wished to prevail.

The actions and objectives of the Federal Reserve System and the Treasury were, naturally, of a fiscal and financial nature. Suggested changes in their policies were mainly proposed by economists—actually, by that smaller group that may be described as financial economists. Notwithstanding their differences of opinion on many points, we may assume that this group of technical experts, inside and outside the government were, on the whole, competent to interpret the Treasury and Federal Reserve policies, both actual and suggested, and were able to indicate with reasonable accuracy the results that would follow one or another course of action, if allowance is made for the more intemperate claims advanced in the heat of argument.

The issues at stake, however, were and are momentous. The decisions made will have far-reaching consequences, and will in many ways influence the conditions under which all of us live. Consequently, such decisions should not and probably cannot be made by the technical experts alone. Because of their magnitude, because the welfare of the entire population will be affected by them, the decisions are essentially political in their nature. Under these circumstances the choices should be made by the people and in the end will be made by them.

The chief effect of the debt was to raise issues that cannot be determined solely by financial theory, and that cannot be resolved by administrative action directed toward manipulating economic forces. Ultimately they must, and will, be settled by political decisions.

PART III

COMMITTEE REPORT

Chapter 13

FEDERAL DEBT MANAGEMENT FOR STEADY
ECONOMIC GROWTH

THIS REPORT DEALS with one of our great national economic facts—
the federal debt. The main concern of the report is with the
direct, interest-bearing debt of $255 billion, but the additional $250
billion of guarantees and indirect liabilities also has an influence on
debt management, and one that cannot be ignored.

A federal debt of these huge proportions raises grave issues of
public policy. The way these issues are handled affects every individual through employment and prices. These issues are:

1. The *size* of the debt in relation to the national product. This
in turn raises questions as to the carrying cost of the debt and the
timing and rate of its repayment.

2. The *ownership* of the debt and the effects of the debt contracts
on different kinds of savers.

3. The arrangements of *maturities* of the debt, as they relate to the
Treasury's task of handling it.

4. The structure of *interest rates* that is appropriate under changing economic conditions.

The Twentieth Century Fund Committee on the Federal Debt has
concerned itself mainly with the first of these issues—the size and
the burden of the direct federal debt—because this bears most directly on the economic progress and stability of the nation's economy.
The other issues, and the effects of the indirect federal debt, are dealt
with more generally to the extent that they influence America's
economic growth.

SIZE OF THE DEBT

The total debt of the federal government is a mass of obligations,
guarantees and commitments. The size and variety of these obliga-

tions can be seen from the following list (figures of the Bureau of
the Budget, as of June 30, 1951, in millions) :

Direct federal debt	$255,222
Unpaid obligations against appropriations	47,178
Issued on the credit of U.S. Postal Savings	2,905
Federal Reserve Notes	22,975
Loan guarantees for housing, business, farm and defense loans	19,378
Insurance in force, including life insurance, crop insurance and deposit insurance	154,592
Subscription to the capital stock of the International Bank for Reconstruction and Development	2,540
Other	108
Total federal obligations and contingent liabilities	$504,898[1]

The total federal debt is therefore much larger than most people
think it is. The direct federal debt is customarily thought of as the
major, preponderant part of the government's obligations. True,
some of the other obligations are contingent liabilities. But the significant facts about the total federal debt that are often overlooked
are these: (1) the direct federal debt has become a smaller proportion of the total obligations over the years; and (2) a great many
different federal agencies are entrusted with the administration of
various phases of the federal debt.

Some of the agencies involved in the handling of the total federal
debt are: the Treasury, Federal Reserve Board, Post Office, Federal
Housing Administration, Federal National Mortgage Association,
Farmers Home Administration, Commodity Credit Corporation,
Reconstruction Finance Corporation, Export-Import Bank, Veterans
Administration, Federal Crop Insurance Corporation, Federal Deposit
Insurance Corporation, Federal Savings and Loan Insurance Corpo-
ration, Mutual Security Administration, Maritime Administration.
Many of these agencies seek or influence funds in the private capital
market, sometimes at cross purposes.

Although the main concern of this report is with the direct federal
debt of $255 billion, the indirect obligations of the federal govern-

1. This figure and the discussion herein go much farther toward recognition of the
facts of the national commitments than most current statements, but I think the total
magnitude of the commitments is understated even here. For example, the Budget
Bureau figures apparently exclude the massive obligations for future payments under
the Social Security System and various other programs. The truth seems to be that,
despite the tremendous importance of the subject, no serious attempt has anywhere
been made to determine the total magnitude and nature of commitments the federal
government has made for the future. This is a job that needs to be done, and certainly
should be done before significant additions are made. It would be important to add
to the analysis those made by other governmental units and by private organizations.—
DONALD B. WOODWARD

ment all too often set up competition for funds from private or institutional investors.

Growth of the Direct Federal Debt

The federal debt has not always been an important feature of American economic life, or even regarded as a permanent one. We are not, even yet, a nation with settled or fixed ideas about it.

During the century from 1817 to 1917 there were few occasions to expand the direct federal debt. The big borrowings that helped fight the Civil War and the smaller borrowing that helped build the Panama Canal were mostly repaid. Through the whole course of our history, we have retired debt in far more years than we have increased it.

We entered the fiscal year 1916-1917 with a gross debt of $1.2 billion, or half of one per cent of the present direct debt. We entered the depression year 1930-1931 with a debt of $16.2 billion, or 6 per cent of the present debt, as a legacy from World War I. We entered the World War II period in mid-1940 with a debt of $43.0 billion, which grew to $263 billion by V-J Day. This had been reduced to $260 billion by February 1952. In short, 80 per cent of the total was created in fighting World War II, and practically all of it either in fighting wars or overcoming depression. It was not deliberately incurred.

The committee preparing this report will not review at length the history of the debt, nor will it waste time bewailing its existence—much as every American would wish it gone. Nor will it be so rash as to predict its extinction within our lifetime. It sees its tasks as something else—to argue that the size of the debt may at least be whittled down[2] and to insist that in the meantime we must organize it so as to promote financial stability and economic progress. In other words, we must master the problem of managing the debt rather than let it manage us.

OWNERSHIP OF THE DEBT

How is the federal debt "organized" today? This is best reflected in the following survey of its ownership by various significant groups in 1944 and 1952, rounded off to the nearest billion dollars.

2. We cannot now be sure, however, that the circumstances will make debt reduction desirable on the principles that are later enumerated in this report.—NEIL H. JACOBY

	1944	1952
Debt held for the benefit of individual savers		
Individuals		
Savings bonds	$36	$49
Other securities	17	16
Financial institutions		
Mutual savings banks	8	10
Insurance companies	20	16
Savings and loan institutions, corporate pension funds, international accounts, colleges, hospitals, other nonprofit institutions and endowments	7	10
U.S. government accounts—social security, trust funds, etc.	19	43
	$107	$144
Debt held as a liquid asset		
Federal Reserve Banks	$15	$23
Commercial banks	78	60
Corporations	21	23
State and local governments	4	10
	$118	$116
Total	$225	$260

The $144 billion shown as the first subtotal for 1952 is owned by individuals. Thus savings banks, corporate pension funds, colleges, the Federal Old-Age and Survivors Insurance Trust Fund, all hold their government bonds on a permanent basis to yield income for the benefit of particular depositors, pensioners, or teachers and students. Moreover, savings bank deposits, pension funds and E-bonds are all financial assets of lower-income groups. Such groups thus acquire a substantial interest in the national debt, and all society gains from this widespread personal interest. It testifies to the fact that our society is productive, so that savings are increasingly being made by our workers from their own earnings. Pensions and investment incomes are thereby being created for the years of retirement.[3]

This type of debt ownership promotes a larger middle-class, democratic capitalism and thereby solidifies not only the debt structure itself but also the nation's economic foundations. This is not to say that saving by the middle-class groups through federal debt is any more meritorious than through private debt. On the contrary, the investment of savings in private debt normally adds to the productive facilities of the nation. We do, however, consider the existence of some interest-bearing federal debt as a positive advantage in pro-

3. The general point made by this paragraph is true, but it applies more widely. Many savings accounts are held in commercial banks and are not different in any significant way from those in mutual savings banks. Also among the financial assets of lower-income groups, life insurance is one of the most important of all.—DONALD B. WOODWARD

viding a versatile medium for savings of the public. Most small savers do not have the knowledge and skill to manage their funds. While it is true that present financial institutions offer adequate facilities for lodging and administering small savings, the federal debt offers additional variety and encouragement to savers. As long as the national debt must remain outstanding in large amounts, we think it is important to work toward its ownership by this class of true saver.

MATURITIES

The maturity of the federal debt refers to the time when specific issues of the debt must be paid, or new bonds sold in place of ones retired. Because the Treasury has many different issues of debt outstanding, each issue designed to meet the need of a particular class of buyers, there are in fact many maturity dates.

This report will not attempt to review the specific issues comprising the federal debt in order to present the arrangement of maturities; instead, a grouping of issues into time periods is shown below. The marketable interest-bearing debt and the savings bonds are by far the largest portion. Their maturities in mid-1952 were as follows (figures in billions):

Number of Years within Which Due or Callable	Marketable Interest-Bearing Securities	Savings Bonds
Due within 1 year	$71	$ 3
1 to 5 years	30	26
5 to 10 years	11	24
10 to 15 years	21	4
15 to 20 years	9	0
Over 20 years	0	0
	$142	$57

The most important fact about the maturities of federal debt issues is that 50 per cent of the marketable securities are due within one year. The effect of this upon the Treasury is twofold: (1) it makes a repeated handling and turning over of the debt necessary and (2) it makes the Treasury very sensitive to prevailing interest rates. Since the Treasury must constantly be in the market to place new issues of the federal debt, the slightest change in interest rates is of grave concern and consequence. There is reason to believe, as will be developed later, that this pointed concern over prevailing interest rates—caused by short-term nature of maturities—has operated to the detriment of sound debt management.

A flexible arrangement of maturities, in place of the unremitting concentration on short-term issues, is a need for the future. The stability of the economy and of prices would be improved by placing issues of long-term maturity during the early phases of a boom, by abstaining from the market as much as possible or retiring debt during periods of rising prices, and by resorting to short-term borrowing only during recessions.

INTEREST RATES

There is a sense in which the commercial slogan, "the more you get, the more you want," applies to government debt. It was even possible to finance the vast expansion of debt in World War II at unprecedentedly low interest rates. From 1941 to 1945 the 90-day Treasury bills were sold on a ⅜ of one per cent yield basis; the very popular one-year certificate of indebtedness brought ⅞ of one per cent; and the longest 25-year marketable bond brought 2½ per cent. It was said that we were fighting a "2½ per cent war." The market carried these rates even lower when the war ended, for by April 1946, the longest-term issues sold in December 1945, had appreciated until their yield was 2¼ per cent. The bonds had been issued at par, but were then selling as high as 106²⁹⁄₃₂.

The extraordinarily low interest rates paid by the federal government during World War II made for a low direct expense to the taxpayer in paying interest charges on the debt, but this was not without serious costs of another sort. The low interest pattern could be maintained only by inflating the money supply and constantly driving prices higher and higher. The "saving" on interest was, therefore, a costly illusion for which pensioners, aged persons, teachers, white-collar workers and many other citizens have since paid heavily through a lower standard of living. Even the Treasury suffered by paying *dollars* in higher prices for goods and services purchased by the government as a result of saving *cents* in interest disbursements.

Rates on Short-Term Money

The most striking feature of this interest rate structure during World War II was the extraordinarily low yield on short-term money. Later on, while long-term money was still yielding little more than 2½ per cent, the whole rate curve swung around on this "fixed hinge" of 2½ per cent to bring short-term rates a good deal higher than they had been in 1945.

The interest rate on short-term money has, historically, been higher than that on long-term money. This relation held good, on the average, for decades up to 1930. After 1930 a startling shift in the interest pattern took place, due primarily to the lack of commercial borrowing in the depth of the depression but also to the influence of gold revaluation.

The effect of the depression on the banks (those that survived) was to force them to liquidate their assets. They had to collect on loans and turn them into cash, reserves or short-term obligations in order to meet the possibility of demands by the public through withdrawal of deposits. At the same time that the banks were becoming more heavily loaded with short-term funds, business was less inclined to borrow through short loans. Much of the short-term borrowing is for the purpose of financing the purchase of inventory or carrying accounts receivable. Businessmen did not generally expect rising prices or expanding sales, both of which would enlarge their needs for inventory or accounts receivable. Indeed, through much of this period the borrowing of short-term money was hazardous because of the probability of declining prices and declining sales. This is one reason why short-term funds in the hands of the banks tended to go unused and short-term interest rates declined.

Influence of Gold Revaluation

Another profound influence on short-term interest rates can be found in the revaluation of gold. On January 30, 1934, the Gold Reserve Act set the price of an ounce of pure gold at the Treasury at $35 as against the previous $20.67. In other words, the United States raised its offering price for gold, to anybody and everybody, by 69.3 per cent. At this time wholesale prices had dropped to about 75 per cent of their predepression level. Whoever turned in gold to the Treasury got a dollar payment the purchasing power of which was, therefore, more than twice what it would have been before 1929. This was truly a golden opportunity.

Partly because of the higher price of gold, and partly because conditions abroad were more uncertain than here, there was a very substantial flow of gold into the United States. The monetary gold stock increased very rapidly, owing both to its revalued price and to the new imports of gold. The revaluation automatically raised our monetary gold stock, which had been $4 billion in 1929, to $7 billion. To these $7 billion were now to be added $10 billion more which people all over the world mined and melted and unburied in order to cash in on the high price offered at Washington. Practically every dollar that was paid for this gold went right into someone's bank deposit. The American banking system, with this high-powered money coming into its possession, soon had *excess* reserves, $7 billion, equal to its *required* reserves, also $7 billion.

The banks naturally tried to put the money to use wherever it was safe to do so. The safest place of all was in 90-day Treasury bills. The yield on these securities at one time fell to $9/100$ of one percent— not quite the vanishing point, but very close to it. When $3/8$ of one per cent was later decided upon "for the duration," bankers were able to say that the rate represented a 400 per cent improvement over the previous yield.

Meanwhile the yield on longer-term bonds that were nearing their final maturity became at times negative. The reason was that holders of such bonds were given a priority in the purchase of newly issued longer-term securities. Since new securities were always issued at 100, and since the prevailing money market ease frequently made them appreciate quickly above that figure, it was often worth while to buy maturing bonds on which one would incur an actual loss in order to be allotted new bonds on which one could take a quick profit.

Financing World War II

It was thus largely a historical accident that Pearl Harbor found our money rates low enough to permit the Treasury to finance the war with the greatest of ease. The memory of the unsettlement of bond prices after World War I made people feel that financial preparedness this time required interest rates to be frozen for the duration. This worked well enough during the war itself. Patriotic urges went along with such a policy, and no wartime project that was ever launched had to be delayed for lack of ability to finance it.

Not only did we finance government and industry throughout the war, but we were able to put out additional billions of hand-to-hand currency, fully backed at the traditional reserve ratios. The historic Federal Reserve ratio of gold to note issue, 40 per cent, was never breached, even though Congress willingly approved a reduction to 25 per cent early in 1945.

Besides the sale of securities to large investors, the issuance of savings bonds in large amounts brought in the money of small investors at an interest rate and on terms that they could understand and appreciate. The guarantee of the government that these bonds could be redeemed at any time at their purchase price or higher created an obligation for the Treasury which was the penalty paid to secure their sale.

Finally, although lip service was given to the notion that government bonds should not be sold to banks, because of the potentially inflationary consequences, banks did increase their bondholdings from less than $20 billion to more than $90 billion at the peak. These securities were mostly short-term ones. Again the Treasury accepted the obligation of quick redemption, for banks treat their securities as a readily available source of cash.

CONSEQUENCES OF PAST DEBT MANAGEMENT

Management of the federal debt is closely tied to tax policy. Thus the tax policy in three wars has been an influential factor on the federal debt. From 1917 to 1919 we paid only 39 per cent of federal expenses out of tax receipts. This record was improved slightly in World War II, when taxes covered 46 per cent of expenses. Granted that the present war production effort has not reached its maximum annual expenditure level, it is nevertheless significant that taxes covered 94 per cent of federal expenditures in the second year of the Korean conflict.

The increasing realization of the need to meet expenditures out of taxes instead of adding to the debt indicates a growing financial maturity on the part of the American people. A similar understanding of the implications, dangers and opportunities of the *existing* national debt is much to be desired. It is to such an understanding that the present committee hopes to contribute. To appreciate the problems and dangers of the existing debt, we would do well to examine the consequences of past debt management.

Inflating the Money Supply

The negative side of the easy financing of World War II was the inflationary increases in the money supply. Demand deposits nearly trebled between 1939 and 1946, while savings deposits doubled and cash in circulation quadrupled. This increase in deposits was the direct result of the huge purchases of government securities by the banks. Each such purchase gave the government a credit on the books of the banking system which it could spend, and which was eventually transformed into deposits in the name of the ultimate recipients of these expenditures.[4]

Such additional bank deposits, in addition to the large amounts of paper money paid out by banks to their customers to meet their transaction needs, would have been impossible without adequate bank reserves in the form of deposits at the Federal Reserve Banks. These reserves were provided through the purchase of government bonds by the Federal Reserve System itself: between 1939 and 1946 it added $21 billion to its portfolio. Whether a central bank buys direct from the Treasury (and this is normally prohibited in order to have at least the façade of arm's-length dealings) or from a member bank or from an individual, it gives a credit on its own books to the seller of the bonds, and this credit quickly becomes part of the basic reserves of the banking system.

Government Double Talk

Consequently, as the government needed more funds, the country experienced a species of double talk. The Treasury repeatedly professed that it did not want the banks to buy bonds, for this would inflate the money supply. It wanted its securities bought only by savers, since these would reduce their personal expenditures as the government increased its own. It is true that even when savers bought bonds, they received relatively liquid assets, which they might later decide to redeem or sell in order to do their deferred spending; but the Treasury planned to face this issue when it should arise—after the end of the war.

4. One of the most curious and significant aspects of war finance was this huge increase in demand deposits and currency. The growth was much more rapid than the rise of transactions requirements. The balance of the rise in effect represented a non-interest-bearing loan. The holders could instead have bought government securities or have placed these funds in the institutions which would have paid interest on them. If any of these courses had been taken, the money supply would have increased that much less, and so the inflation base would have been restricted. Apparently the rate of interest then offered was an insufficient reward for giving up liquidity, or the alternative possibilities were not sufficiently convenient, or there was not enough solicitation— or something else was lacking. But certainly the consequences would have been far happier if those funds held as non-interest-bearing cash had been invested.—DONALD B. WOODWARD

Unfortunately for this theory, the desire of the government for easy financing required that the banks possess excess reserves. These were kept close to $2 billion throughout the war, although by the end of 1945 they were down to $1.4 billion. But banks with excess reserves naturally seek the liquidity and income that come from investing them in government securities. They therefore steadily bought bonds. This process reduced the excess reserves, for part of them now became "required" reserves against the new bank deposits thus created—whereupon the Federal Reserve System stepped in with its own bond purchases to restore excess reserves to the $2 billion level.

The net result was that the money supply increased from $65 billion in 1939 to $165 billion in 1946. We had a new and sophisticated kind of greenbackism in the form of deposits that, if ever drawn on in a buying wave, could catapult us into inflation. Harry C. Scherman, in his *The Promises Men Live By,* rightly called them "dangerous dollars."

The Delayed Price Effect

Prices at first showed only a moderate increase—less than 10 per cent during the war years. They were restrained by the spirit of patriotism, by the energetic efforts of the Office of Price Administration, by the almost complete lack of durable consumer goods, and by some unexpected assistance from business costs. As industrial output grew, fixed costs per unit of output became smaller. The OPA did not, therefore, have to permit even as much of an increase in prices as would have been warranted by the rise in variable costs (labor and raw materials).

Thus we had a condition of "suppressed inflation." The money supply was inflated, but prices were suppressed. There was no question but that, when the war was over and controls were removed, prices would rise. To be sure, the public was in a buying mood after the war, and drew on its savings. But the basic cause of the postwar inflation was the time bomb laid during the war in the form of inflationary financing. By 1944 it had become very clear that our supplies of goods were not increasing and that we had, as Leon Henderson called it, an increasing amount of "money rattling around with no place to go." Taxation and the sale of bonds to true savers would have forestalled this situation. It is important that our wartime experience be kept in mind as a warning for the future. The fiscal authorities should not again pursue the easy course of borrowing from the banks.

The abandonment of direct controls on prices, wages, and supply of materials in 1946 was not a mistake—except in the sense that better stabilizing measures were not substituted. Freeing the economy was in itself a desirable step. The resulting price rise and outlook for higher profits gave a clear and unmistakable signal to business to produce to the limit. Some may feel that the signal was actually too loud, but after the deep depression of the 1930's and the decline in the spirit of enterprise that resulted from it, loud signals may have been needed. Moreover, the highest circles in Washington had expected a recession after the war, and a real stimulus to prices and profits was not out of place if it would ensure against this danger.

Stabilization Measures: Used and Unused

This does not mean that a 33 per cent rise in prices, such as followed between 1945 and 1948, was inevitable. But it does mean that true stabilization measures adapted to the causes of the boom, and not mere ceilings, should have been applied. The central pillars of the 1948 boom were business expenditures for capital investment, residential construction, and business expenditures for additions to inventory. The first two of these could have been restrained without undue difficulty by a rise in interest rates—or, more accurately, by a tightening of credit supplies, which has as its price an advance in interest rates. Controlling the expansion in business capital and in residential construction would in turn have removed much of the reason for the third form of expansion, that of inventories.[5]

In the relatively new and untested field of fiscal policy, on the other hand, an adequate policy was in fact enforced. Huge surpluses, amounting to nearly $6 billion in the calendar year 1947 and to $8 billion in 1948, were realized in the cash budget.

The failure of monetary policy is explained by the inhibitions that

5. While it is generally accepted as desirable that business capital outlay should be curtailed as part of boom restraint, the subject seems to me to need more exploration. Business capital investment is the most clearly identified way to increase income of the economy over time, and to restrain any inflationary tendencies over time. The investment choked off to curtail a boom may be lost forever, and with it the higher income that might have been achieved. Curtailment of other types of expenditure would be a more desirable method of boom restraint.—DONALD B. WOODWARD

arose from the existence of so large an outstanding national debt. Our attitude became one of keeping bonds at par value at all costs, although we now realize that any possible damage from a decline in bond prices would have been less than the damage done by a 33 per cent rise in commodity prices. The predominant opinion was that if government bonds declined in price, the decline must be kept "orderly." This policy requires the central banking authorities to buy securities lest the decline become disorderly. The effect of such buying is, as we have seen, to give the banks additional surplus reserves. This, in turn, means that pressure on the bond market would have ceased, for banks possessing surplus reserves simply do not sell bonds in a declining market.

"Reason May Deceive Us"

One of the founding fathers urged: "Let us be guided by experience, reason may deceive us." Our reasoning has deceived us in the field of monetary policy. Because such policy was ineffective in stimulating recovery in the 1930's, we reasoned that it was just simply ineffective. We forgot the lesson of long experience, that a policy incapable of creating a boom can nevertheless restrain one.[6] Monetary policy needs to be rescued from the "innocuous desuetude" in which it has been resting.

Monetary policy has had an honorable history for more than two centuries. It is one means of control that is compatible with freedom. It can be used to limit the extent of the price boom resulting from enlargement of the money supply, and it was finally so used in 1951 in concert with other remedies. Here at last there was one fortunate departure from the rule of "too little and too late," for it was "late" but, when used, became of real assistance.

DEBT RETIREMENT

Can We Retire the Debt?

Must the debt remain outstanding in such large amounts? Would it not be better to keep our national government, on which our safety as a people depends, unencumbered so that it may be able to borrow again in large amounts with great ease at any emergency? Even though the committee recognizes the impossibility of complete debt

---

6. I do not agree with the implication that monetary policy is ineffective in stimulating recovery under all conditions.—DONALD B. WOODWARD

retirement within generations, it does argue for whittling down the debt whenever possible.[7]

This process would involve some investment shifts. We would have to seek some equally desirable repository for the savings that average citizens have lodged in the federal debt today. Such a repository might well be one of the many investment institutions, since the average citizen often does not have a highly cultivated ability to manage the investment of his funds. High-grade corporation bonds with serial maturity also offer the necessary safety and liquidity.

Furthermore, although the subject might seem beyond the purview of this committee, there are important values in a more widely spread ownership of common stocks than prevails in the United States today. It must be recognized that the risk of capital loss to the individual is greater in owning stocks than in owning bonds. But there are other "risks" to be considered. The danger of loss in purchasing power by holding bonds has been an even more serious risk in recent years. The purchasing power of common-stock investments has been much more satisfactory. Gains in soundness and vigor in our capitalist economy would be additional advantages from wider stock ownership. In fact, there are circumstances under which the risk of *not* having a wide distribution of common shares may be found much greater than the risk of letting them be owned by groups not used to their behavior.[8]

This committee proposes that a program be developed for the retirement of the government debt. Such a program must be flexible, and the committee recognizes that it must be improvised to mesh with the economic conditions of the times. Nevertheless, a fairly specific objective or formula is needed if consistent progress is to be made toward the goal of retirement.

7. For "possible" I would substitute "consistent with high employment and stable prices," to make the point more explicit.—NEIL H. JACOBY

8. Common stocks are appropriate holdings for some investors some of the time under certain conditions: investors who are not likely to need the funds on short notice; who have made reasonable provision for emergency needs and death and sickness and accident contingencies; who do not "load up" at periods of high prices; and who are either reasonably well informed on stocks themselves or who have and utilize access to someone who has. The more popular thesis that "common stocks are a hedge against inflation" is undemonstrated and the experience of the British investor over recent years should serve as a stern warning. And even in those periods when common stocks as measured by the averages have seemed a hedge against inflation, this has not necessarily been true of those stocks investors actually bought. It is possible to be too enthusiastic about common stocks as well as too cautious about them.—DONALD B. WOODWARD

Specifically, it is proposed that the Congress declare by resolution its intention to reduce the public debt as rapidly as consistent with the maintenance of stable prices and high levels of production and employment. The President should be left the discretion necessary to conform with this directive in formulating his taxation, expenditure and budgetary policies. An automatic 10 per cent rise in the rate of withholding tax when employment is high might be a principal feature of such a policy.

The annual amount of retirement, or increase, of debt must depend on the balance of other forces that are to be offset. As a guide, however, the congressional resolution might perhaps set an objective of retiring 3 per cent of the total debt in any year, provided unemployment is less than 5 per cent of the labor force, and provided the consumer price index has not declined by more than one per cent in the preceding six months.

Encouragement to state and local government capital expansion, as well as to private capital expansion, would do much to create the prosperous climate of high employment and stable prices that would make debt retirement possible.

Debt Retirement and Debt Ownership

The test of the desirability of such debt reduction lies in part in its effect on the ownership groups, mentioned in the second section of this report. In general, that retirement is most desirable which reduces the debt in banks, where the debt has been serving merely as a liquid asset—more or less temporary—and augmenting the money supply.

Debt reduction may also have the unintended effect of retiring debt owned by individuals. Care needs to be taken not to make it hard for true savers to keep their funds invested. When bonds held directly or indirectly by individual savers are retired, the test is surely the availability of alternative investment outlets for the same groups. In fact, as the American economy becomes richer, these groups are going to save more, not less. Alternative investment outlets, therefore, become all the more important.

Satisfactory investment outlets are to be found only when business is active and brisk, so that a flow of new stocks, bonds and mortgages is coming on the market. If this flow is adequate to absorb *future* savings, it will be eminently desirable, especially if foreign as well as domestic investment can be encouraged. If private demand is still larger, so that individuals may find large enough outlets for funds hitherto reposed in federal securities, that too is desirable. Certainly it is only in times of high employment that such a transfer from public to private holdings will be feasible.

When private investment demand is as high as this, there is always the danger that it will speed on into inflation. This is the result when unrestrained bidding for labor, materials and money, running up against the existing supply, finally causes their prices to break away in an upward direction. We have done well to establish a progressive tax structure, which puts brakes on the ensuing rise in incomes and spending. At the same time, these taxes are capable of producing an excess of funds, from time to time, with which the government can retire debt held by individuals. This does not mean, however, that the present high rates of income tax are to be recommended as permanent additions to our tax structure. Indeed, tax reduction will be needed to provide incentive and stimulus in the future to private investment and demand.

Debt Retirement and National Security

The possibility of debt retirement, which is already in view because of our rapid growth in population and private investment, will become all the greater if world tension can be relaxed. If we achieve military and political security, part of the funds not devoted to defense at home and abroad can be diverted to debt retirement—corresponding to the simultaneous switch of our national energies from defense production to civilian production financed by issues of private securities. This private financing will be all the easier to achieve if taxes are cut (insofar as the needs of debt retirement permit) when defense spending goes down.

Nevertheless, the committee wishes to emphasize that our national objectives are, first, the preservation of the nation and our freedom, and only second, economic security and welfare and progress. If there is any threat to our national existence, calling for greatly enlarged national expenditures, a policy of debt retirement cannot be sustained. Similarly, debt retirement may have to be abandoned temporarily if private investment should be so low as to fail to sustain employment. National debt is an instrument that can be used along with others to defend both political and military security and employment and high productive output.

Debt Retirement and Employment

The criterion for relating debt to employment is found in our statistics. Except for a short period in 1949-1950, unemployment has remained down around two million since very early in the 1940's. This seems to be a minimum if we are to maintain tolerable fluidity and mobility—geographic, seasonal and occupational—in our labor supply. It is difficult for a mass of workers to change areas or jobs without a transitional period of unemployment.

Employment has remained high in the postwar period. We have demonstrated a remarkable ability to put large numbers of people efficiently to work in the private segment of the economy in short periods of time. This is extraordinarily important as a guide in meeting any big threat of unemployment in any future years—for instance, when defense industries are demobilized.

There have also been years in which our employment has been overfull. Such years were 1947 and 1948, when weekly wages in manufacturing rose by 10 per cent without either appreciable diminution in unemployment or increase in employment. In other words, we were unable to make the full gain in national output that we were attempting, and in an effort to do so we forced up wages and prices. This is not to say that the advance in wages itself is the most important cause of inflation, but merely to argue that it does at times indicate the presence of excess demand which has not been neutralized.

It is at such times that retirement of public debt can serve its most effective purpose, whether accomplished by increased taxation, by reduced government expenditures or, preferably, by both.

Debt Owned by Federal Reserve Banks

We turn now to that 45 per cent of the total debt that is not owned by genuine savers but is held as a more or less liquid asset. To what extent can this debt prudently be retired? We begin with the Federal Reserve Banks, owners of $23 billion of government securities.

The Reserve-held debt serves two major functions. First, it is the instrument by which the country is provided with its hand-to-hand currency. Second, and to a much smaller degree, it is the means of controlling the reserves of our commercial banks—or at least those that are members of the Federal Reserve System.

Our hand-to-hand currency consists chiefly of Federal Reserve notes. A portion of these came into being in the process of purchasing the government securities now held by the Reserve Banks. Retiring the $23 billion of securities would cut the foundation from under the $25 billion of Federal Reserve notes outstanding. Then one of two things would happen. The commercial banks might have to become indebted to the Federal Reserve Banks on a large scale to obtain currency. This could cause a tightening of credit, which might be too severe if done rapidly. Second, the government might replace the hand-to-hand currency by issuing fiat money. This would raise undesirable emotional responses such as could endanger our economic security.

Turning to the use of bondholdings to control bank reserves, the success of such use can be measured by observing the commodity price level. If the price level is advancing in the face of previously existing full employment of national resources, we have inflation. This is a clear proof that the Federal Reserve Banks should be reducing their bond portfolios so as to sop up some of the excess purchasing power of the buyers of bonds.

But this does not mean that there is any call to reduce the Federal Reserve portfolios in large amounts at the present time. Despite the excessive issue of national debt from 1941 to 1945, which contributed to the substantial price inflation from 1946 to 1948, we have grown up to the money supply—partly by a more productive economy and partly by adjusting to a higher price level. This has given us greater price stability since 1948. It is very difficult, of course, to adjust again to a lower price level. Except for the two intense but brief periods of consumer purchasing following the Korean outbreak and the Chinese intervention, we have had what seems to this committee a fairly workable wage and price structure.[9] At least, it will not be made more workable by deliberately trying to reduce the level of wages and prices through debt reduction.

9. The wage and price structure during this whole period has been supported by the accumulation of deferred demands, very large government outlays, very high family formation, and has existed in a world economy not viable. Whether the wage and price structure of such a period can be judged "fairly workable" is open to question.—DONALD B. WOODWARD

Debt should be retired, rather, when prices will remain stable despite the extinction of money based on federal debt.

In short, there is but limited scope for reduction in the bonds held by the Federal Reserve if we want to avoid the risks of currency contraction and price deflation. Such retirements as are made would necessarily be small and gradual.

Commercial Banks as Bondholders

The bond portfolios of corporations and of state and local governments serve special purposes—anticipating tax requirements of the former, raising cash to begin expensive projects of the latter— or other corporate and public functions with which there is no reason to interfere. We shall therefore confine the rest of our discussion of the effect of retirement on debt owners to the case of the commercial banks. These, with their $60 billion, constitute the largest class of holders.

Since the peak of commercial bank holding, after the final $26 billion victory bond drive in December 1945, the debt ownership of this class has been reduced by a full $30 billion. Much of this one-third reduction was synthetic and imaginary, however. It resulted from directing excessive federal government bank balances to the formal retirement of debt.

We need a further, *real* reduction in the debt owned by banks. When bank deposits are swollen as a result of bank purchases of government bonds, there is an inflationary potential in the money supply of the country. Inflation cannot be fought successfully as long as government bonds are sold to commercial banks. We need a national conscience to tell us that such sales are undermining our people's very security for old age. By raising the money supply and therefore the price of goods, such sales have the consequence that dollars laid aside for old age will buy too little to keep the pensioner or annuitant in comfort.

Treasury Policy and the Banks Today

We think this warning is of great importance at the present time, because, over the remainder of the 1952-1954 period, we may expect rising government expenditures without an increase in tax levies.[10]

10. That government expenditures will continue to rise during 1953 and 1954 is uncertain.—DONALD B. WOODWARD

If it is the national decision not to increase tax rates, and if the buoyancy of tax revenues becomes less than it has fortunately been in the last two years, this will mean further federal borrowing.

We urge that the future borrowing schedules of the Treasury should be directed with all the intensity required toward securing funds from individuals and savings institutions. This will mean that private spending is reduced as federal spending rises: our price level will be held in check and the old-age security of the people protected. To secure this end, a high enough rate of interest must be offered to make saving seem to the average man more attractive than additional spending.

Even if people are saving money, they do not necessarily have to buy government bonds—and this applies especially to large savers and savings institutions. The Treasury will have to grant lenders attractive enough terms to secure the funds it needs. The principle it should follow in regard to interest rates can be put quite simply: to "meet the market." The "market" should not, it is true, be left entirely to itself. But any attempt to influence it should be that of the monetary authority of the nation, the Federal Reserve System, and should be guided by the state of employment and the movement of prices. The "needs" of the Treasury for low-cost funds should not be the determinant of federal monetary policy in peacetime; rather the Treasury should be obliged to compete for funds in the monetary market.

The committee is disturbed that, in face of one unsatisfactory outcome of an offered bond issue in the spring of 1952, the Treasury at once took the easy course of inviting bank subscriptions to another issue in the same month. This device did succeed in producing subscriptions equal to more than three times the amount of contemplated borrowing. It is fortunate that the Treasury can secure the funds it needs and can recover from ill successes. But if the final outcome is that bank holdings of bonds, and consequently bank deposits, are enlarged, with all their inflationary potential, the successes will have been bought at a high price.

Looking back at World War II, it appears that the efforts made to avoid such direct credit inflation were either not well enough conceived or not strenuously enough applied to be successful. Since its conclusion we have learned more effective ways of covering increases in federal expenditures by taxation. If we now throw over these lessons and return to the easy course of borrowing from banks, it will be a retrograde step in the history of American public debt management.

Bank Liquidity and the Debt

We cannot leave the commercial banks without mentioning one very substantial advantage accruing to the nation from their ownership of federal bonds. The pages of America's financial history are strewn with the records of bank collapse and failure. In sheer numbers, more banks have failed than have succeeded. In most other modern countries there are a few, large banks with many branches each. It is implicit in such countries that the banking system has the support of the national government behind it. This has not been so in the United States. We have chosen to conceive and retain a flexible, independent, changeable unit banking system. But a price must be paid for this independence. Such banks, lacking the support of the government and of large resources and many branches of their own, must either keep their loans in a highly liquid condition or hold a substantial amount of impeccable federal securities of short-term maturity.

The great improvement in our banking liquidity since 1920 can be quickly indicated. In 1920 a typical country bank had only 10 per cent of its deposit liabilities in cash reserves. The remaining 90 per cent was invested in loans. Many of these, even if not directly "slow" in collection, were quickly made slow if precipitous collection was attempted. Other loans were soon frozen outright. Whenever wholesale collection was attempted, the local community was quickly immersed in deflation and bad times.

Today these banks have a liquidity ratio hovering close to 50 per cent, of which about half is in cash and reserves and the rest in government securities. The loan component is somewhat below 50 per cent in agricultural areas and above it in industrial areas. This is the consequence both of the cautious borrowing policies of farmers and of the great improvement in the prices at which they sell compared to those at which they buy. Debt today tends to be a "city-bred habit."

Our point has been that the amount of debt owned by central and commercial banks is not as far out of line with today's price level and need of liquidity as to call for severe measures. It suggests that we can, without much difficulty, achieve a well-organized national debt.

DEBT MANAGEMENT FOR THE FUTURE

The beginning of wisdom on the subject of debt management is in distinguishing between the immediate interests of the Treasury as an operating institution and the broader interests of the American people as a whole.

The Treasury has the direct responsibility for debt management, and it is not unnatural that it may feel itself bound by the necessity of selling securities as cheaply as possible. It feels itself to be the guardian of Uncle Sam's money. Secretary of the Treasury John W. Snyder has explained the Treasury's conception of its responsibility along these lines in forceful manner before congressional committees.

One of the strongest points in the Treasury's position is that the interest rate that is required to induce a needed amount of savings is unknown. Only experience in the market and the offering of a sufficient inducement to save can answer this question.[11] Naturally the Treasury shuns the prospect of an uncertain venture in offering higher and higher interest rates, for fear of the criticism that might come if a very high interest rate proved necessary to elicit large sums of savings. But uncertainty in the level of interest rates is a smaller matter, from the point of view of the public interest, compared with the certainty of the heavy toll of inflation.

A second possible approach to the debt problem is to place primary emphasis on debt management in terms of its effect on our national economic life. The best expression of our peacetime economic aims, though it is not a perfect one and may have an inflationary bias, is in the Employment Act of 1946. Insofar as the particular interests of the Treasury and its present conception of its responsibilities as defined by law may clash with this broader ideal, the present committee favors the broader policy. It chooses, therefore, to treat the debt from the point of view of maintaining over-all financial stability and promoting over-all economic progress.

Even more fundamental than these issues of debt *management*

11. And this rate is likely to be different under different conditions.—DONALD B. WOODWARD

is the issue of the *debt itself*. Debt created to fight a war represents a deadweight loss—though one well worth incurring for the nation's survival. Similarly, debt created by government merely to pump out purchasing power during a depression is in itself a deadweight loss —although the price is worth paying to achieve recovery.[12] Private debt can, like government debt, be deadweight when it is incurred for nonproductive purposes.

The committee maintains that any debt, public or private, is a drag on the economy unless it increases the productive abilities of the nation. A productive asset is the source of new goods and new income that flow out to the community. The income generated by the productive asset pays interest charges and amortizes the principal of the debt. Contrariwise, a debt arising from a nonproductive expenditure can be serviced as to interest charges and repayments only by garnering and diverting income from some productive resource elsewhere.

Business Debt versus Government Debt

Business debt can be a deadweight drag on the economy, like much of government debt. But most business borrowing is for the creation of productive assets. Business, like government, wants to be in a liquid position and wants to keep down its debt and its fixed charges. Nevertheless, a sacrifice in liquidity or a higher debt is often the price of economic progress.

This can best be seen in the balance sheet and income consequences of the construction of a large modern plant. Such an industrial plant is being built on the banks of the Delaware River below Trenton, New Jersey, by the United States Steel Corporation. Paying the costs of this construction will denude the corporation of some of its liquid assets. The corporation may have to increase its debt to restore liquidty. But in this plant there will be a trebling of per worker output, raising it from the average of 109 tons a year in all hitherto existing plants of the corporation to 333 tons in the new mill. On the balance sheet of the United States Steel Corporation there will be plant assets and either reduced liquid assets or increased debt. For the nation as a whole there will be increased capacity and efficiency in the production of steel, as well

12. Some increase in debt may be appropriate in depression, but this statement is too unrestricted and unqualified. Both the quality of the debt and the quality of the recovery need consideration.—DONALD B. WOODWARD

as greater opportunities for employment and the creation of outlets for the investment funds of the nation's savers.

On balance, the advantages accruing from the construction and operation of the new plant are very great, both to the company and to the community. The corporation acted wisely in incurring the debt to build the new facility.

National debt may also be incurred for the creation of valuable assets—highways, dams, harbors, river valley development—with the same social advantages. Even with federal debt, which is a mere heritage from war and does not purchase physical assets that add to the productivity of the economy, wise management can make it an advantageous medium for the investment of the public's savings.

RECOMMENDATIONS

1. The committee recommends that *the Employment Act of 1946 be amended to include a directive that attention be given to maintenance of the value of money,* along with the other objectives it now contains.

2. The committee recommends that better coordination be established between the many federal lending agencies. A common policy objective for management of all the federal debt should be established by congressional directive. *All agencies dealing with federal obligations, commitments, guarantees and insurance should operate consistently with the Employment Act, and in matters of monetary policy should follow the lead of the Federal Reserve Board.* Numerous federal credit agencies now engage in very large operations, which may serve to neutralize or defeat the debt retirement or expansion operations of the Treasury; yet all these lending operations are derived from the credit of the United States government. Thus, it is possible that the real estate loan guarantees of the FHA have had a more profound effect on the economy during some recent years than the Treasury's debt operations.

3. We urge the *adoption of a regular program of extinguishing part of the federal debt* whenever employment is at or below a frictional level and prices are stable or rising. Such a retirement program should be halted whenever business turns definitely downward. Fortunately, the retirement since the end of 1945 of one third of the $90 billion of federal debt owned by the commercial banking

system means that our debt is now much better organized for financial stability and economic progress than it would otherwise have been.

4. It is recommended that *the proportion of debt taking the form of short-term maturities be reduced* as the first step in debt retirement. Short-term federal securities are "near-money," a volatile element in the debt structure, adding to the inflationary potential of the economy.

5. To avoid the risk of bunched-up or untimely due dates, *maturities should be distributed over time,* with emphasis on longer-term issues. This will help reduce the dependency of the Treasury on current interest rates and its continuous worry and concern over immediate market conditions.

6. *Federal debt management should use the market place more and the fruitless and risky gadgetry of special-purpose issues less.* The proper principle for federal borrowing is to use marketable issues, bearing whatever rates of interest and terms of payment are necessary to elicit funds from individuals and from each particular type of savings institution.

7. We recommend a concerted program on the part of the Treasury directed toward *transferring as much as possible of the debt from commercial banks and other less permanent holders* into the hands of true savers and savings institutions. We cannot always rely on some of the pieces of good fortune that have come our way since victory was won in 1945. The rate of defense expenditures declined much more precipitously after victory than almost anyone had thought possible. The results were that the $26 billion obtained in the final war bond drive of December 1945 was never required and that the budget came into balance at about May 1946 without any very conscious effort. The cash surpluses of the fiscal years 1947, 1948, 1950 and 1951 were of great aid in fighting inflation and meant also a considerable transfer of government securities out of unstable hands into the trust funds and social security funds.

8. *We should not retire that portion of the debt which backs our hand-to-hand currency.* With the growth of population and productivity, the percentage of the debt devoted to this purpose and held accordingly in banking hands may be expected to increase.

9. *We do not recommend such a heroic debt reduction as to threaten us with deflation of the price level.* The degree of stability

that we do have, and the rate of current economic progress, suggest that our present price level is one we should want to defend.

10. We must *recognize the potentiality of the national debt as a tool to maintain high employment.* We must not be afraid of the debt, for if properly handled it is a resource of great power and usefulness. Sound fiscal policy and sound debt policy can achieve far greater financial stability and can add to our assurance of the economic future of our own country and of the free world.

11. The committee recommends that *monetary policy be installed as a regular weapon in the arsenal of economic stabilization.* The Federal Reserve System should be free to deal with the money market on the basis of its effects on employment and prices, and not on the basis of the needs of the Treasury for securing low-cost funds. A rise in interest rates and a tightening of credit supplies should be employed whenever the flow of credit is too great. Granted, this will involve at such times a decline in the price of existing government securities. The Treasury should nevertheless come to see that the saving in costs of all expenditures by the United States government, when a rise in prices of goods and services it buys is prevented, far exceeds the cost of such prevention in the form of higher interest rates. Interest, after all, amounted to only 9 per cent of federal expenditures in the last fiscal year.

ARTHUR R. UPGREN, *Chairman*
HENRY H. HEIMANN
NEIL H. JACOBY
E. B. MACNAUGHTON
EARL B. SCHWULST
LOUIS STULBERG
DONALD B. WOODWARD

APPENDIX TABLES

TABLE 1

GROWTH OF THE NATIONAL DEBT COMPARED WITH THE NATIONAL INCOME, 1939-1948[a]

(In Billions)

Year	Federal Securities Outstanding —Direct and Guaranteed	National Income
1939	$ 45.9	$ 72.5
1940	48.5	81.3
1941	55.3	103.8
1942	77.0	137.1
1943	140.8	169.7
1944	202.6	183.8
1945	259.1	182.7
1946	269.9	179.6
1947	258.4	201.7
1948	252.4	226.2

Sources: Debt: 1939-1940, *Treasury Bulletin,* September 1947, p. 22; 1941-1948, *ibid.,* August 1949, p. 15. National income: *Survey of Current Business,* July 1949, p. 10.

a. For fiscal years, 1939-1948. These figures exclude guaranteed securities held by the U.S. Treasury.

TABLE 2

ASSETS OF FINANCIAL INSTITUTIONS, END OF DECEMBER, 1939-1948

(In Billions)

Year	Federal Reserve Banks (1)	All Commercial Banks (2)	Mutual Savings Banks (3)	Life Insurance Companies (4)
1939	$19.0	$ 40.7	$10.2	$29.2
1940	23.3	43.9	10.2	30.8
1941	24.4	50.7	10.4	32.7
1942	29.0	67.4	10.8	34.9
1943	34.0	85.1	11.9	37.8
1944	40.3	105.5	13.9	41.1
1945	45.1	124.0	16.2	44.8
1946	45.0	114.0	17.7	48.2
1947	47.7	116.3	18.6	51.7
1948	50.0	114.3	19.4	55.6

Sources: Col. 1: for 1939-1946 figures, *Survey of Current Business,* Statistical Supplement, July 1947, p. 72; for 1947-1948 figures, *ibid.,* January and July 1949, p. S-15; cols. 2 and 3: *Federal Reserve Bulletin,* January 1949, p. 42, and July 1949, p. 815; col. 4: *Life Insurance Fact Book, 1949,* Institute of Life Insurance, New York, 1950, p. 46.

TABLE 3

LIQUID ASSET HOLDINGS OF INDIVIDUALS AND TRUST FUNDS, NONFINANCIAL CORPORATIONS, UNINCORPORATED BUSINESSES, AND TOTAL NET ASSETS OF INVESTMENT COMPANIES, ANNUAL TOTALS, 1939-1948

Year	Personal Holdings[a] (1)	Nonfinancial Corporations (2)	Unincorporated Businesses (3)	Investment Companies (4)
	In Billions			In Millions
1939	$ 49.6	$11.3	$ 6.4	—
1940	52.4	13.2	7.3	$1,062
1941	59.5	15.2	8.5	925
1942	76.8	24.6	12.3	1,044
1943	100.5	35.5	17.3	1,362
1944	128.4	40.9	22.8	1,621
1945	154.5	40.3	27.9	2,255
1946	165.2	34.5	27.4	2,163
1947	172.3	33.9	26.5	2,180
1948	174.8	34.2	25.3	2,246

Sources: Cols. 1, 2, 3: *Federal Reserve Bulletin,* July 1949, p. 794; col. 4: "Investment Company Statistics," National Association of Investment Companies, New York, 1940-1948.

a. Includes trust funds and holdings of farmers and professional persons.

TABLE 4

YIELDS OF TAXABLE TREASURY SECURITIES, SEPTEMBER 29, 1945[a]

(Yield in Per Cent Per Annum)

Class of Security	Mean	Yield to Earliest Call Date	Class of Security	Yield to Earliest Call Date
Certificates of indebtedness			Bank-eligible Treasury bonds	
⅞% G— 10/1/45	—		2% 3/15/48-50	1.12%
" H— 12/1/45	.68%		1¾ 6/15/48	1.18
" A— 2/1/46	.80		2 6/15/49-51	1.31
" B— 3/1/46	.81		2 9/15/49-51	1.33
" C— 4/1/46	.82		2 12/15/49-51	1.34
" D— 5/1/46	.82		2 3/15/50-52	1.38
" E— 6/1/46	.83		2 9/15/50-52	1.40
" F— 8/1/46	.84		1½ 12/15/50	1.24
" G— 9/1/46	.84		2 9/15/51-53	1.46
" H— 10/1/46	.86		2 12/15/51-55	1.46
			2½ 3/15/52-54	1.55
			2 6/15/52-54	1.51
			2¼ 6/15/52-55	1.56
			2 12/15/52-54	1.54
			2½ 3/15/56-58	1.72
			2¼ 9/15/56-59	1.82
			2½ 9/15/67-72	2.21

TABLE 4 (continued)

Class of Security	Mean	Yield to Earliest Call Date	Class of Security	Yield to Earliest Call Date
Treasury notes			Bank-restricted Treasury bonds	
¾% B— 12/15/45		.75		
.90 C— 1/ 1/46		.78	2¼% 6/15/59-62	2.20%
1 A— 3/15/46		.86	2½ 6/15/62-67	2.29
.90 D— 7/ 1/46		.85	2½ 12/15/63-68	2.35
1½ B— 12/15/46		.95	2½ 6/15/64-69	2.38
1¼ B— 3/15/47		.99	2½ 12/15/64-69	2.39
1½ A— 9/15/47		1.03	2½ 3/15/65-70	2.40
1¼ C— 9/15/47		1.02	2½ 3/15/66-71	2.40
1½ A— 9/15/48		1.16	2½ 6/15/67-72	2.46

Source: *Treasury Bulletin*, November 1945, p. 55.
a. Based on mean of closing bid and asked quotations.

TABLE 5

COMPUTED ANNUAL INTEREST CHARGE ON THE PUBLIC DEBT AND GUARANTEED OBLIGATIONS, SEPTEMBER 1945–DECEMBER 1948

(In Millions)

Date	1945	1946	1947	1948
January	—	$5,472	$5,327	$5,472
February	—	5,487	5,336	5,471
March	—	5,445	5,319	5,435
April	—	5,430	5,318	5,433
May	—	5,424	5,344	5,435
June	—	5,357	5,376	5,457
July	—	5,368	5,424	5,517
August	—	5,371	5,464	5,517
September	$5,051	5,358	5,449	5,513
October	5,052	5,349	5,456	5,536
November	5,133	5,344	5,462	5,544
December	5,424	5,304	5,451	5,552

Source: *Treasury Bulletin*, October 1945–March 1949.

TABLE 6

GENERAL FUND BALANCE OF THE U.S. TREASURY AND PORTIONS HELD IN SPECIAL DEPOSITORIES AND IN FEDERAL RESERVE BANKS, SEPTEMBER 1945–DECEMBER 1948

(In Millions)

Date	1945			1946			1947			1948		
	General Fund Balance	Special Depositories	Federal Reserve Banks	General Fund Balance	Special Depositories	Federal Reserve Banks	General Fund Balance	Special Depositories	Federal Reserve Banks	General Fund Balance	Special Depositories	Federal Reserve Banks
January	—	—	—	$25,427	$24,030	$1,011	$4,711	$2,736	$1,620	$4,648	$ 959	$2,256
February	—	—	—	25,961	24,447	1,209	7,134	3,363	2,561	4,318	1,434	1,571
March	—	—	—	24,367	21,776	2,160	6,909	3,292	2,369	5,353	1,972	1,972
April	—	—	—	20,935	19,502	1,124	4,312	2,317	842	4,612	2,156	1,236
May	—	—	—	18,536	16,949	1,230	4,066	1,807	989	4,946	2,007	1,714
June	—	—	—	14,238	12,993	1,006	3,308	962	1,202	4,932	1,773	1,928
July	—	—	—	12,029	10,961	702	3,069	958	884	5,074	2,081	1,755
August	—	—	—	11,040	9,842	872	3,400	1,362	884	4,832	1,741	1,919
September	$16,134	$13,989	$1,755	10,171	8,377	1,445	3,952	1,618	749[a]	5,583	2,703	1,664
October	12,813	11,389	1,124	8,070	6,936	773	4,107	1,437	1,091	4,802	1,976	1,608
November	14,445	12,694	1,372	6,665	5,487	824	3,935	1,417	1,393	4,385	1,621	1,601
December	26,003	24,044	1,674	3,502	2,570	682	3,097	968	866	4,208	1,909	1,123

Source: Federal Reserve Bulletin, October 1945–March 1949.
a. Change in classification.

TABLE 7

TOTAL FEDERAL RESERVE CREDIT OUTSTANDING AND FEDERAL RESERVE
BANK HOLDINGS OF U.S. GOVERNMENT SECURITIES, END OF MONTH,
SEPTEMBER 1945–DECEMBER 1948

(In Billions)

Year and Month	Total Credit Outstanding	Holdings of U.S. Government Securities
1945		
September	$24.1	$22.3
October	24.0	23.3
November	24.7	23.5
December	25.1	24.3
1946		
January	24.0	23.3
February	23.6	22.9
March	23.6	22.6
April	23.4	22.7
May	23.5	22.9
June	24.5	23.8
July	24.2	23.6
August	24.7	23.9
September	24.6	24.0
October	24.1	23.5
November	24.8	23.9
December	24.1	23.3
1947		
January	24.8	23.9
February	24.8	24.1
March	23.4	22.6
April	22.2	21.9
May	22.7	22.1
June	22.2	21.9
July	21.9	21.5
August	22.8	22.2
September	22.7	22.3
October	22.9	22.2
November	23.0	22.2
December	23.2	22.6
1948		
January	22.8	21.9
February	22.1	21.0
March	21.6	20.9
April	20.9	20.3
May	21.6	20.7
June	21.9	21.4
July	22.0	21.3
August	22.1	21.6
September	24.1	23.4
October	23.9	23.0
November	23.9	23.2
December	24.1	23.3

Source: Federal Reserve Bulletin, October 1945–March 1949.

TABLE 8
INTEREST RATES ON U.S. GOVERNMENT SECURITIES, SEPTEMBER 1945–DECEMBER 1948

(Per Cent Per Annum)

Month	*1945*	*1946*	*1947*	*1948*
Taxable Bonds—15 Years and Over				
January	—	2.21	2.21	2.45
February	—	2.12	2.21	2.45
March	—	2.09	2.19	2.45
April	—	2.08	2.19	2.44
May	—	2.19	2.19	2.42
June	—	2.16	2.22	2.41
July	—	2.18	2.25	2.44
August	—	2.23	2.24	2.45
September	2.37	2.28	2.24	2.45
October	2.35	2.26	2.27	2.45
November	2.33	2.25	2.36	2.44
December	2.33	2.24	2.39	2.44
Notes				
January	—	1.10	1.26	1.63
February	—	1.03	1.26	1.63
March	—	.99	1.24	1.60
April	—	1.12	1.24	1.58
May	—	1.18	1.27	1.51
June	—	1.15	1.29	1.49
July	—	1.13	1.33	1.56
August	—	1.14	1.31	1.65
September	1.19	1.22	1.28	1.69
October	1.17	1.24	1.35	1.71
November	1.14	1.22	1.47	1.69
December	1.15	1.22	1.54	1.64
Certificates				
January	—	.79	.84	1.09
February	—	.76	.85	1.10
March	—	.79	.82	1.09
April	—	.81	.83	1.10
May	—	.83	.85	1.09
June	—	.83	.85	1.09
July	—	.84	.85	1.10
August	—	.84	.85	1.15
September	.84	.85	.87	1.18
October	.83	.83	.97	1.23
November	.84	.84	.99	1.22
December	.84	.85	1.04	1.21
Bills[a]				
January	—	.375	.376	.977
February	—	.375	.376	.996
March	—	.375	.376	.996
April	—	.375	.376	.997
May	—	.375	.376	.997
June	—	.375	.376	.998
July	—	.375	.703	.997

TABLE 8 (continued)

(Per Cent Per Annum)

Month	1945	1946	1947	1948
August	—	.375	.748	1.053
September	.375	.375	.804	1.090
October	.375	.375	.857	1.120
November	.375	.376	.932	1.144
December	.375	.375	.950	1.154

Source: Federal Reserve Bulletin, October 1945–March 1949.
a.   Rate on new issues offered within the period.

TABLE 9

YIELDS TO EARLIEST CALL DATE OF TAXABLE ISSUES OF
U.S. TREASURY BANK-ELIGIBLE BONDS, AS OF
DECEMBER 31, 1945, 1946, 1947, 1948

(Per Cent Per Annum)

Class of Security	Yield			
	1945	1946	1947	1948
2%—3/15/48-50	1.02	.97	.90	—
1¾%—6/15/48	1.05	1.03	.98	—
2%—6/15/49-51	1.08	1.12	1.17	1.09
2%—9/15/49-51	1.12	1.14	1.29	1.19
2%—12/15/49-51	1.16	1.14	1.32	1.24
2%—3/15/50-52	1.17	1.20	1.33	1.31
2%—9/15/50-52	1.22	1.29	1.44	1.36
1½%—12/15/50	1.17	1.18	1.36	1.35
2%—9/15/51-53	1.26	1.39	1.60	1.51
2%—12/15/51-55	1.24	1.38	1.63	1.53
2½%—3/15/52-54	1.32	1.48	1.72	1.57
2%—6/15/52-54	1.30	1.46	1.70	1.59
2¼%—6/15/52-55	1.33	1.50	1.74	1.63
2%—12/15/52-54	1.33	1.49	1.75	1.63
2½%—3/15/56-58	1.46	1.66	2.13	1.92
2¼%—9/15/56-59	1.61	1.66	2.09	1.92
2½%—9/15/67-72	1.99	2.13	2.43	2.37

Source: Treasury Bulletin, various issues.

TABLE 10

ALL COMMERCIAL BANKS: TOTAL DEPOSITS AND HOLDINGS OF
U.S. GOVERNMENT SECURITIES, SEMIANNUALLY,
JUNE 1945–DECEMBER 1950

(In Billions)

Year and Month	Total Deposits	Holdings of U.S. Government Securities	Year and Month	Total Deposits	Holdings of U.S. Government Securities
1945			1948		
June	$136.6	$84.1	June	$138.1	$64.8
December	150.2	90.6	December	142.8	62.6
1946			1949		
June	142.9	84.5	June	137.5	63.2
December	139.0	74.8	December	145.2	67.0
1947			1950		
June	135.9	70.5	June	143.8	65.8
December	144.1	69.2	December	155.3	62.0

Source: Federal Reserve Bulletin, November 1946–July 1951.

TABLE 11

PERSONAL HOLDINGS, INCLUDING TRUST FUNDS: ESTIMATED LIQUID ASSET
HOLDINGS AND HOLDINGS OF U.S. GOVERNMENT SECURITIES,
SEMIANNUALLY, 1945-1946, ANNUALLY, 1947-1950

(In Billions)

Year and Month	Liquid Asset Holdings	Holdings of U.S. Government Securities	Year and Month	Liquid Asset Holdings	Holdings of U.S. Government Securities
1945			1948		
June	$140.6	$51.5	June	—	—
December	154.5	55.6	December	$174.5	$60.3
1946			1949		
June	158.9	55.2	June	—	—
December	165.2	55.6	December	176.7	62.0
1947			1950		
June	—	—	June	—	—
December	172.3	58.4	December	182.1	63.9

Source: "Estimated Liquid Asset Holdings of Individuals and Businesses," Federal Reserve Bulletin, July 1951, p. 808.

TABLE 12

U.S. CORPORATIONS, EXCLUDING BANKS AND INSURANCE COMPANIES:
TOTAL CURRENT ASSETS AND HOLDINGS OF U.S. GOVERNMENT
SECURITIES, QUARTERLY, JUNE 1945–DECEMBER 1950

(In Billions)

Year and Month	Total Current Assets	Holdings of U.S. Government Securities	Year and Month	Total Current Assets	Holdings of U.S. Government Securities
			1948		
1945			March 31	$121.4	$13.7
June 30	$99.1	$22.3	June 30	121.7	13.0
Sept. 30	99.0	20.7	Sept. 30	126.8	13.4
Dec. 31	97.7	21.1	Dec. 31	126.7	13.9
1946			1949		
March 31	95.6	19.8	March 31	125.0	14.0
June 30	95.7	17.6	June 30	123.3	14.8
Sept. 30	98.9	16.2	Sept. 30	124.6	15.6
Dec. 31	104.5	15.0	Dec. 31	124.1	15.7
1947			1950		
March 31	106.2	14.1	March 31	129.3	17.4
June 30	107.4	13.0	June 30	134.2	18.3
Sept. 30	110.7	12.9	Sept. 30	143.0	19.5
Dec. 31	116.0	13.7	Dec. 31	150.5	19.9

Source: Securities and Exchange Commission Statistical Series, Releases No. 762,
June 13, 1946; No. 775, May 6, 1947; No. 797, June 6, 1948; No. 876, July 19, 1949;
No. 945, July 5, 1950; No. 1024, July 20, 1951.

TABLE 13

FEDERAL RESERVE BANK HOLDINGS OF U.S. GOVERNMENT SECURITIES,
QUARTERLY, JUNE 1945–DECEMBER 1950

(In Billions)

Date	1945	1946	1947	1948	1949	1950
March	—	$22.5	$23.0	$20.6	$21.6	$17.7
June	$21.3	23.2	21.7	20.8	19.4	17.8
September	22.9	23.6	22.0	21.6	17.4	18.9
December	23.7	23.8	21.9	23.0	18.3	20.3

Source: Federal Reserve Bulletin, November 1946–July 1951. Averages of daily
figures.

TABLE 14
LIFE INSURANCE COMPANIES: ADMITTED ASSETS AND HOLDINGS OF U.S. GOVERNMENT SECURITIES, QUARTERLY, JUNE 1945–DECEMBER 1950

(In Billions)

Year and Month	Admitted Assets	Holdings of U.S. Government Securities	Year and Month	Admitted Assets	Holdings of U.S. Government Securities
1945			**1948**		
			March	$47.1	$17.7
June	$34.9	$15.8	June	47.9	17.1
September	35.4	16.0	September	48.6	16.1
December	36.3	17.4	December	49.5	15.2
1946			**1949**		
March	36.9	18.0	March	50.3	15.0
June	37.6	18.3	June	51.1	14.3
September	38.1	18.4	September	51.8	13.9
December	38.8	18.2	December	52.9	13.8
1947			**1950**		
March	39.4	17.9	March	53.7	13.7
June	40.1	17.7	June	54.5	13.3
September	45.5	18.9	September	55.4	12.8
December	46.3	18.3	December	56.5	12.0

Source: Survey of Current Business, December 1945–March 1951. Life Insurance Association of America data: through June 1947 includes 36 companies which had about 81 per cent of total admitted assets of all United States legal reserve companies; thereafter includes 49 companies which accounted for about 90 per cent of the total admitted assets of all legal reserve companies at the end of 1946.

TABLE 15
ALL MUTUAL SAVINGS BANKS: TIME DEPOSITS AND HOLDINGS OF U.S. GOVERNMENT SECURITIES, SEMIANNUALLY, JUNE 1945–DECEMBER 1950

(In Billions)

Year and Month	Time Deposits	Holdings of U.S. Government Securities	Year and Month	Time Deposits	Holdings of U.S. Government Securities
1945			**1948**		
June	$14.4	$ 9.6	June	$18.2	$12.0
December	15.4	10.7	December	18.4	11.5
1946			**1949**		
June	16.3	11.4	June	18.9	11.7
December	16.9	11.8	December	19.3	11.4
1947			**1950**		
June	17.4	12.1	June	19.9	11.6
December	17.7	12.0	December	20.0	10.9

Source: Federal Reserve Bulletin, November 1946–March 1951.

HOLDINGS OF U.S. GOVERNMENT SECURITIES[a] BY U.S. GOVERNMENT AGENCIES AND TRUST FUNDS AND FEDERAL RESERVE BANKS, BY CALL CLASS, OCTOBER 1945–DECEMBER 1950

(In Millions)

Year and Call Class	Jan.	Feb.	March	April	May	June	July	Aug.	Sept.	Oct.	Nov.	Dec.
1945												
Due or first becoming callable:												
Within 1 year	—	—	—	—	—	—	—	—	—	$22,313	$22,485	$23,476
1 to 5 years	—	—	—	—	—	—	—	—	—	1,398	1,392	1,100
5 to 10 years	—	—	—	—	—	—	—	—	—	1,018	1,010	997
10 to 15 years	—	—	—	—	—	—	—	—	—	544	543	617
15 to 20 years	—	—	—	—	—	—	—	—	—	2,329	2,330	2,253
Over 20 years	—	—	—	—	—	—	—	—	—	1,813	1,811	2,820
Various years[b]	—	—	—	—	—	—	—	—	—	7	7	7
Total										$29,422	$29,576	$31,271
1946												
Due or first becoming callable:												
Within 1 year	$22,490	$22,142	$21,815	$21,920	$22,130	$22,810	$22,688	$22,993	$23,098	$22,650	$23,042	$22,443
1 to 5 years	1,090	1,087	1,090	1,110	1,110	1,239	1,223	1,223	1,378	1,305	1,304	1,407
5 to 10 years	988	990	1,036	1,037	1,031	851	815	812	783	732	717	600
10 to 15 years	620	623	571	571	571	552	524	501	314	314	314	314
15 to 20 years	2,257	2,259	2,936	2,934	2,933	2,930	2,866	2,840	2,812	2,751	2,742	2,738
Over 20 years	2,825	2,825	2,162	2,165	2,166	2,160	2,143	2,133	2,144	2,140	2,136	2,139
Various years[b]	7	8	8	8	9	9	9	9	9	9	9	9
Total	$30,278	$29,934	$29,617	$29,746	$29,950	$30,551	$30,269	$30,510	$30,538	$29,902	$30,264	$29,652
1947												
Due or first becoming callable:												
Within 1 year	$23,077	$23,233	$21,919	$21,183	$21,423	$21,204	$20,851	$21,483	$21,785	$21,773	$21,577	$20,075
1 to 5 years	1,409	1,414	1,267	1,225	1,157	1,167	1,140	1,083	933	760	846	1,722
5 to 10 years	600	600	551	544	543	463	464	455	424	419	536	796
10 to 15 years	315	315	315	315	315	455	455	454	454	458	474	840
15 to 20 years	2,738	2,737	2,738	2,726	2,594	2,998	2,589	2,424	2,459	2,452	2,578	4,387
Over 20 years	2,145	2,146	2,146	2,131	1,976	993	838	751	660	657	737	—
Various years[b]	9	9	9	9	10	2	1	1	1	1	—	—
Total	$30,293	$30,454	$28,945	$28,135	$28,017	$27,281	$26,338	$26,652	$26,717	$26,520	$26,748	$27,820

Table 16 (continued)

Year and Call Class	Jan.	Feb.	March	April	May	June	July	Aug.	Sept.	Oct.	Nov.	Dec.
1948												
Due or first becoming callable:												
Within 1 year	$17,562	$15,852	$15,518	$14,404	$14,557	$15,347	$14,800	$14,024	$14,019	$11,998	$11,947	$12,653
1 to 5 years	2,169	2,343	2,402	2,892	3,046	2,954	2,970	3,093	3,634	4,007	3,985	3,485
5 to 10 years	864	873	870	848	814	861	855	852	843	827	802	747
10 to 15 years	1,266	1,552	1,651	1,651	1,650	1,575	1,700	1,904	2,226	2,522	2,631	3,158
15 to 20 years	5,378	5,904	6,010	6,021	6,015	6,031	6,448	7,146	8,173	9,189	9,332	8,767
Over 20 years	—	—	—	—	—	—	—	—	—	—	—	—
Various years[b]	c	c	c	c	c	c	c	c	c	c	c	c
Total	$27,240	$26,524	$26,451	$25,815	$26,082	$26,768	$26,772	$27,019	$28,894	$28,542	$28,698	$28,810
1949												
Due or first becoming callable:												
Within 1 year	$12,315	$12,980	$13,080	$13,156	$12,262	$12,360	$11,519	$10,532	$11,509	$10,796	$11,185	$12,114
1 to 5 years	3,231	3,164	3,032	2,600	2,426	2,332	2,332	2,332	1,844	1,844	1,844	2,108
5 to 10 years	569	561	490	476	392	1,116	1,116	1,115	1,115	1,115	1,112	1,956
10 to 15 years	3,021	2,924	2,645	2,458	2,274	1,600	1,601	1,602	1,603	1,603	1,603	1,205
15 to 20 years	8,493	8,285	8,054	7,966	7,844	7,307	7,307	7,311	7,316	7,312	7,306	6,828
Over 20 years	—	—	—	—	—	—	—	—	—	—	—	—
Various years[b]	—	—	c	—	—	—	—	—	—	—	—	c
Total	$27,628	$27,914	$27,302	$26,656	$25,198	$24,717	$23,876	$22,893	$23,387	$22,671	$23,050	$24,212
1950												
Due or first becoming callable:												
Within 1 year	$11,177	$11,194	$10,693	$10,700	$10,492	$9,836	$10,227	$14,384	$11,039	$10,698	$15,737	$16,084
1 to 5 years	2,116	2,272	3,114	3,545	3,680	5,443	5,402	1,968	6,348	5,951	1,109	1,474
5 to 10 years	1,940	1,827	1,574	1,575	1,575	1,571	1,441	1,310	1,379	1,397	1,364	1,394
10 to 15 years	1,179	1,147	2,177	2,175	2,171	2,171	2,148	2,145	2,233	2,288	2,284	2,278
15 to 20 years	6,772	6,676	5,420	5,182	4,834	4,660	4,902	3,854	3,937	4,266	4,507	4,912
Over 20 years	—	—	—	—	—	—	—	—	—	—	—	—
Various years[b]	—	—	—	—	—	—	—	—	c	c	c	c
Total	$23,184	$23,117	$22,977	$23,177	$22,752	$23,681	$23,310	$23,662	$24,938	$24,601	$25,000	$26,142

Source: *Treasury Bulletin*, January 1946–March 1951.
a. Interest-bearing public marketable securities, par values.
b. Federal Housing Administration debentures.

236

TABLE 17

HOLDINGS OF U.S. GOVERNMENT SECURITIES[a] BY U.S. GOVERNMENT AGENCIES AND TRUST FUNDS AND FEDERAL RESERVE BANKS, BY TYPE OF SECURITY, OCTOBER 1945–DECEMBER 1950

(In Millions)

Year and Type of Security	Jan.	Feb.	March	April	May	June	July	Aug.	Sept.	Oct.	Nov.	Dec.
1945												
Issued by U.S. government:												
Treasury bills	—	—	—	—	—	—	—	—	—	$13,193	$12,611	$12,836
Certificates	—	—	—	—	—	—	—	—	—	7,283	7,862	8,402
Treasury notes	—	—	—	—	—	—	—	—	—	2,000	2,173	2,128
Treasury bonds—bank-eligible	—	—	—	—	—	—	—	—	—	{6,903	{6,888	2,683
Treasury bonds—bank-restricted[b]	—	—	—	—	—	—	—	—	—			5,179
Postal savings and Panama Canal bonds	—	—	—	—	—	—	—	—	—	35	36	36
Guaranteed by U.S. government[c]	—	—	—	—	—	—	—	—	—	7	7	7
Total										$29,422	$29,576	$31,271
1946												
Issued by U.S. government:												
Treasury bills	$12,872	$13,052	$13,289	$13,669	$13,903	$14,469	$14,413	$14,746	$14,715	$14,601	$15,031	$14,747
Certificates	8,098	7,604	7,027	6,574	6,470	6,871	7,959	7,930	7,972	7,516	7,387	7,560
Treasury notes	1,413	1,380	1,472	1,672	1,751	1,757	603	603	676	729	849	361
Treasury bonds—bank-eligible	2,662	2,661	2,577	2,577	2,571	2,202	2,098	2,072	2,159	2,097	2,047	2,034
Treasury bonds—bank-restricted[b]	5,190	5,195	5,208	5,210	5,209	5,208	5,151	5,114	4,972	4,914	4,905	4,905
Postal savings and Panama Canal bonds	35	35	36	36	36	36	36	36	36	36	36	36
Guaranteed by U.S. government[c]	7	8	8	8	9	9	9	9	9	9	9	9
Total	$30,278	$29,934	$29,617	$29,746	$29,950	$30,551	$30,269	$30,510	$30,538	$29,902	$30,264	$29,652

TABLE 17 (continued)

Year and Type of Security	Jan.	Feb.	March	April	May	June	July	Aug.	Sept.	Oct.	Nov.	Dec.
1947												
Issued by U.S. government:												
Treasury bills	$15,661	$15,739	$15,105	$15,119	$14,984	$14,506	$13,903	$14,208	$14,055	$13,583	$12,560	$11,451
Certificates	7,280	7,268	6,486	5,737	6,094	6,328	6,594	6,929	7,161	7,128	7,286	6,827
Treasury notes	361	455	363	364	381	376	375	369	474	814	1,427	1,480
Treasury bonds—bank-eligible	2,033	2,032	2,030	1,976	1,848	1,790	1,733	1,660	1,597	1,572	1,852	3,363
Treasury bonds—bank-restricted[b]	4,913	4,914	4,914	4,893	4,665	4,243	3,695	3,448	3,393	3,387	3,586	4,662
Postal savings and Panama Canal bonds	36	36	36	36	36	36	36	36	36	36	36	37
Guaranteed by U.S. government[c]	9	9	9	9	10	2	1	1	1	—	—	—
Total	$30,293	$30,454	$28,945	$28,135	$28,017	$27,281	$26,338	$26,652	$26,717	$26,520	$26,748	$27,820
1948												
Issued by U.S. government:												
Treasury bills	$ 9,782	$ 9,292	$ 8,940	$ 8,001	$ 8,256	$ 8,592	$ 7,611	$ 7,076	$ 7,102	$ 5,195	$ 5,261	$ 5,557
Certificates	5,916	4,426	4,517	4,264	4,167	4,630	5,078	4,982	5,199	6,172	6,075	6,101
Treasury notes	1,546	1,738	1,887	1,964	1,959	1,968	1,953	1,808	1,954	871	803	798
Treasury bonds—bank-eligible	3,942	4,210	4,046	4,513	4,626	4,483	4,490	4,611	4,753	5,111	5,107	4,899
Treasury bonds—bank-restricted[b]	6,018	6,821	7,026	7,036	7,037	7,058	7,603	8,506	9,850	11,157	11,416	11,419
Postal savings and Panama Canal bonds	36	36	36	36	37	37	36	36	36	37	37	37
Guaranteed by U.S. government[c]	a	a	a	a	—	—	—	—	—	a	a	—
Total	$27,240	$26,524	$26,451	$25,815	$26,082	$26,768	$26,772	$27,019	$28,894	$28,542	$28,698	28,810
1949												
Issued by U.S. government:												
Treasury bills	$ 5,129	$ 5,421	$ 5,327	$ 4,959	$ 4,323	$ 4,410	$ 3,815	$ 3,545	$ 4,410	$ 3,756	$ 4,052	$ 4,840
Certificates	6,444	6,816	6,909	6,965	6,782	6,883	6,644	5,983	5,856	5,798	5,898	6,324
Treasury notes	444	407	433	438	412	406	398	348	339	339	332	577

Year and Type of Security	Jan.	Feb.	March	April	May	June	July	Aug.	Sept.	Oct.	Nov.	Dec.
Treasury bonds—bank-eligible	4,410	4,342	4,197	4,134	3,806	3,495	3,495	3,488	3,246	3,246	3,242	2,976
Treasury bonds—bank-restricted[b]	11,165	10,892	10,400	10,124	9,839	9,486	9,487	9,493	9,499	9,495	9,489	9,458
Postal savings and Panama Canal bonds	36	36	36	37	37	37	36	36	36	36	37	37
Guaranteed by U.S. government[c]	—	[d]	[d]	—	—	—	—	—	—	[d]	—	[d]
Total	$27,628	$27,914	$27,302	$26,656	$25,198	$24,717	$23,876	$22,893	$23,387	$22,671	$23,050	$24,212
1950												
Issued by U.S. government:												
Treasury bills	$ 3,811	$ 3,909	$ 3,991	$ 4,400	$ 4,084	$ 3,860	$ 4,151	$ 2,305	$ 1,569	$ 801	$ 1,121	$ 1,331
Certificates	6,433	6,351	5,885	5,780	5,887	5,364	2,796	4,853	4,976	70	718	2,334
Treasury notes	560	716	1,403	1,538	1,674	3,529	6,160	4,446	9,316	14,252	13,509	12,538
Treasury bonds—bank-eligible	2,969	2,904	2,775	2,773	2,771	2,771	2,766	4,955	1,727	1,722	1,683	1,552
Treasury bonds—bank-restricted[b]	9,376	9,201	8,887	8,649	8,298	8,121	7,400	7,066	7,314	7,719	7,933	8,351
Postal savings and Panama Canal bonds	36	36	36	37	37	37	36	36	36	36	37	37
Guaranteed by U.S. government[c]	—	—	—	—	—	—	—	—	[d]	[d]	[d]	[d]
Total	$23,184	$23,117	$22,977	$23,177	$22,752	$23,681	$23,310	$23,662	$24,938	$24,601	$25,000	$26,142

Source: Treasury Bulletin, January 1946–March 1951.

a. Interest-bearing public marketable securities, par values.
b. Issues that commercial banks may not acquire before a specified date.
c. Excludes guaranteed securities held by the Treasury.
d. Less than $500,000.

TABLE 18

HOLDINGS OF U.S. GOVERNMENT SECURITIES[a] BY COMMERCIAL BANKS, BY CALL CLASS, OCTOBER 1945–DECEMBER 1950

(In Millions)

Year and Call Class	Jan.	Feb.	March	April	May	June	July	Aug.	Sept.	Oct.	Nov.	Dec.
1945												
Due or first becoming callable:												
Within 1 year	—	—	—	—	—	—	—	—	—	$26,161	$26,496	$30,504
1 to 5 years	—	—	—	—	—	—	—	—	—	25,438	25,653	25,096
5 to 10 years	—	—	—	—	—	—	—	—	—	20,978	21,694	20,891
10 to 15 years	—	—	—	—	—	—	—	—	—	2,032	2,097	3,465
15 to 20 years	—	—	—	—	—	—	—	—	—	1,034	1,045	67
Over 20 years	—	—	—	—	—	—	—	—	—	1,471	1,530	2,354
Various years[b]	—	—	—	—	—	—	—	—	—	12	13	11
Total										$77,127	$78,528	$82,390
1946												
Due or first becoming callable:												
Within 1 year	$31,632	$31,876	$29,319	$28,564	$26,779	$23,443	$21,996	$20,368	$21,353	$20,478	$18,605	$16,710
1 to 5 years	25,196	25,339	24,148	24,190	24,133	25,223	25,270	25,244	28,222	27,854	27,801	28,388
5 to 10 years	21,359	21,394	22,487	22,795	22,952	21,820	21,977	22,122	17,516	17,719	17,795	16,535
10 to 15 years	3,533	3,566	2,876	2,888	2,926	2,982	3,070	3,106	2,118	2,128	2,129	2,134
15 to 20 years	66	66	138	137	142	142	141	140	138	135	134	142
Over 20 years	2,442	2,474	2,412	2,421	2,466	2,479	2,517	2,519	2,546	2,539	2,571	2,563
Various years[b]	12	12	13	10	13	13	12	12	12	11	12	12
Total	$84,240	$84,727	$81,393	$81,006	$79,411	$76,103	$74,982	$73,511	$71,905	$70,864	$69,047	$66,484
1947												
Due or first becoming callable:												
Within 1 year	$16,085	$15,096	$15,729	$15,791	$14,911	$16,237	$16,314	$15,529	$15,836	$17,682	$17,227	$16,816
1 to 5 years	28,252	28,109	26,924	26,911	26,792	29,824	29,876	29,886	29,447	27,197	27,182	33,307
5 to 10 years	16,743	16,809	16,291	16,361	16,416	11,477	11,606	11,715	11,913	12,038	12,069	6,019
10 to 15 years	2,137	2,152	2,159	2,163	2,172	2,200	2,236	2,249	2,254	2,291	2,291	2,150
15 to 20 years	132	130	129	135	136	208	217	205	2,196	2,200	2,206	2,620
Over 20 years	2,584	2,584	2,562	2,540	2,606	2,548	2,594	2,640	661	661	653	—
Various years[b]	14	15	13	12	12	12	10	11	12	10	10	13

Year and Call Class	Jan.	Feb.	March	April	May	June	July	Aug.	Sept.	Oct.	Nov.	Dec.
1948												
Due or first becoming callable:												
Within 1 year	$19,242	$18,207	$16,328	$17,541	$17,010	$16,793	$16,834	$16,747	$13,859	$14,898	$14,395	$17,403
1 to 5 years	31,340	31,039	30,934	30,590	30,491	30,467	30,590	30,461	31,352	30,954	30,951	27,941
5 to 10 years	5,980	5,996	5,971	6,023	6,100	6,167	6,187	6,195	6,193	6,184	6,196	6,233
10 to 15 years	2,121	2,072	2,058	2,060	2,052	1,383	1,383	1,364	1,349	1,325	1,330	1,334
15 to 20 years	2,444	2,373	2,342	2,338	2,354	2,350	2,339	2,276	2,148	2,073	2,064	2,048
Over 20 years												
Various years[b]	9	11	11	11	9	9	5	5	6	6	5	4
Total	$61,136	$59,698	$57,643	$58,563	$58,017	$57,170	$57,337	$57,048	$54,907	$55,440	$54,942	$54,962
1949												
Due or first becoming callable:												
Within 1 year	$17,091	$16,464	$16,152	$18,985	$19,353	$19,355	$20,782[c]	$22,307	$26,117	$26,855	$26,219	$24,060
1 to 5 years	28,123	28,193	26,812	25,216	25,506	26,209	26,414	26,518	22,636	22,648	22,759	24,907
5 to 10 years	6,461	6,504	6,658	6,738	6,917	6,500	6,650	6,670	6,693	6,754	6,798	6,995
10 to 15 years	1,351	1,382	1,406	1,423	1,420	1,348	1,417	1,420	1,448	1,449	1,453	1,294
15 to 20 years	2,174	2,191	2,216	2,233	2,308	2,438	2,541	2,575	2,576	2,595	2,600	2,595
Over 20 years												
Various years[b]	4	5	4	4	4	4	5	6	5	5	5	5
Total	$55,205	$54,739	$53,247	$54,509	$55,507	$55,853	$57,809	$59,496	$59,476	$60,305	$59,834	$59,856
1950												
Due or first becoming callable:												
Within 1 year	$24,403	$22,508	$18,406	$16,074	$16,558	$16,068	$16,546	$16,232	$19,515	$20,376	$19,878	$20,088
1 to 5 years	25,115	26,014	30,312	32,917	32,938	33,127	31,595	31,136	25,907	24,703	24,426	24,534
5 to 10 years	7,047	7,119	5,473	5,499	5,536	5,675	5,750	5,924	6,062	6,069	6,086	7,329
10 to 15 years	1,309	1,312	1,377	1,388	1,397	1,409	1,415	1,418	1,420	1,424	1,424	181
15 to 20 years	2,625	2,651	2,625	2,663	2,682	2,685	2,688	2,736	2,754	2,765	2,746	2,753
Over 20 years												
Various years[b]	5	5	5	7	7	7	6	7	7	8	8	9
Total	$60,504	$59,610	$58,198	$58,548	$59,118	$58,972	$58,000	$57,454	$55,665	$55,346	$54,569	$54,893

Source: Treasury Bulletin, January 1946–March 1951.
a. Interest-bearing public marketable securities, par values.
b. Federal Housing Administration debentures.
c. Beginning with July 1949, stock savings banks were included with commercial banks.

241

TABLE 19

HOLDINGS OF U.S. GOVERNMENT SECURITIES[a] BY COMMERCIAL BANKS, BY TYPE OF SECURITY, OCTOBER 1945–DECEMBER 1950

(In Millions)

Year and Type of Security	Jan.	Feb.	March	April	May	June	July	Aug.	Sept.	Oct.	Nov.	Dec.
1945												
Issued by U.S. government:												
Treasury bills	—	—	—	—	—	—	—	—	—	$ 1,977	$ 2,305	$ 2,476
Certificates	—	—	—	—	—	—	—	—	—	16,195	16,333	18,065
Treasury notes	—	—	—	—	—	—	—	—	—	15,795	15,640	15,664
Treasury bonds—bank-eligible	—	—	—	—	—	—	—	—	—	43,132	44,221	44,626
Treasury bonds—bank-restricted[b]	—	—	—	—	—	—	—	—	—			1,532
Postal savings and Panama Canal bonds	—	—	—	—	—	—	—	—	—	16	16	16
Guaranteed by U.S. government[c]	—	—	—	—	—	—	—	—	—	12	13	11
Total										$77,127	$78,528	$82,390
1946												
Issued by U.S. government:												
Treasury bills	$ 2,387	$ 2,395	$ 1,509	$ 1,874	$ 1,715	$ 1,141	$ 1,224	$ 924	$ 938	$ 1,125	$ 847	$ 1,187
Certificates	21,352	21,687	20,589	19,566	18,126	16,651	17,588	16,316	14,505	13,318	11,807	11,196
Treasury notes	13,616	13,589	12,259	12,036	11,793	11,360	8,904	8,810	8,674	8,436	8,323	6,090
Treasury bonds—bank-eligible	45,318	45,510	45,473	45,984	46,073	45,260	45,589	45,782	46,399	46,616	46,719	46,647
Treasury bonds—bank-restricted[b]	1,540	1,519	1,537	1,522	1,677	1,663	1,651	1,654	1,363	1,343	1,323	1,339
Postal savings and Panama Canal bonds	15	14	14	14	15	15	15	14	15	15	15	13
Guaranteed by U.S. government[c]	12	12	13	10	13	13	12	12	12	11	12	12
Total	$84,240	$84,727	$81,393	$81,006	$79,411	$76,103	$74,982	$73,511	$71,905	$70,864	$69,047	$66,484

Year and Type of Security	Jan.	Feb.	March	April	May	June	July	Aug.	Sept.	Oct.	Nov.	Dec.
1947												
Issued by U.S. government:												
Treasury bills	$ 519	$ 538	$ 680	$ 928	$ 590	$ 787	$ 1,060	$ 684	$ 767	$ 1,066	$ 1,404	$ 2,052
Certificates	11,176	10,196	9,974	9,820	9,322	8,520	8,269	7,880	7,745	7,678	7,417	6,530
Treasury notes	6,141	6,066	5,105	5,033	4,913	4,839	4,826	4,829	4,748	4,437	3,955	5,315
Treasury bonds—bank-eligible	46,777	46,768	46,744	46,841	46,920	47,068	47,400	47,559	47,785	47,571	47,566	45,807
Treasury bonds—bank-restricted[b]	1,305	1,297	1,278	1,266	1,274	1,267	1,273	1,259	1,248	1,303	1,273	1,195
Postal savings and Panama Canal bonds	14	15	13	13	14	13	15	14	13	13	12	15
Guaranteed by U.S. government[e]	14	15	13	12	12	12	10	11	12	10	10	13
Total	$65,946	$64,895	$63,807	$63,913	$63,044	$62,506	$62,852	$62,235	$62,319	$62,078	$61,637	$60,925
1948												
Issued by U.S. government:												
Treasury bills	$ 3,087	$ 2,824	$ 1,978	$ 3,013	$ 2,518	$ 2,342	$ 2,783	$ 2,836	$ 2,189	$ 3,373	$ 2,877	$ 2,788
Certificates	6,704	6,299	7,119	7,204	7,260	8,532	8,106	7,898	7,453	8,693	8,690	9,045
Treasury notes	5,154	4,926	4,537	4,615	4,511	4,519	4,558	4,614	4,329	2,958	2,964	3,093
Treasury bonds—bank-eligible	45,095	44,642	43,031	42,766	42,775	40,788	40,924	40,780	40,080	39,606	39,561	39,252
Treasury bonds—bank-restricted[b]	1,073	983	955	941	930	965	946	903	835	791	831	766
Postal savings and Panama Canal bonds	14	14	13	13	14	15	15	13	14	13	13	13
Guaranteed by U.S. government[e]	9	11	11	11	9	9	5	5	6	6	5	4
Total	$61,136	$59,698	$57,643	$58,563	$58,017	$57,170	$57,337	$57,048	$54,907	$55,440	$54,942	$54,962
1949												
Issued by U.S. government:												
Treasury bills	$ 2,976	$ 2,794	$ 1,774	$ 2,608	$ 2,775	$ 2,812	$ 3,617	$ 4,219	$ 3,730	$ 4,087	$ 3,471	$ 3,514
Certificates	9,822	9,377	8,817	8,850	9,058	9,530	10,023	10,857	11,965	12,181	12,141	11,520
Treasury notes	1,937	1,925	1,799	1,801	1,812	1,798	1,841	1,894	1,909	1,937	1,948	5,569

243

TABLE 19 (continued)

Year and Type of Security	Jan.	Feb.	March	April	May	June	July	Aug.	Sept.	Oct.	Nov.	Dec.
Treasury bonds—bank-eligible	39,704	39,862	40,061	40,458	41,074	40,906	41,383	41,583	40,924	41,158	41,337	38,331
Treasury bonds—bank-restricted[b]	748	762	780	776	772	791	927	922	928	924	920	904
Postal savings and Panama Canal bonds	13	13	12	13	13	14	14	13	15	13	14	13
Guaranteed by U.S. government[c]	4	5	4	4	4	4	5	6	5	5	5	5
Total	$55,205	$54,739	$53,247	$54,509	$55,507	$55,853	$57,809	$59,496	$59,476	$60,305	$59,834	$59,856
1950												
Issued by U.S. government:												
Treasury bills	$ 4,122	$ 3,455	$ 2,409	$ 2,732	$ 3,174	$ 3,703	$ 2,992	$ 3,641	$ 3,774	$ 3,939	$ 3,374	$ 3,888
Certificates	11,287	9,935	8,128	7,712	7,723	5,354	3,986	2,937	2,438	1,970	2,017	1,544
Treasury notes	5,669	6,648	9,472	9,800	9,736	11,204	12,283	13,479	13,982	14,041	13,982	15,833
Treasury bonds—bank-eligible	38,495	38,644	37,260	37,372	37,543	37,746	37,729	36,409	34,459	34,380	34,205	32,637
Treasury bonds—bank-restricted[b]	913	905	912	913	918	945	994	970	995	996	971	970
Postal savings and Panama Canal bonds	13	16	11	13	16	13	11	10	11	12	12	13
Guaranteed by U.S. government[c]	5	5	5	7	7	7	6	7	7	8	8	9
Total	$60,504	$59,610	$58,198	$58,548	$59,118	$58,972	$58,000	$57,454	$55,665	$55,346	$54,569	$54,893

Source: *Treasury Bulletin*, January 1946–March 1951.

a. Interest-bearing public marketable securities, par values.
b. Issues that commercial banks may not acquire before a specified date.
c. Excludes guaranteed securities held by the Treasury.

HOLDINGS OF U.S. GOVERNMENT SECURITIES[a] BY FIRE, CASUALTY AND MARINE INSURANCE COMPANIES, BY CALL CLASS, OCTOBER 1945–DECEMBER 1950

(In Millions)

Year and Call Class	Jan.	Feb.	March	April	May	June	July	Aug.	Sept.	Oct.	Nov.	Dec.
1945												
Due or first becoming callable:												
Within 1 year	—	—	—	—	—	—	—	—	—	$ 343	$ 303	$ 291
1 to 5 years	—	—	—	—	—	—	—	—	—	568	563	530
5 to 10 years	—	—	—	—	—	—	—	—	—	770	739	705
10 to 15 years	—	—	—	—	—	—	—	—	—	484	487	746
15 to 20 years	—	—	—	—	—	—	—	—	—	320	313	204
Over 20 years	—	—	—	—	—	—	—	—	—	126	132	284
Various years[b]	—	—	—	—	—	—	—	—	—	1	1	1
Total										$2,611	$2,538	$2,761
1946												
Due or first becoming callable:												
Within 1 year	$ 288	$ 263	$ 282	$ 280	$ 276	$ 242	$ 239	$ 250	$ 311	$ 348	$ 329	$ 337
1 to 5 years	537	541	498	496	495	564	543	547	652	637	645	677
5 to 10 years	685	680	684	673	669	606	610	607	634	626	624	594
10 to 15 years	762	782	785	775	777	794	814	844	657	660	663	667
15 to 20 years	204	219	244	264	263	263	271	255	256	259	265	286
Over 20 years	327	339	318	324	336	345	348	355	358	370	375	378
Various years[b]	1	1	1	1	c	c	c	1	1	1	1	1
Total	$2,805	$2,824	$2,813	$2,813	$2,816	$2,815	$2,824	$2,858	$2,869	$2,901	$2,902	$2,939
1947												
Due or first becoming callable:												
Within 1 year	$ 331	$ 322	$ 343	$ 348	$ 349	$ 383	$ 390	$ 403	$ 413	$ 498	$ 520	$ 508
1 to 5 years	681	674	674	675	679	764	764	766	742	663	662	892
5 to 10 years	594	600	586	589	581	467	469	473	472	464	458	307
10 to 15 years	679	704	710	714	723	790	809	817	805	800	799	789
15 to 20 years	289	295	290	291	305	399	417	423	499	576	589	916
Over 20 years	386	399	401	407	426	301	320	325	318	326	330	—
Various years[b]	1	1	1	1	c	1	1	1	1	1	2	1
Total	$2,961	$2,995	$3,005	$3,026	$3,064	$3,104	$3,170	$3,208	$3,250	$3,327	$3,360	$3,413

TABLE 20 (continued)

Year and Call Class	Jan.	Feb.	March	April	May	June	July	Aug.	Sept.	Oct.	Nov.	Dec.
1948												
Due or first becoming callable:												
Within 1 year	$ 663	$ 714	$ 705	$ 718	$ 713	$ 729	$ 691	$ 700	$ 706	$ 730	$ 744	$ 835
1 to 5 years	863	874	895	880	893	925	933	962	1,049	1,103	1,125	1,042
5 to 10 years	306	322	331	342	345	381	383	395	402	440	459	478
10 to 15 years	757	736	739	742	751	693	694	686	654	617	606	697
15 to 20 years	877	832	824	827	832	837	840	829	790	745	733	649
Over 20 years	—	—	—	—	—	—	—	—	—	—	—	—
Various years[b]	1	1	1	1	1	1	c	c	c	c	c	c
Total	$3,468	$3,478	$3,495	$3,509	$3,535	$3,567	$3,541	$3,571	$3,601	$3,635	$3,668	$3,701
1949												
Due or first becoming callable:												
Within 1 year	$ 830	$ 806	$ 816	$ 919	$ 906	$ 899	$ 904	$ 876	$ 999	$ 991	$ 996	$ 878
1 to 5 years	1,074	1,078	1,025	913	920	942	936	941	774	773	767	829
5 to 10 years	470	462	455	445	436	748	759	768	776	781	768	1,005
10 to 15 years	725	756	775	811	840	618	627	625	631	644	651	564
15 to 20 years	665	680	718	729	744	678	686	697	713	737	754	634
Over 20 years	—	—	—	—	—	—	—	—	—	—	—	—
Various years[b]	c	c	c	c	c	c	c	c	c	c	c	c
Total	$3,763	$3,781	$3,789	$3,816	$3,847	$3,884	$3,913	$3,906	$3,893	$3,926	$3,936	$3,910
1950												
Due or first becoming callable:												
Within 1 year	$ 888	$ 840	$ 747	$ 640	$ 621	$ 614	$ 633	$ 631	$ 769	$ 803	$ 789	$ 799
1 to 5 years	830	883	1,063	1,117	1,121	1,112	1,037	1,012	825	778	765	744
5 to 10 years	987	993	897	912	913	926	955	989	991	1,001	1,001	1,042
10 to 15 years	580	591	722	728	743	758	761	782	789	793	863	842
15 to 20 years	669	676	570	589	624	636	679	705	716	727	694	689
Over 20 years	—	—	—	—	—	—	—	—	—	—	—	—
Various years[b]	c	c	c	c	c	c	c	c	c	c	c	c
Total	$3,953	$3,984	$3,999	$3,986	$4,022	$4,046	$4,065	$4,119	$4,090	$4,101	$4,111	$4,116

Source: *Treasury Bulletin*, January 1946–March 1951
a. Interest-bearing public marketable securities, par values.
b. Federal Housing Administration debentures.
c. Less than $500,000.

TABLE 21

HOLDINGS OF U.S. GOVERNMENT SECURITIES[a] BY FIRE, CASUALTY AND MARINE INSURANCE COMPANIES, BY TYPE OF SECURITY, OCTOBER 1945–DECEMBER 1950

(In Millions)

Year and Type of Security	Jan.	Feb.	March	April	May	June	July	Aug.	Sept.	Oct.	Nov.	Dec.
1945												
Issued by U.S. government:												
Treasury bills										—	—	$ 1
Certificates										$ 230	$ 181	176
Treasury notes										200	215	195
Treasury bonds—bank-eligible[b]										} 2,180	} 2,140	1,450
Treasury bonds—bank-restricted[b]												937
Postal savings and Panama Canal bonds										1	1	1
Guaranteed by U.S. government[c]										1	1	1
Total										$2,611	$2,536	$2,761
1946												
Issued by U.S. government:												
Treasury bills	—	—	$ 4	—	—	—	—	—	—	—	—	—
Certificates	$ 180	$ 170[d]	171	$ 174[d]	$ 171[d]	$ 164[d]	$ 175	$ 187[d]	$ 185	$ 195	$ 182[d]	$ 196
Treasury notes	190	183	173	173	172	180	164	169	173	177	177	156
Treasury bonds—bank-eligible[b]	1,432	1,417	1,386	1,362	1,347	1,301	1,263	1,271	1,416	1,417	1,404	1,399
Treasury bonds—bank-restricted[b]	1,001	1,053	1,077	1,103	1,125	1,170	1,220	1,230	1,094	1,111	1,138	1,186
Postal savings and Panama Canal bonds	a	a	d	d	1	a	2	a	1	1	a	a
Guaranteed by U.S. government[e]	1	1	1	1	a	a	a	a	1	1	1	1
Total	$2,805	$2,824	$2,813	$2,813	$2,816	$2,815	$2,824	$2,858	$2,869	$2,901	$2,902	$2,939

Table 21 (continued)

Year and Type of Security	Jan.	Feb.	March	April	May	June	July	Aug.	Sept.	Oct.	Nov.	Dec.
1947												
Issued by U.S. government:												
Treasury bills	$ 1	—	$ 5	[a]	—	$ 1	—	—	[a]	$ 10	$ 10	$ 16
Certificates	199	$ 194	202	$ 211	$ 206	198	$ 202	$ 210	$ 210	217	227	212
Treasury notes	149	149	124	118	123	128	130	131	127	153	161	221
Treasury bonds—bank-eligible	1,400	1,397	1,423	1,424	1,416	1,425	1,430	1,440	1,432	1,387	1,385	1,398
Treasury bonds—bank-restricted[b]	1,211	1,254	1,250	1,271	1,316	1,350	1,406	1,425	1,479	1,559	1,574	1,565
Postal savings and Panama Canal bonds	[a]	[a]	[a]	[a]	1	1	1	1	[a]	[a]	1	[a]
Guaranteed by U.S. government[c]	1	1	1	1	1	1	1	1	1	1	2	1
Total	$2,961	$2,995	$3,005	$3,026	$3,064	$3,104	$3,170	$3,208	$3,250	$3,327	$3,360	$3,413
1948												
Issued by U.S. government:												
Treasury bills	$ 31	$ 63	$ 68	$ 58	$ 46	$ 55	$ 43	$ 24	$ 50	$ 58	$ 54	$ 42
Certificates	278	299	341	374	386	431	407	413	450	553	570	586
Treasury notes	233	232	219	206	209	209	207	229	231	155	159	158
Treasury bonds—bank-eligible	1,446	1,475	1,469	1,472	1,481	1,450	1,460	1,513	1,544	1,630	1,667	1,694
Treasury bonds—bank-restricted[b]	1,479	1,407	1,397	1,397	1,410	1,421	1,423	1,391	1,324	1,237	1,217	1,222
Postal savings and Panama Canal bonds	[a]	1	1	[a]	[a]	[a]	[a]	1	1	2	1	[a]
Guaranteed by U.S. government[c]	1	1	1	1	1	1	[a]	[a]	[a]	[a]	[a]	[a]
Total	$3,468	$3,478	$3,495	$3,509	$3,535	$3,567	$3,541	$3,571	$3,601	$3,635	$3,668	$3,701
1949												
Issued by U.S. government:												
Treasury bills	$ 45	$ 44	$ 52	$ 47	$ 36	$ 38	$ 37	$ 36	$ 47	$ 54	$ 54	$ 43
Certificates	632	598	553	553	551	551	561	543	532	507	516	497
Treasury notes	101	105	104	103	103	103	100	99	98	94	91	207

Year and Type of Security	Jan.	Feb.	March	April	May	June	July	Aug.	Sept.	Oct.	Nov.	Dec.
Treasury bonds—bank-eligible	1,731	1,733	1,701	1,689	1,686	1,656	1,648	1,635	1,586	1,582	1,559	1,415
Treasury bonds—bank-restricted[b]	1,253	1,300	1,378	1,424	1,468	1,534	1,564	1,591	1,629	1,688	1,715	1,747
Postal savings and Panama Canal bonds	1	1	1	1	1	1	2	1	1	1	1	1
Guaranteed by U.S. government[c]	d	d	d	d	d	d	d	d	d	d	d	d
Total	$3,763	$3,781	$3,789	$3,816	$3,847	$3,884	$3,913	$3,906	$3,893	$3,926	$3,936	$3,910
1950												
Issued by U.S. government:												
Treasury bills	$ 54	$ 53	$ 69	$ 44	$ 46	$ 64	$ 51	$ 61	$ 79	$ 94	$ 92	$ 83
Certificates	496	463	395	377	350	274	215	181	148	113	97	52
Treasury notes	203	235	301	302	294	337	387	446	479	480	465	542
Treasury bonds—bank-eligible	1,394	1,402	1,366	1,340	1,347	1,334	1,287	1,222	1,147	1,142	1,142	1,098
Treasury bonds—bank-restricted[b]	1,805	1,830	1,867	1,921	1,983	2,035	2,122	2,208	2,236	2,271	2,314	2,339
Postal savings and Panama Canal bonds	1	1	1	1	1	1	1	1	1	1	2	1
Guaranteed by U.S. government[c]	d	d	d	d	d	d	d	d	d	d	d	d
Total	$3,953	$3,984	$3,999	$3,986	$4,022	$4,046	$4,065	$4,119	$4,090	$4,101	$4,111	$4,116

Source: *Treasury Bulletin,* January 1946–March 1951.

a. Interest-bearing public marketable securities, par values.
b. Issues that commercial banks may not acquire before a specified date.
c. Excludes guaranteed securities held by the Treasury.
d. Less than $500,000.

Table 22

Holdings of U.S. Government Securities[a] by Life Insurance Companies, by Call Class, October 1945–December 1950

(In Millions)

Year and Call Class	Jan.	Feb.	March	April	May	June	July	Aug.	Sept.	Oct.	Nov.	Dec.
1945												
Due or first becoming callable:												
Within 1 year	—	—	—	—	—	—	—	—	—	$ 463	$ 469	$ 306
1 to 5 years	—	—	—	—	—	—	—	—	—	1,327	1,311	1,211
5 to 10 years	—	—	—	—	—	—	—	—	—	2,329	2,251	2,194
10 to 15 years	—	—	—	—	—	—	—	—	—	1,737	1,729	2,042
15 to 20 years	—	—	—	—	—	—	—	—	—	8,073	8,071	8,005
Over 20 years	—	—	—	—	—	—	—	—	—	4,948	4,995	6,650
Various years[b]	—	—	—	—	—	—	—	—	—	13	13	13
Total										$18,890	$18,839	$20,422
1946												
Due or first becoming callable:												
Within 1 year	$ 307	$ 457	$ 727	$ 704	$ 796	$ 830	$ 844	$ 839	$ 869	$ 790	$ 770	$ 755
1 to 5 years	1,209	1,208	967	948	940	941	938	940	1,470	1,464	1,377	1,425
5 to 10 years	2,111	2,059	2,412	2,321	2,275	2,214	2,162	2,097	2,330	2,292	2,272	2,233
10 to 15 years	2,086	2,019	1,647	1,761	1,811	1,856	1,876	1,882	1,043	1,044	1,043	1,056
15 to 20 years	8,020	8,021	9,620	9,623	9,641	9,635	9,706	9,680	9,676	9,691	9,698	9,701
Over 20 years	7,208	7,294	5,809	5,879	5,938	5,981	6,031	6,072	6,159	6,188	6,208	6,224
Various years[b]	12	12	12	12	12	13	13	13	13	13	13	13
Total	$20,953	$21,071	$21,195	$21,247	$21,413	$21,470	$21,569	$21,523	$21,560	$21,481	$21,381	$21,407
1947												
Due or first becoming callable:												
Within 1 year	$ 729	$ 712	$ 419	$ 409	$ 407	$ 403	$ 336	$ 290	$ 165	$ 151	$ 131	$ 231
1 to 5 years	1,428	1,457	1,485	1,480	1,473	1,908	1,898	1,899	1,871	1,805	1,734	2,157
5 to 10 years	2,206	2,202	2,153	2,180	2,165	1,535	1,464	1,392	1,292	1,218	1,195	573
10 to 15 years	1,047	1,040	1,036	1,018	1,011	2,079	2,040	2,025	2,034	2,010	1,999	1,954
15 to 20 years	9,720	9,713	9,711	9,736	9,751	11,869	11,931	11,951	12,120	12,059	12,021	14,553
Over 20 years	6,235	6,242	6,239	6,235	6,235	3,058	3,069	3,058	2,865	2,860	2,819	
Various years[b]	14	14	14	14	14	14	13	13	13	13	13	13
Total	$21,378	$21,379	$21,056	$21,071	$21,056	$20,865	$20,751	$20,629	$20,360	$20,118	$19,912	$19,482

Year and Call Class	Jan.	Feb.	March	April	May	June	July	Aug.	Sept.	Oct.	Nov.	Dec.
1948												
Due or first becoming callable:												
Within 1 year	$ 467	$ 400	$ 318	$ 232	$ 167	$ 134	$ 165	$ 164	$ 416	$ 404	$ 341	$ 250
1 to 5 years	2,078	2,033	1,982	1,955	1,888	1,865	1,797	1,746	1,637	1,617	1,549	1,459
5 to 10 years	536	535	536	535	534	530	523	520	520	519	518	519
10 to 15 years	1,895	1,867	1,851	1,842	1,835	1,817	1,801	1,741	1,682	1,653	1,633	2,770
15 to 20 years	14,201	14,124	14,116	13,964	13,934	13,782	13,474	13,145	12,780	12,410	12,320	11,114
Over 20 years												
Various years[b]	12	12	12	12	12	10	6	6	6	6	6	6
Total	$19,189	$18,971	$18,815	$18,540	$18,369	$18,138	$17,765	$17,323	$17,041	$16,609	$16,367	$16,118
1949												
Due or first becoming callable:												
Within 1 year	$ 247	$ 221	$ 273	$ 234	$ 176	$ 151	$ 91	$ 98	$ 266	$ 223	$ 183	$ 295
1 to 5 years	1,448	1,441	1,292	1,223	1,209	1,182	1,168	1,089	858	858	822	812
5 to 10 years	520	519	519	513	511	984	983	985	973	949	941	1,224
10 to 15 years	2,770	2,767	2,770	2,774	2,769	3,744	3,730	3,719	3,743	3,734	3,743	4,776
15 to 20 years	11,065	11,041	10,993	10,888	10,744	9,139	8,995	8,936	8,894	8,861	8,837	7,511
Over 20 years												
Various years[b]	6	6	6	6	6	6	6	6	6	6	7	7
Total	$16,056	$15,995	$15,852	$15,637	$15,415	$15,206	$14,973	$14,834	$14,741	$14,632	$14,533	$14,625
1950												
Due or first becoming callable:												
Within 1 year	$ 267	$ 270	$ 246	$ 273	$ 259	$ 218	$ 235	$ 223	$ 399	$ 343	$ 436	$ 655
1 to 5 years	791	758	772	766	654	619	603	537	421	404	404	398
5 to 10 years	1,224	1,231	1,233	1,224	1,216	1,129	1,072	1,006	925	913	905	906
10 to 15 years	4,789	4,794	6,885	6,840	6,800	6,761	6,732	6,631	6,526	6,390	6,187	5,947
15 to 20 years	7,514	7,501	5,391	5,370	5,350	5,353	5,416	5,426	5,365	5,220	5,031	4,832
Over 20 years												
Various years[b]	5	6	6	6	6	6	5	6	9	9	9	9
Total	$14,590	$14,560	$14,532	$14,479	$14,285	$14,086	$14,062	$13,829	$13,644	$13,279	$12,971	$12,746

Source: *Treasury Bulletin*, January 1946–March 1951.

a. Interest-bearing public marketable securities, par values.
b. Federal Housing Administration debentures.

TABLE 23

HOLDINGS OF U.S. GOVERNMENT SECURITIES[a] BY LIFE INSURANCE COMPANIES, BY TYPE OF SECURITY, OCTOBER 1945–DECEMBER 1950

(In Millions)

Year and Type of Security	Jan.	Feb.	March	April	May	June	July	Aug.	Sept.	Oct.	Nov.	Dec.
1945												
Issued by U.S. government:												
Treasury bills	—	—	—	—	—	—	—	—	—		$ 1	[a]
Certificates	—	—	—	—	—	—	—	—	—	$ 323	380	$ 185
Treasury notes	—	—	—	—	—	—	—	—	—	391	392	381
Treasury bonds—bank-eligible	—	—	—	—	—	—	—	—	—	} 18,163	} 18,053	4,081
Treasury bonds—bank-restricted[b]	—	—	—	—	—	—	—	—	—			15,762
Postal savings and Panama Canal bonds	—	—	—	—	—	—	—	—	—	[a]	[a]	[a]
Guaranteed by U.S. government[c]	—	—	—	—	—	—	—	—	—	13	13	13
Total										$18,890	$18,839	$20,422
1946												
Issued by U.S. government:												
Treasury bills	$ —	$ —	$ 2	$ —	$ 1	$ 1	[a]	[a]	[a]			$ 10
Certificates	210	361	402	375	408	412	428	423	420	$ 326	$ 296	294
Treasury notes	356	356	347	354	412	443	440	440	456	459	471	447
Treasury bonds—bank-eligible	3,929	3,834	3,777	3,661	3,632	3,532	3,468	3,377	4,129	4,091	3,971	3,979
Treasury bonds—bank-restricted[b]	16,445	16,509	16,655	16,846	16,948	17,070	17,220	17,269	16,543	16,592	16,630	16,662
Postal savings and Panama Canal bonds	1	[a]	[a]	[a]	[a]	[a]	1	[a]	[a]	1	1	1
Guaranteed by U.S. government[c]	12	12	12	12	12	13	13	13	13	13	13	13
Total	$20,953	$21,071	$21,195	$21,247	$21,413	$21,470	$21,569	$21,523	$21,560	$21,481	$21,381	$21,407

Year and Type of Security	Jan.	Feb.	March	April	May	June	July	Aug.	Sept.	Oct.	Nov.	Dec.
1947												
Issued by U.S. government:												
Treasury bills	—	—	1	—	—	—	1	4	3	16	46	138
Certificates	$ 278	$ 260	$ 247	$ 236	$ 233	$ 164	$ 120	$ 84	$ 83	$ 82	$ 48	$ 57
Treasury notes	447	449	155	158	159	157	131	124	8	10	12	24
Treasury bonds—bank-eligible	3,951	3,976	3,964	3,982	3,936	3,777	3,661	3,569	3,425	3,251	3,134	2,825
Treasury bonds—bank-restricted[b]	16,687	16,681	16,674	16,681	16,714	16,753	16,824	16,835	16,828	16,746	16,658	16,425
Postal savings and Panama Canal bonds	[d]	[d]	[d]	[d]	[d]	[d]	1	[d]	[d]	[d]	[d]	[d]
Guaranteed by U.S. government[c]	14	14	14	14	14	14	13	13	13	13	13	13
Total	$21,378	$21,379	$21,056	$21,071	$21,056	$20,865	$20,751	$20,629	$20,360	$20,118	$19,912	$19,482
1948												
Issued by U.S. government:												
Treasury bills	$ 326	$ 278	$ 205	$ 142	$ 87	$ 57	$ 99	$ 34	$ 224	$ 222	$ 169	$ 42
Certificates	73	66	69	57	55	48	36	89	122	128	123	86
Treasury notes	38	28	25	16	14	14	14	24	31	14	14	8
Treasury bonds—bank-eligible	2,723	2,672	2,612	2,582	2,505	2,483	2,415	2,363	2,276	2,257	2,182	2,174
Treasury bonds—bank-restricted[b]	16,017	15,915	15,891	15,731	15,696	15,526	15,194	14,807	14,382	13,981	13,874	13,802
Postal savings and Panama Canal bonds	[d]	[d]	[d]	[d]	[d]	[d]	1	[d]	[d]	[d]	[d]	[d]
Guaranteed by U.S. government[c]	12	12	12	12	12	10	6	6	6	6	6	6
Total	$19,189	$18,971	$18,815	$18,540	$18,369	$18,138	$17,765	$17,323	$17,041	$16,609	$16,367	$16,118

TABLE 23 (continued)

Year and Type of Security	Jan.	Feb.	March	April	May	June	July	Aug.	Sept.	Oct.	Nov.	Dec.
1949												
Issued by U.S. government:												
Treasury bills	$ 27	$ 15	$ 30	$ 34	$ 9	$ 22	$ 5	$ 4	$ 4	$ 5	$ 4	$ 27
Certificates	105	92	63	55	50	51	37	46	65	65	69	137
Treasury notes	2	2	1	1	1	1	1	d	d	d	d	38
Treasury bonds—bank-eligible	2,162	2,155	2,069	1,957	1,912	1,837	1,784	1,699	1,615	1,567	1,483	1,459
Treasury bonds—bank-restricted[b]	13,753	13,724	13,682	13,584	13,436	13,288	13,140	13,079	13,050	12,987	12,969	12,958
Postal savings and Panama Canal bonds	d	d	d	d	2	d	1	d	1	1	1	d
Guaranteed by U.S. government[c]	6	6	6	6	6	6	6	6	6	6	7	7
Total	$16,056	$15,995	$15,852	$15,637	$15,415	$15,206	$14,973	$14,834	$14,741	$14,632	$14,533	$14,625
1950												
Issued by U.S. government:												
Treasury bills	$ 36	$ 43	$ 42	$ 59	$ 20	$ 26	$ 35	$ 59	$ 204	$ 154	$ 248	$ 391
Certificates	104	125	120	132	156	107	77	74	31	28	28	1
Treasury notes	38	13	55	56	32	66	92	73	64	61	61	165
Treasury bonds—bank-eligible	1,437	1,397	1,347	1,327	1,237	1,104	1,015	792	687	668	662	650
Treasury bonds—bank-restricted[b]	12,970	12,976	12,962	12,898	12,833	12,776	12,837	12,823	12,650	12,359	11,964	11,529
Postal savings and Panama Canal bonds	d	d	d	d	d	d	d	d	d	d	d	d
Guaranteed by U.S. government[c]	5	6	6	6	6	6	5	6	9	9	9	9
Total	$14,590	$14,560	$14,532	$14,479	$14,285	$14,086	$14,062	$13,829	$13,644	$13,279	$12,971	$12,746

Source: Treasury Bulletin, January 1946–March 1951.

a. Interest-bearing public marketable securities, par values.
b. Issues that commercial banks may not acquire before a specified date.
c. Excludes guaranteed securities held by the Treasury.
d. Less than $500,000.

TABLE 24

HOLDINGS OF U.S. GOVERNMENT SECURITIES[a] BY MUTUAL SAVINGS BANKS, BY CALL CLASS, OCTOBER 1945–DECEMBER 1950

(In Millions)

Year and Call Class	Jan.	Feb.	March	April	May	June	July	Aug.	Sept.	Oct.	Nov.	Dec.
1945												
Due or first becoming callable:												
Within 1 year	—	—	—	—	—	—	—	—	—	$ 302	$ 246	$ 156
1 to 5 years	—	—	—	—	—	—	—	—	—	905	811	701
5 to 10 years	—	—	—	—	—	—	—	—	—	2,478	2,265	2,056
10 to 15 years	—	—	—	—	—	—	—	—	—	2,882	2,928	3,275
15 to 20 years	—	—	—	—	—	—	—	—	—	2,151	2,214	2,249
Over 20 years	—	—	—	—	—	—	—	—	—	1,127	1,119	2,051
Various years[b]	—	—	—	—	—	—	—	—	—	2	3	3
Total										$ 9,847	$ 9,587	$10,491
1946												
Due or first becoming callable:												
Within 1 year	$ 171	$ 197	$ 310	$ 333	$ 340	$ 362	$ 366	$ 409	$ 483	$ 495	$ 440	$ 439
1 to 5 years	698	678	652	685	698	709	714	719	965	976	1,016	1,047
5 to 10 years	1,826	1,731	1,744	1,662	1,623	1,609	1,576	1,528	2,135	2,046	2,039	2,042
10 to 15 years	3,410	3,459	3,337	3,407	3,367	3,391	3,398	3,383	2,401	2,445	2,463	2,506
15 to 20 years	2,297	2,292	2,551	2,578	2,606	2,635	2,695	2,750	2,792	2,830	2,819	2,798
Over 20 years	2,321	2,512	2,359	2,357	2,449	2,509	2,586	2,630	2,670	2,691	2,679	2,687
Various years[b]	3	3	3	3	3	3	3	3	3	3	3	4
Total	$10,726	$10,871	$10,955	$11,026	$11,087	$11,220	$11,337	$11,422	$11,449	$11,487	$11,459	$11,521
1947												
Due or first becoming callable:												
Within 1 year	$ 441	$ 449	$ 528	$ 546	$ 530	$ 624	$ 545	$ 533	$ 492	$ 495	$ 442	$ 491
1 to 5 years	1,086	1,122	1,247	1,243	1,256	1,573	1,536	1,528	1,506	1,424	1,410	1,876
5 to 10 years	2,048	2,037	1,794	1,751	1,705	1,244	1,194	1,143	1,110	1,077	1,018	575
10 to 15 years	2,521	2,525	2,522	2,546	2,522	2,944	2,922	2,909	2,896	2,938	3,002	3,008
15 to 20 years	2,790	2,798	2,808	2,809	2,914	3,806	4,026	4,128	4,237	4,244	4,223	5,599
Over 20 years	2,706	2,731	2,786	2,798	1,809	1,650	1,664	1,647	1,587	1,588	1,547	—
Various years[b]	4	4	4	4	4	4	4	4	4	4	3	3
Total	$11,595	$11,667	$11,689	$11,696	$11,740	$11,845	$11,891	$11,892	$11,833	$11,769	$11,646	$11,552

TABLE 24 (continued)

Year and Call Class	Jan.	Feb.	March	April	May	June	July	Aug.	Sept.	Oct.	Nov.	Dec.
1948												
Due or first becoming callable:												
Within 1 year	$ 657	$ 693	$ 680	$ 647	$ 566	$ 546	$ 465	$ 458	$ 545	$ 572	$ 516	$ 539
1 to 5 years	1,908	1,954	1,982	1,924	1,904	1,829	1,816	1,826	1,853	1,890	1,855	1,769
5 to 10 years	570	571	565	555	511	506	508	520	525	548	546	520
10 to 15 years	2,967	2,927	2,928	2,933	2,963	2,963	2,925	2,884	2,794	2,726	2,707	3,207
15 to 20 years	5,490	5,442	5,466	5,546	5,583	5,676	5,674	5,615	5,430	5,300	5,283	4,841
Over 20 years												
Various years[b]	2	2	2	2	2	2	c	c	c	c	c	c
Total	$11,593	$11,590	$11,624	$11,608	$11,529	$11,522	$11,388	$11,303	$11,148	$11,037	$10,907	$10,877
1949												
Due or first becoming callable:												
Within 1 year	$ 501	$ 489	$ 510	$ 558	$ 521	$ 455	$ 444	$ 425	$ 529	$ 492	$ 449	$ 423
1 to 5 years	1,755	1,692	1,555	1,413	1,344	1,279	1,259	1,277	1,144	1,130	1,090	1,121
5 to 10 years	507	480	432	378	313	2,002	2,010	1,988	1,972	1,977	1,968	2,640
10 to 15 years	3,231	3,245	3,411	3,492	3,575	2,981	2,990	2,976	2,959	2,938	2,916	3,078
15 to 20 years	4,977	5,069	5,121	5,183	5,249	4,312	4,287	4,297	4,319	4,321	4,322	3,510
Over 20 years												
Various years[b]	c	c	1	1	1	1	1	1	1	1	1	1
Total	$10,971	$10,975	$11,030	$11,024	$11,003	$11,029	$10,991	$10,964	$10,924	$10,860	$10,745	$10,772
1950												
Due or first becoming callable:												
Within 1 year	$ 428	$ 387	$ 357	$ 323	$ 280	$ 249	$ 226	$ 203	$ 369	$ 371	$ 304	$ 270
1 to 5 years	1,086	1,080	1,079	1,087	1,052	1,058	951	884	639	617	575	568
5 to 10 years	2,662	2,658	2,681	2,575	2,524	2,439	2,382	2,304	2,230	2,180	2,158	2,125
10 to 15 years	3,106	3,138	3,726	3,749	3,769	3,824	3,823	3,889	3,933	3,987	4,039	4,219
15 to 20 years	3,566	3,569	3,033	3,157	3,255	3,306	3,415	3,417	3,359	3,233	3,143	2,961
Over 20 years												
Various years[b]	1	1	1	1	1	1	c	c	1	1	1	1
Total	$10,849	$10,833	$10,876	$10,891	$10,881	$10,877	$10,797	$10,697	$10,531	$10,389	$10,220	$10,144

Source: *Treasury Bulletin*, January 1946–March 1951.
a. Interest-bearing public marketable securities, par values.
b. Federal Housing Administration debentures.

TABLE 25

HOLDING OF U.S. GOVERNMENT SECURITIES[a] BY MUTUAL SAVINGS BANKS, BY TYPE OF SECURITY, OCTOBER 1945–DECEMBER 1950

(In Millions)

Year and Type of Security	Jan.	Feb.	March	April	May	June	July	Aug.	Sept.	Oct.	Nov.	Dec.
1945												
Issued by U.S. government:												
Treasury bills										$ 6	$ 14	[d]
Certificates										221	171	$ 91
Treasury notes										258	223	179
Treasury bonds—bank-eligible[b]										9,360	9,176	2,847
Treasury bonds—bank-restricted[b]										(braced with above)	(braced with above)	7,370
Postal savings and Panama Canal bonds										[d]	[d]	[d]
Guaranteed by U.S. government[c]										2	3	3
Total										$ 9,847	$ 9,587	$10,491
1946												
Issued by U.S. government:												
Treasury bills	$ 1	[d]	$ 2	$ 8	$ 1	$ 3	$ 1	[d]	$ 1	$ 1	$ 1	[d]
Certificates	101	119	179	205	211	243	272	302	261	252	210	257
Treasury notes	176	184	211	211	224	227	206	222	254	273	263	211
Treasury bonds—bank-eligible	2,599	2,466	2,399	2,344	2,322	2,347	2,263	2,210	3,133	3,048	3,084	3,149
Treasury bonds—bank-restricted[b]	7,846	8,099	8,162	8,255	8,325	8,396	8,592	8,683	7,797	7,910	7,899	7,900
Postal savings and Panama Canal bonds	[d]	[d]	[d]	[d]	[d]	[d]	[d]	[d]	[d]	[d]	[d]	1
Guaranteed by U.S. government[c]	3	3	3	3	3	3	3	3	3	3	3	4
Total	$10,726	$10,871	$10,955	$11,026	$11,087	$11,220	$11,337	$11,422	$11,449	$11,487	$11,459	$11,521

TABLE 25 (continued)

Year and Type of Security	Jan.	Feb.	March	April	May	June	July	Aug.	Sept.	Oct.	Nov.	Dec.
1947												
Issued by U.S. government:												
Treasury bills	$ [d]	[a]	3	1	1	1	2	2	5	7	8	$ 25
Certificates	273	291	292	293	266	249	195	187	221	213	198	200
Treasury notes	197	188	154	162	171	183	174	177	116	81	71	98
Treasury bonds—bank-eligible	3,163	3,199	3,193	3,168	3,157	3,107	2,978	2,904	2,836	2,753	2,671	2,696
Treasury bonds—bank-restricted[b]	7,957	7,985	8,043	8,068	8,141	8,300	8,538	8,618	8,650	8,712	8,694	8,530
Postal savings and Panama Canal bonds	[d]	[d]	[d]	[d]	1	[d]	[d]	[d]	[d]	[d]	[d]	[d]
Guaranteed by U.S. government[c]	4	4	4	4	4	4	4	4	4	4	3	3
Total	$11,595	$11,667	$11,689	$11,696	$11,740	$11,845	$11,891	$11,892	$11,833	$11,769	$11,646	$11,552
1948												
Issued by U.S. government:												
Treasury bills	$ 39	60	78	67	58	58	34	35	69	78	66	$ 50
Certificates	275	308	356	354	313	317	256	245	240	331	290	256
Treasury notes	129	134	133	124	116	98	104	106	165	96	87	84
Treasury bonds—bank-eligible	2,786	2,828	2,762	2,688	2,590	2,509	2,519	2,575	2,633	2,763	2,738	2,703
Treasury bonds—bank-restricted[b]	8,363	8,259	8,292	8,372	8,447	8,538	8,475	8,341	8,040	7,768	7,727	7,783
Postal savings and Panama Canal bonds	[d]	[d]	2	1	2	[d]	[d]	1	1	[d]	[d]	[d]
Guaranteed by U.S. government[e]	2	2	2	2	2	2	[d]	[d]	[d]	[d]	[d]	[d]
Total	$11,593	$11,590	$11,624	$11,608	$11,529	$11,522	$11,388	$11,303	$11,148	$11,037	$10,907	$10,877

Year and Type of Security	Jan.	Feb.	March	April	May	June	July	Aug.	Sept.	Oct.	Nov.	Dec.
1949												
Issued by U.S. government:												
Treasury bills	$ 44	$ 26	$ 18	$ 17	$ 14	$ 13	$ 16	$ 19	$ 18	$ 15	$ 11	$ 15
Certificates	259	255	241	232	214	207	193	179	187	168	149	169
Treasury notes	70	72	63	61	59	41	40	39	38	37	32	107
Treasury bonds—bank-eligible	2,650	2,535	2,381	2,249	2,048	1,886	1,836	1,830	1,761	1,728	1,653	1,547
Treasury bonds—bank-restricted[b]	7,949	8,086	8,326	8,464	8,667	8,881	8,906	8,897	8,919	8,910	8,899	8,932
Postal savings and Panama Canal bonds	d	d	d	1	1	d	d	d	d	1	d	d
Guaranteed by U.S. government[c]	d	d	1	1	1	1	1	1	1	1	1	1
Total	$10,971	$10,975	$11,030	$11,024	$11,003	$11,029	$10,991	$10,964	$10,924	$10,860	$10,745	$10,772
1950												
Issued by U.S. government:												
Treasury bills	$ 42	$ 38	$ 28	$ 36	$ 21	$ 35	$ 15	$ 25	$ 50	$ 72	$ 44	$ 33
Certificates	159	145	142	144	124	64	49	47	33	18	10	7
Treasury notes	117	120	144	139	130	154	142	151	148	146	124	136
Treasury bonds—bank-eligible	1,480	1,453	1,353	1,290	1,247	1,223	1,141	1,006	913	909	841	804
Treasury bonds—bank-restricted[b]	9,052	9,077	9,207	9,281	9,357	9,401	9,449	9,467	9,386	9,243	9,201	9,163
Postal savings and Panama Canal bonds	d	—	1	d	d	1	a	a	1	1	1	—
Guaranteed by U.S. government[c]	1	1	1	1	1	1			1	1	1	1
Total	$10,849	$10,833	$10,876	$10,891	$10,881	$10,877	$10,797	$10,697	$10,531	$10,389	$10,220	$10,144

Source: *Treasury Bulletin*, January 1946–March 1951.

a. Interest-bearing public marketable securities, par values.
b. Issues that commercial banks may not acquire before a specified date.
c. Excludes guaranteed securities held by the Treasury.
d. Less than $500,000.

TABLE 26

HOLDINGS OF U.S. GOVERNMENT SECURITIES[a] BY STOCK SAVINGS BANKS, BY CALL CLASS, OCTOBER 1945–JUNE 1949

(In Millions)

Year and Call Class	Jan.	Feb.	March	April	May	June	July	Aug.	Sept.	Oct.	Nov.	Dec.
1945												
Due or first becoming callable:												
Within 1 year	—	—	—	—	—	—	—	—	—	$ 43	$ 32	$ 34
1 to 5 years	—	—	—	—	—	—	—	—	—	69	68	67
5 to 10 years	—	—	—	—	—	—	—	—	—	121	120	117
10 to 15 years	—	—	—	—	—	—	—	—	—	83	82	111
15 to 20 years	—	—	—	—	—	—	—	—	—	61	61	47
Over 20 years	—	—	—	—	—	—	—	—	—	44	44	63
Various years[b]	—	—	—	—	—	—	—	—	—	c	c	c
Total										$420	$407	$440
1946												
Due or first becoming callable:												
Within 1 year	$ 35	$ 36	$ 49	$ 51	$ 50	$ 44	$ 45	$ 43	$ 55	$ 53	$ 53	$ 50
1 to 5 years	68	66	55	49	49	62	63	63	75	74	74	79
5 to 10 years	115	114	122	122	122	114	115	115	126	127	126	122
10 to 15 years	117	120	112	112	113	115	118	119	85	85	85	85
15 to 20 years	49	49	60	66	67	67	69	70	71	72	72	72
Over 20 years	77	79	69	70	70	72	73	71	71	71	71	69
Various years[b]	c	c	c	1	1	1	1	1	1	1	1	1
Total	$460	$465	$468	$471	$473	$475	$483	$482	$485	$483	$482	$478
1947												
Due or first becoming callable:												
Within 1 year	$ 43	$ 40	$ 31	$ 31	$ 30	$ 32	$ 32	$ 29	$ 25	$ 32	$ 30	$ 31
1 to 5 years	77	79	77	78	79	97	96	94	95	87	89	110
5 to 10 years	127	120	123	122	123	100	100	99	100	96	95	70
10 to 15 years	90	80	80	80	79	84	85	87	89	93	93	93
15 to 20 years	71	72	73	73	73	94	96	96	99	100	101	140
Over 20 years	70	69	70	71	71	46	46	45	43	42	39	—
Various years[b]	1	1	1	1	2	2	2	2	2	2	2	2

260

Year and Call Class	Jan.	Feb.	March	April	May	June	July	Aug.	Sept.	Oct.	Nov.	Dec.
1948												
Due or first becoming callable:												
Within 1 year	$ 40	$ 42	$ 42	$ 38	$ 39	$ 39	$ 39	$ 39	$ 37	$ 39	$ 40	$ 45
1 to 5 years	114	116	116	115	113	113	111	111	116	116	114	104
5 to 10 years	73	76	76	76	75	84	82	82	82	82	81	81
10 to 15 years	89	84	83	80	78	66	65	61	59	57	55	60
15 to 20 years	134	130	125	124	125	125	121	120	118	114	110	100
Over 20 years	—	—	—	—	—	—	—	—	—	—	—	—
Various years[b]	2	2	2	2	2	2	c	c	c	c	c	c
Total	$452	$451	$444	$435	$432	$429	$417	$413	$411	$408	$399	$391
1949												
Due or first becoming callable:												
Within 1 year	$ 46	$ 48	$ 54	$ 56	$ 56	$ 52	d	—	—	—	—	—
1 to 5 years	104	104	100	95	94	95	—	—	—	—	—	—
5 to 10 years	82	82	75	71	71	87	—	—	—	—	—	—
10 to 15 years	60	58	64	70	69	69	—	—	—	—	—	—
15 to 20 years	101	101	101	99	99	81	—	—	—	—	—	—
Over 20 years	—	—	—	—	—	—	—	—	—	—	—	—
Various years[b]	c	c	c	c	c	c	—	—	—	—	—	—
Total	$393	$393	$394	$391	$389	$384						

Source: *Treasury Bulletin*, January 1946–October 1949.

a. Interest-bearing public marketable securities, par values.
b. Federal Housing Administration debentures.
c. Less than $500,000.
d. Beginning with July 1949, stock savings banks were included with commercial banks.

TABLE 27

HOLDINGS OF U.S. GOVERNMENT SECURITIES[a] BY STOCK SAVINGS BANKS, BY TYPE OF SECURITY, OCTOBER 1945–JUNE 1949

(In Millions)

Year and Type of Security	Jan.	Feb.	March	April	May	June	July	Aug.	Sept.	Oct.	Nov.	Dec.
1945												
Issued by U.S. government:												
Treasury bills	—	—	—	—	—	—	—	—	—	$ 1	$ 1	$ 1[d]
Certificates	—	—	—	—	—	—	—	—	—	35	25	$ 26
Treasury notes	—	—	—	—	—	—	—	—	—	39	38	37
Treasury bonds—bank-eligible	—	—	—	—	—	—	—	—	—	{345	343}	215
Treasury bonds—bank-restricted[b]	—	—	—	—	—	—	—	—	—			162
Postal savings and Panama Canal bonds	—	—	—	—	—	—	—	—	—	[d]	[d]	[d]
Guaranteed by U.S. government[c]	—	—	—	—	—	—	—	—	—	[d]	[d]	[d]
Total										$420	$407	$440
1946												
Issued by U.S. government:												
Treasury bills	[d]	$ 1	$ 3	$ 1	$ 1	$ 1	$ 1	$ 1	$ 1	$ 1	$ 1	$ 1
Certificates	$ 28	29	29	32	31	25	28	26	27	25	24	25
Treasury notes	36	36	33	35	35	36	34	33	33	33	30	30
Treasury bonds—bank-eligible	206	205	200	192	192	196	195	197	220	219	220	219
Treasury bonds—bank-restricted[b]	189	195	204	210	213	216	225	223	204	205	206	204
Postal savings and Panama Canal bonds	[d]	[d]	[d]	[d]	[d]	[d]	[d]	[d]	[d]	[d]	[d]	[d]
Guaranteed by U.S. government[c]	[d]	[d]	[d]	1	1	1	1	1	1	1	1	1
Total	$460	$465	$468	$471	$473	$475	$483	$482	$485	$483	$482	$478

Year and Type of Security	Jan.	Feb.	March	April	May	June	July	Aug.	Sept.	Oct.	Nov.	Dec.
1947												
Issued by U.S. government:												
Treasury bills	$ 1	$ 1	$ 1	a	—	—	—	—	$ 1	$ 1	$ 1	$ —
Certificates	19	16	17	17	14	16	13	13	9	9	9	8
Treasury notes	27	30	17	18	20	16	18	14	15	15	12	12
Treasury bonds—bank-eligible	226	214	218	219	220	220	219	218	218	213	216	214
Treasury bonds—bank-restricted[b]	205	199	201	201	200	201	204	206	209	211	209	209
Postal savings and Panama Canal bonds	a	a	a	a	a	a	a	a	a	a	a	a
Guaranteed by U.S. government[c]	1	1	1	1	2	2	2	2	2	2	2	2
Total	$480	$460	$456	$455	$456	$455	$456	$452	$454	$451	$448	$445
1948												
Issued by U.S. government:												
Treasury bills	$ 5	$ 6	$ 6	$ 4	$ 3	$ 3	$ 1	a	$ 2	$ 5	$ 6	$ 6
Certificates	8	7	9	13	16	20	22	22	21	26	24	27
Treasury notes	14	19	19	13	12	12	12	12	12	7	6	6
Treasury bonds—bank-eligible	224	226	223	222	220	215	210	211	213	212	212	206
Treasury bonds—bank-restricted[b]	198	190	185	181	179	178	172	168	163	158	151	148
Postal savings and Panama Canal bonds	a	a	a	a	a	a	a	a	a	a	a	a
Guaranteed by U.S. government[c]	2	2	2	2	2	2	a	a	a	a	a	a
Total	$452	$451	$444	$435	$432	$429	$417	$413	$411	$408	$399	$391

TABLE 27 (continued)

Year and Type of Security	Jan.	Feb.	March	April	May	June	July	Aug.	Sept.	Oct.	Nov.	Dec.
1949												
Issued by U.S. government:												
Treasury bills	$ 6	$ 7	$ 7	$ 7	$ 6	$ 5	•	—	—	—	—	—
Certificates	30	29	31	32	31	31	—	—	—	—	—	—
Treasury notes	3	3	3	2	3	3		—		—	—	—
Treasury bonds—bank-eligible	208	207	200	193	193	184	—	—	—	—	—	—
Treasury bonds—bank-restricted[b]	147	147	153	157	156	161	—	—	—	—	—	—
Postal savings and Panama Canal bonds	d	d	d	d	d	d	—	—	—	—	—	—
Guaranteed by U.S. government[e]	d	d	d	d	d	d	—	—	—	—	—	—
Total	$393	$393	$394	$391	$389	$384						

Source: Treasury Bulletin, January 1946–October 1949.

a. Interest-bearing public marketable securities, par values.
b. Issues that commercial banks may not acquire before a specified date.
c. Excludes guaranteed securities held by the Treasury.
d. Less than $500,000.
e. Beginning with July 1949, stock savings banks were included with commercial banks.

Holdings of U.S. Government Securities[a] by "All Other Investors," by Call Class, October 1945–December 1950

(In Millions)

Year and Call Class	Jan.	Feb.	March	April	May	June	July	Aug.	Sept.	Oct.	Nov.	Dec.
1945												
Due or first becoming callable:												
Within 1 year	—	—	—	—	—	—	—	—	—	$15,586	$15,181	$15,778
1 to 5 years	—	—	—	—	—	—	—	—	—	6,312	6,220	6,685
5 to 10 years	—	—	—	—	—	—	—	—	—	7,967	7,583	6,064
10 to 15 years	—	—	—	—	—	—	—	—	—	4,694	5,210	6,982
15 to 20 years	—	—	—	—	—	—	—	—	—	5,312	5,247	4,972
Over 20 years	—	—	—	—	—	—	—	—	—	4,636	6,234	10,559
Various years[b]	—	—	—	—	—	—	—	—	—	4	3	6
Total										$44,512	$45,679	$51,046
1946												
Due or first becoming callable:												
Within 1 year	$15,555	$15,407	$17,046	$15,712	$15,601	$14,359	$13,904	$13,933	$15,048	$15,143	$14,727	$14,218
1 to 5 years	6,580	6,459	6,021	5,951	6,005	6,318	6,306	6,321	6,641	6,335	6,428	6,550
5 to 10 years	5,941	6,057	5,989	5,864	5,801	5,632	5,592	5,567	5,387	5,368	5,337	5,155
10 to 15 years	6,822	6,831	6,632	6,446	6,396	6,321	6,213	6,177	4,589	4,531	4,509	4,445
15 to 20 years	4,903	4,889	5,727	5,674	5,624	5,555	5,478	5,492	5,481	5,488	5,497	5,489
Over 20 years	10,405	10,309	9,245	9,158	8,948	8,826	8,675	8,593	8,424	8,374	8,333	8,314
Various years[b]	4	4	3	6	4	4	5	5	5	5	6	5
Total	$50,210	$49,957	$50,663	$48,811	$48,379	$47,015	$46,174	$46,088	$45,574	$45,243	$44,837	$44,177
1947												
Due or first becoming callable:												
Within 1 year	$14,079	$13,899	$14,171	$12,905	$12,955	$13,559	$13,782	$13,863	$13,076	$14,417	$14,417	$12,582
1 to 5 years	6,639	6,717	6,583	6,646	6,821	7,189	7,212	7,266	7,820	6,386	6,400	9,884
5 to 10 years	4,962	4,914	4,759	4,710	4,725	3,646	3,634	3,654	3,621	3,620	3,561	1,928
10 to 15 years	4,420	4,392	4,385	4,373	4,384	4,774	4,779	4,785	4,794	4,736	4,668	4,493
15 to 20 years	5,487	5,482	5,478	5,455	5,454	7,702	7,799	7,848	8,180	8,160	8,074	13,266
Over 20 years	8,247	8,201	8,169	8,190	8,250	5,810	5,875	5,938	5,555	5,555	5,563	—
Various years[b]	3	1	4	5	4	4	3	2	1	3	3	1
Total	$43,838	$43,606	$43,549	$42,284	$42,594	$42,685	$43,085	$43,357	$43,048	$42,878	$42,686	$42,154

TABLE 28 (continued)

Year and Call Class	Jan.	Feb.	March	April	May	June	July	Aug.	Sept.	Oct.	Nov.	Dec.
1948												
Due or first becoming callable:												
Within 1 year	$14,796	$15,361	$16,257	$15,806	$16,347	$16,281	$16,089	$16,526	$15,958	$16,500	$16,969	$17,353
1 to 5 years	7,942	8,055	8,102	8,058	8,078	7,971	7,908	7,925	8,788	8,740	8,848	8,253
5 to 10 years	1,940	1,896	1,922	1,890	1,891	1,935	1,927	1,898	1,899	1,864	1,860	1,885
10 to 15 years	4,231	4,089	4,016	4,018	3,997	3,911	3,840	3,767	3,642	3,507	3,445	4,012
15 to 20 years	12,956	12,674	12,598	12,660	12,637	12,679	12,586	12,348	12,043	11,650	11,639	11,130
Over 20 years	1	c	c	c	2	3	3	3	2	2	3	4
Various years[b]												
Total	$41,866	$42,075	$42,895	$42,433	$42,952	$42,779	$42,353	$42,467	$42,331	$42,264	$42,764	$42,637
1949												
Due or first becoming callable:												
Within 1 year	$17,527	$17,335	$18,320	$18,786	$19,334	$19,030	$18,373	$18,468	$19,506	$19,285	$19,614	$18,617
1 to 5 years	8,318	8,380	8,274	7,035	6,994	7,136	7,065	7,018	5,793	5,796	5,767	5,290
5 to 10 years	1,855	1,857	1,835	1,842	1,823	3,630	3,549	3,541	3,537	3,491	3,480	4,716
10 to 15 years	4,080	4,107	4,166	4,211	4,290	3,356	3,350	3,374	3,330	3,347	3,348	3,167
15 to 20 years	11,174	11,283	11,448	11,552	11,662	10,933	11,072	11,071	11,070	11,062	11,069	9,972
Over 20 years								c				
Various years[b]	1	1	2	2	2	2	1		2	2	3	2
Total	$42,956	$42,982	$44,045	$43,429	$44,105	$44,087	$43,410	$43,472	$43,239	$42,982	$43,282	$41,764
1950												
Due or first becoming callable:												
Within 1 year	$18,912	$18,887	$18,750	$16,920	$17,121	$15,463	$17,534	$19,073	$20,076	$21,179	$21,857	$20,117
1 to 5 years	5,150	6,000	7,881	9,178	9,165	10,442	9,120	7,819	6,409	5,496	5,418	5,661
5 to 10 years	4,677	4,708	4,068	4,141	4,163	4,186	4,326	4,393	4,338	4,366	4,411	4,615
10 to 15 years	3,120	3,101	4,394	4,402	4,401	4,358	4,402	4,416	4,379	4,398	4,484	4,329
15 to 20 years	9,905	9,976	8,815	8,892	9,108	9,213	9,564	9,715	9,721	9,640	9,733	9,706
Over 20 years												
Various years[b]	3	3	3	2	2	2	2	2	1	2	2	2
Total	$41,767	$42,675	$43,911	$43,535	$43,959	$43,664	$44,948	$45,418	$44,924	$45,082	$45,906	$44,430

Source: Treasury Bulletin, January 1946–March 1951.

a. Interest-bearing public marketable securities, par values.
b. Federal Housing Administration debentures.

TABLE 29

HOLDINGS OF U.S. GOVERNMENT SECURITIES[a] BY "ALL OTHER INVESTORS," BY TYPE OF SECURITY, OCTOBER 1945–DECEMBER 1950

(In Millions)

Year and Type of Security	Jan.	Feb.	March	April	May	June	July	Aug.	Sept.	Oct.	Nov.	Dec.
1945												
Issued by U.S. government:												
Treasury bills	—	—	—	—	—	—	—	—	—	$ 1,850	$ 2,094	$ 1,723
Certificates	—	—	—	—	—	—	—	—	—	10,735	10,070	11,211
Treasury notes	—	—	—	—	—	—	—	—	—	4,815	4,817	4,383
Treasury bonds—bank-eligible	—	—	—	—	—	—	—	—	—	12,306		
Treasury bonds—bank-restricted[b]	—	—	—	—	—	—	—	—	—	21,273	26,964	28,551
Postal savings and Panama Canal bonds	—	—	—	—	—	—	—	—	—	144	144	144
Guaranteed by U.S. government[c]	—	—	—	—	—	—	—	—	—	4	3	6
Total										$44,512	$45,679	$51,046
1946												
Issued by U.S. government:												
Treasury bills	$ 1,783	$ 1,584	$ 2,239	$ 1,502	$ 1,421	$ 1,424	$ 1,384	$ 1,352	$ 1,352	$ 1,260	$ 1,121	$ 1,088
Certificates	11,532	11,442	12,003	11,483	11,410	10,439	11,270	11,289	11,108	11,846	10,569	10,459
Treasury notes	3,764	3,824	3,765	3,779	3,874	4,258	3,000	3,074	3,087	3,245	3,238	2,796
Treasury bonds—bank-eligible	12,061	12,116	11,907	11,598	11,580	11,026	10,988	10,955	12,232	12,199	12,241	12,260
Treasury bonds—bank-restricted[b]	20,939	20,858	20,616	20,314	19,961	19,738	19,400	19,285	17,663	17,562	17,535	17,440
Postal savings and Panama Canal bonds	127	128	129	129	128	127	126	128	127	127	127	128
Guaranteed by U.S. government[c]	4	4	3	6	4	4	5	5	5	5	6	5
Total	$50,210	$49,957	$50,663	$48,811	$48,379	$47,015	$46,174	$46,088	$45,574	$45,243	$44,837	$44,177

TABLE 29 (continued)

Year and Type of Security	Jan.	Feb.	March	April	May	June	July	Aug.	Sept.	Oct.	Nov.	Dec.
1947												
Issued by U.S. government:												
Treasury bills	$ 892	$ 769	$ 1,243	$ 562	$ 427	$ 480	$ 790	$ 837	$ 893	$ 1,050	$ 1,306	$ 1,455
Certificates	10,566	10,559	10,574	9,980	10,158	9,821	9,729	9,723	9,464	9,481	9,315	7,386
Treasury notes	2,767	2,754	2,224	2,289	2,376	2,445	2,487	2,498	2,351	2,330	2,201	4,224
Treasury bonds—bank-eligible	12,136	12,101	12,113	12,076	12,190	12,299	12,265	12,337	12,395	12,180	12,103	11,924
Treasury bonds—bank-restricted[b]	17,359	17,308	17,275	17,257	17,436	17,522	17,698	17,846	17,829	17,719	17,642	17,051
Postal savings and Panama Canal bonds	115	114	116	116	113	114	112	113	115	115	115	113
Guaranteed by U.S. government[c]	3	1	4	5	4	4	3	2	1	3	3	1
Total	$43,838	$43,606	$43,549	$42,284	$42,594	$42,685	$43,085	$43,357	$43,048	$42,878	$42,686	$42,154
1948												
Issued by U.S. government:												
Treasury bills	$ 1,568	$ 1,915	$ 2,670	$ 2,463	$ 2,793	$ 2,651	$ 2,696	$ 2,833	$ 2,991	$ 3,676	$ 3,987	$ 3,739
Certificates	7,423	7,514	7,920	7,798	7,867	8,610	8,388	8,644	8,810	10,106	10,236	10,424
Treasury notes	4,261	4,298	4,556	4,436	4,552	4,556	4,525	4,581	4,501	3,030	3,098	2,984
Treasury bonds—bank-eligible	12,011	12,174	11,745	11,646	11,689	10,898	10,807	10,773	10,876	10,795	10,908	10,876
Treasury bonds—bank-restricted[b]	16,488	16,061	15,891	15,977	15,937	15,949	15,824	15,521	15,041	14,544	14,421	14,497
Postal savings and Panama Canal bonds	114	113	112	113	111	112	111	112	111	111	112	113
Guaranteed by U.S. government[c]	1	a	a	a	2	3	3	3	2	2	3	4
Total	$41,866	$42,075	$42,895	$42,433	$42,952	$42,779	$42,353	$42,467	$42,331	$42,264	$42,764	$42,637

Year and Type of Security	Jan.	Feb.	March	April	May	June	July	Aug.	Sept.	Oct.	Nov.	Dec.
1949												
Issued by U.S. government:												
Treasury bills	$ 3,907	$ 3,828	$ 4,439	$ 3,871	$ 4,380	$ 4,237	$ 4,040	$ 4,300	$ 4,107	$ 4,401	$ 4,729	$ 3,880
Certificates	12,338	12,266	12,188	12,024	12,024	12,175	11,788	11,638	11,836	11,435	11,381	10,990
Treasury notes	1,039	1,082	1,193	1,191	1,205	1,245	1,216	1,215	1,211	1,188	1,193	1,752
Treasury bonds—bank-eligible	10,937	10,968	11,194	11,124	11,085	10,824	10,644	10,555	10,364	10,216	10,222	9,393
Treasury bonds—bank-restricted[b]	14,622	14,725	14,918	15,107	15,299	15,495	15,613	15,654	15,611	15,632	15,645	15,636
Postal savings and Panama Canal bonds	112	112	112	110	109	110	109	110	107	109	109	110
Guaranteed by U.S. government[c]	1	1	2	2	2	2	1	[d]	2	2	3	2
Total	$42,956	$42,982	$44,045	$43,429	$44,105	$44,087	$43,410	$43,472	$43,239	$42,982	$43,282	$41,764
1950												
Issued by U.S. government:												
Treasury bills	$ 4,267	$ 4,837	$ 5,795	$ 5,352	$ 5,676	$ 5,846	$ 6,398	$ 7,545	$ 7,961	$ 8,569	$ 8,730	$ 7,901
Certificates	10,836	10,303	9,729	9,292	9,196	7,255	5,694	4,724	3,995	3,174	2,502	1,434
Treasury notes	1,684	2,457	3,415	3,751	3,719	5,114	6,689	7,160	7,700	7,968	8,808	10,044
Treasury bonds—bank-eligible	9,347	9,323	9,058	9,056	9,014	8,981	9,222	8,775	8,101	8,212	8,503	7,658
Treasury bonds—bank-restricted[b]	15,520	15,647	15,801	15,973	16,247	16,358	16,834	17,102	17,056	17,048	17,253	17,284
Postal savings and Panama Canal bonds	110	106	109	109	105	108	109	110	110	109	108	108
Guaranteed by U.S. government[c]	3	3	3	2	2	2	2	2	1	2	2	2
Total	$41,767	$42,675	$43,911	$43,535	$43,959	$43,664	$44,948	$45,418	$44,924	$45,082	$45,906	$44,430

Source: Treasury Bulletin, January 1946–March 1951.
a. Interest-bearing public marketable securities, par values.
b. Issues that commercial banks may not acquire before a specified date.
c. Excludes guaranteed securities held by the Treasury.
d. Less than $500,000.

INDEX

INDEX

The designation (f) following a page number indicates a reference to a figure (chart); the designation (t), a table.